Mac OS X Tiger
KillerTips

Scott Kelby

MAC OS X TIGER KILLER TIPS

The Mac OS X Tiger Killer Tips Team

TECHNICAL EDITORS
Polly Reincheld
Veronica Martin

PRODUCTION EDITOR
Kim Gabriel

PRODUCTION MANAGER
Dave Damstra

COVER DESIGN AND CREATIVE CONCEPTS
Felix Nelson

PUBLISHED BY
New Riders

Copyright © 2006 by Scott Kelby

First edition: August 2005

Composed in Myriad and Helvetica by NAPP Publishing

Trademarks
All terms mentioned in this book that are known to be trademarks or service marks have been appropriately capitalized. New Riders cannot attest to the accuracy of this information. Use of a term in the book should not be regarded as affecting the validity of any trademark or service mark.

Macintosh and Mac are registered trademarks of Apple Computer.
Windows is a registered trademark of Microsoft Corporation.

Warning and Disclaimer
This book is designed to provide information about Mac OS X tips. Every effort has been made to make this book as complete and as accurate as possible, but no warranty of fitness is implied.

The information is provided on an as-is basis. The authors and New Riders shall have neither liability nor responsibility to any person or entity with respect to any loss or damages arising from the information contained in this book or from the use of the discs or programs that may accompany it.

ISBN 0-321-29054-2

9 8 7 6 5 4 3 2 1

Printed in the United States of America

For my amazing wife, Kalebra

"You don't marry someone you can live with.

You marry the person you cannot live without."

—UNKNOWN

ACKNOWLEDGMENTS

Although only one person's name winds up on the spine of this book, it takes a large army of people to put out a book, and without their help, dedication, and tireless efforts, there wouldn't even have been a spine; and to them I'm greatly indebted.

First, I want to thank absolutely just the coolest person I've ever met—my wife, Kalebra. I don't know how I ever got lucky enough to marry her 15 years ago, but it was without a doubt the smartest thing I've ever done, and the greatest blessing God's ever given me. She just flat-out rocks, and at this point, I can't imagine that the crush I've had on her since the first time I met her will ever go away. I love you, Sweetie!

Secondly, I want to thank my son, Jordan. Little Buddy—there's so much of your mom in you, in particular her kind, loving heart, and that's about the best head start anyone could ask for in life. You're the greatest little guy in the world, and thanks so much for making me smile every single day while I was writing this book, and for setting up your iBook next to me so we can "write books together."

I want to thank my team at KW Media Group—they're a unique group of people, with limitless energy and amazing talent, and I'd put them up against anybody in the business. In particular, I want to thank my Creative Director Felix Nelson for his great ideas, cool cover designs, intro artwork, and for his ongoing dedication and consistently amazing attitude. I want to thank my Tech Editors Polly Reincheld and Veronica Martin for making sure everything works the way it should, and for input and ideas that helped to make this a better book from top to bottom. I want to thank the amazing layout master Dave Damstra for making the book look so squeaky clean, and my Production Editor Kim Gabriel for making sure everything came together on time.

As always, a special thanks goes to my very good friend Dave Moser for his unwavering commitment to making sure that everything we do is better than what we've done before. He's an inspiration to everyone on our team; he helps us go places we couldn't go without him, and I'm honored to have him at the helm.

I owe a huge debt of gratitude to my good friend Terry White. Terry is a major Mac OS X tip hound (and president of MacGroup-Detroit, one of the very best Macintosh User Groups anywhere), and he was kind enough to share so many of his cool tips and amazing tricks with me; and this book is far better than it would have been without his help. Thank you, man—I owe you big time! Also, many thanks go to Dave Gales who helped me with the early testing.

I want to thank Jean Kendra for her support and enthusiasm for all my writing projects, and to Pete Kratzenberg for making it all add up. I also want to thank my brother Jeff for letting me constantly "pick his brain," and for his many ideas, input, support, hard work, and most of all for just being such a great brother to me always.

Of course, I couldn't do any of it without the help of my wonderful assistant, Kathy Siler, and all the "behind-the-scenes" team at KW Media who constantly keep raising the bar.

I want to thank all my "Mac Buddies" who've taught me so much over the years, including Bill Carroll, Jim Goodman, Dick Theriault, Don Wiggins, Dave Gales, Jim Patterson, Larry Becker, Jim Workman, Jon Gales, Jim Nordquist, and a big thanks to my buddy Rod "Mac Daddy" Harlan (President of the DVPA) for his contribution of some very cool iDVD tips.

Thanks to Nancy Ruenzel, Scott Cowlin, and everyone at New Riders and Peachpit for their ongoing commitment to excellence, and for the honor of letting me be one of their "Voices that Matter."

And most importantly, an extra special thanks to God and His son Jesus Christ for always hearing my prayers, for always being there when I need Him, and for blessing me with a wonderful life I truly love, and such a warm, loving family to share it with.

Scott Kelby

Scott is Editor-in-Chief and co-founder of *Layers* magazine (The How-To Magazine for Everything Adobe), Editor-in-Chief of *Photoshop User* magazine, Editor-in-Chief of Nikon's *Capture User*, and president of the National Association of Photoshop Professionals (NAPP), the trade association for Adobe® Photoshop® users. Scott is also president of KW Media Group, Inc., a Florida-based software training and publishing firm.

Scott is the award-winning author of more than 27 books. In 2004, he was the world's best-selling author of computer and technology books. His titles include: *The Mac OS X Conversion Kit, Getting Started with Your Mac and Mac OS X Tiger, Photoshop Classic Effects,* and *The iPod Book: Doing Cool Stuff with the iPod and the iTunes Music Store* from Peachpit Press; *Macintosh: The Naked Truth, Photoshop CS Down & Dirty Tricks, The Photoshop Book for Digital Photographers,* and he is co-author of *Photoshop Killer Tips,* from New Riders. This year Scott also wrote his first non-computer book, about overcoming the fear of fatherhood, called *The Book for Guys Who Don't Want Kids* from Fair Shake Press.

Scott is Training Director for the Adobe Photoshop Seminar Tour, Technical Conference Chair for both the Mac Design Conference and the Photoshop World Conference and Expo, and is a speaker at graphics and photography conferences around the world. Scott is also featured in a series of Adobe Photoshop video training tapes and DVDs and has been training Mac users and graphics professionals since 1993.

For more background info visit www.scottkelby.com.

OTHER BOOKS BY SCOTT KELBY

- *Getting Started with Your Mac and Mac OS X Tiger*

- *Macintosh: The Naked Truth*

- *The iPod Book: Doing Cool Stuff with the iPod and the iTunes Music Store*

- *The Photoshop CS2 Book for Digital Photographers*

- *Photoshop Classic Effects*

- *Photoshop CS Down & Dirty Tricks*

- *Photoshop CS Killer Tips*

- *The Photoshop Elements 3 Book for Digital Photographers*

- *Photoshop Elements 3 Down & Dirty Tricks*

- *InDesign CS Killer Tips*

- *The Book for Guys Who Don't Want Kids*

TABLE OF CONTENTS

TABLE OF CONTENTS

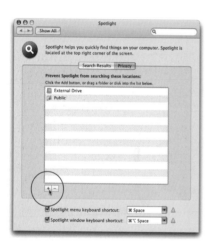

Fly Like an Eagle
Mac OS X Speed Tips

TABLE OF CONTENTS

TABLE OF CONTENTS

TABLE OF CONTENTS

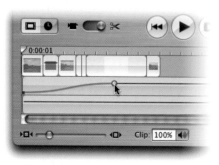

TABLE OF CONTENTS

CHAPTER 13   343

Talking Heads

iChat AV Tips

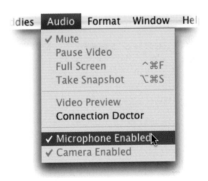

WARNING:
AS MANY AS 7% OF THE PEOPLE
WHO START HERE WILL SUFFER
SPONTANEOUS BLINDNESS

Wait a minute. Is this just a scam to get me to read the book's introduction? Honestly?

Yes. That's exactly what it is, so don't worry; 7% of you aren't going to experience spontaneous blindness. It's really more like 4%. I hate to resort to this kind of hyperbole just to get you to read the introduction, but because this is a totally different kind of Mac book, it's really important that you fully read the introduction (and it wouldn't hurt if you memorized each paragraph, including punctuation, just in case). Look, it's only like three pages long, and quickly reading it will answer a lot of your questions, help you to get the most out of the book, and lead you to a true and lasting inner peace that only comes from becoming "one" with the introduction. Let us begin.

What exactly is a Killer Tips book?

There are two types of people in this world: (1) the type of people who want to understand everything before they do anything. These are the people who buy a new computer, read the entire instruction manual, inventory all the packing items, and only when they feel certain that they have a full and complete understanding of the entire project before them, do they actually remove the Styrofoam cover and pull their new Mac out of the shipping carton. There are no more than 17 of these people using Macs in the world today. This book is not for them.

This book is for (2) the rest of us. People who buy a Mac, tear open the box, set it all up, turn it on, and start messin' around with it. These same people eventually buy computer books, and while casually flipping through them, they stop to read all the sidebar tips first. These are people like you and me. (Well, at least like me, anyway.) I'm an absolute sucker for sidebar tips. I'm hooked on 'em, and whenever I buy a new computer book, the first thing I do is read all those cool little tips scattered throughout the sidebars. Sometimes they're in boxes with a tinted background (like the one shown on the left), sometimes they're on the side of the page, sometimes at the bottom—it doesn't matter. If it says the word "tip," I'm drawn to it like an attorney to a slip-and-fall injury in a Vegas casino.

I finally figured out why I like sidebar tips so much—it's where the "really cool stuff" is. Think about it, if you were writing a computer book and you found some really ingenious technique, some really great undocumented keyboard shortcut, or a closely-guarded inside secret you wanted to share with your readers—you'd want it to stand out and yell, "Hey, there's a very cool thing right over here!" You're not going to bury it inside paragraphs of techno-text. This is exciting stuff. It's intriguing. It's fun. So, you pull it out from the regular text, slap a border around it, add a tint behind it, and maybe even add a special graphic to get the reader's attention. It works. The only problem with sidebar tips is that there's just not enough of 'em.

So I got to thinkin', "Wouldn't it be cool if there was a book where the whole book, cover-to-cover, was nothing but those little sidebar tips?" No long paragraphs explaining the Hierarchical File System. No detailed descriptions of how to configure a LAN, or 16 ways to partition your hard drive—just the fun stuff—just the tips. Well, that's exactly what this is—a book of nothin' but Mac OS X sidebar tips. Without the sidebars.

So what exactly is a "Killer Tip?"

"Double-click on a folder to open it." Technically, that is a tip. It's a very lame tip. It's a boringly obvious tip, and it's definitely not a Killer Tip. If it's a "Killer Tip," it makes you nod and smile when you read it, and you'll be nodding and smiling so much in this book, you're going to look like a bobbing dog in the rear window of a Buick Park Avenue. (I used a Buick Park Avenue as an example because it has a big enough rear window that you can climb up there yourself to test out my prediction. See, I care.) The goal here is to give you tips that are so cool that after reading just a few you have to pick up the phone, call your Mac buddies, and totally tune them up with your newfound Mac OS X power.

Now, I have to tell you, the tips in this book are designed for people who are already using Mac OS X, so there's not much beginner stuff in here. However, if you are a Mac beginner, I have a special bonus for you—a secret special downloadable chapter of beginner tips that I put together just for you. So technically the tips in this downloadable beginners' chapter are not "Killer Tips," they're Mac OS X beginners' tips written in a Killer Tips style, but hey—they're free, I made them especially for you, and all you have to do is download the PDF chapter from **www.scottkelbybooks.com/begtips.html.** You'll also find downloadable chapters on iTunes and using the Classic environment.

Is this book for you?

Is this book for you? Are you kidding? This book is so for you that if you're reading this in a bookstore, and you don't have the money to buy it, you'll shoplift it—risking possible incarceration, just to unlock the secrets its coated pages hold. But you won't have to shoplift it, because if you're reading a Macintosh book, you bought a Macintosh computer, and that probably means you've got lots of money. So buy at least two copies.

Look, although I don't know you personally, I'm willing to bet you love those little sidebar tips just as much as I do. If you didn't, authors would've stopped adding them to their books years ago. But as much as you love those sidebar tips, you still want something more. That's right—you want visuals. As cool as those sidebar tips are, they're usually just a tiny little box with a couple of lines of text (like the sidebar shown at left). So in this book, I thought I'd expand the explanations just enough to make them more accessible, and then add an accompanying screen capture if (a) it helps make the tip easier to understand, or (b) if the page just looks really boring without them.

Is there any UNIX? It scares me.

Mac OS X is built on UNIX, but don't worry—it pretty much stays out of your way. Here's a way to think of it: The pilots of commercial airliners use engines to fly the plane, right? But if they want to start the engines, they don't climb out on each wing and manually crank them up—they do it from up in the cockpit with a flick of a switch. That's kind of like Mac OS X's relationship with UNIX. You're up front in the cockpit running things, you push Macintosh buttons, and UNIX responds (quite brilliantly, I might add), without you having to get your hands dirty.

The vast majority of people who use Mac OS X will never mess with its UNIX "soul" directly (by "mess with," I mean altering their system by writing UNIX command lines. It's not for the faint of heart, because in some cases if you make a mistake while coding, you can seriously mess up your Mac). That's why I decided not to include UNIX tips in the book—I didn't want to have a situation where the vast majority of the book's readers would see a UNIX chapter and go, "Oh, that's not for me." I wanted everybody to have the chance to use every single tip, in every single chapter.

Okay, how do I get started?

My books aren't set up like a novel—you can jump in anywhere and start on any page. That's true for all of my books, with the notable exception of *Macintosh: The Naked Truth*, which is about what life is really like being a Mac user in a PC-dominated world. I'm not going to try to plug that book here (ISBN 0-7357-1284-0 from New Riders Publishing for around $19.99, found anywhere cool Mac books are sold) because that's just tacky (Amazon.com offers discounts on the book—order yours today). Well, with this book you don't have to start at Chapter 1 and read your way through to the back (although there's nothing wrong with that). Actually, you can start in any chapter and immediately try the tips that interest you the most. Also, don't forget to read each chapter's intro page—it's critical to your understanding of what's in that particular chapter (that's totally not true, but it took me a long time to write those intros, so I use little lies like that to get you to read them. Sad, isn't it?).

Wait! One last thing!

I want to let you know, before you go any further, that the only three sidebar tip "boxes" in the entire book appear in this introduction. So, don't go looking for them because (as I said) the book is made up of sidebar tips without the sidebars. Okay tiger—I'm cuttin' you loose. It's time to go get "tipsy."

> **TIP**
>
> *You're doing it again! Stop looking at these sidebars. See, they're intoxicating—you're drawn to them even after you know it's not really a tip. Okay, here's a real tip: if you like sidebar tips, buy this book.*

Window Wonderland

COOL WINDOW TIPS

I have to be honest with you. I have some major concerns about the subhead for this chapter: "Cool Window Tips." My fear is that you

Window Wonderland

cool window tips

might give it a quick glance and accidentally read it as "Cool Windows Tips," which this chapter, in a Mac OS X book, clearly is not. In fact, this couldn't be a chapter on Microsoft Windows, primarily because I don't know Windows. Well, I know where the Start menu is, and I can launch an application (if it's fairly easy to find), but that's as much as I'm willing to admit (at least without a Congressional subpoena). Besides, how could there be anything cool about Windows? So what is this chapter really about? I was hoping you would know. Hmmmm. This is kind of embarrassing. Okay, I'll take a stab at it—it sounds like it's probably filled with tips on using Finder windows, managing your files within them, and other cool window tips that will amuse your friends and absolutely captivate small children and family pets (except, of course, for fish, who are waiting patiently for you to overfeed them).

  INSTANT SLIDE SHOWS WHEREVER YOU ARE

Let's say you open a window and there are 20 photos in that window. Want to see a quick slide show of those photos? Just press Command-A to select all the photos, then Control-click on any photo and from the contextual menu that appears, choose Slideshow. A full-screen slide show of those photos (complete with a nice smooth dissolve transition) will appear onscreen. If you want to see only some of the photos in a slide

show, instead of selecting all the images, just Command-click on the photos you want in your slide show before Control-clicking on one and choosing Slideshow. To quit the slide show in progress, just press the Escape key on your keyboard.

   MAKING TOOLBAR ICONS STICKY

When you shrink a window in an application (like Mail, Safari, TextEdit, etc.), the buttons on the right side of the interface get hidden and wind up in a pop-up menu (if they didn't, they'd just get squashed together). Some of these buttons you probably don't care

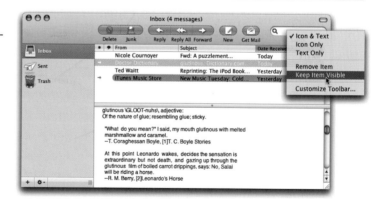

about, but there are others you might prefer stay visible even when shrinking the window quite a bit (for example, when I reduce the size of Mail's window, the Search field gets hidden almost immediately, but I always want that field to stay visible). Luckily, you can decide which icons and tools stay and which get hidden by Control-clicking on the toolbar icon you want to remain visible and choosing Keep Item Visible. Now when you resize the window, that button will stay visible while others are hidden.

SHORTCUT FOR CLOSING THE SIDEBAR

With sidebar

In Panther, where the sidebar was introduced, there was no keyboard shortcut to hide the sidebar, but luckily in Tiger there is—just press Control-Option-Command-T.

Without sidebar

   YOU CAN ALWAYS GO BACK

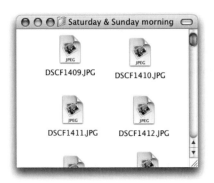

If you have the toolbar hidden in a Finder window, with its all-important Go Back button, you can still go back to the previous window by pressing Command-[(that's the Left Bracket key, which appears diagonally to the left of the Return key on your keyboard).

SEPARATING THE RIFFRAFF IN YOUR TOOLBAR

I remember the first time I saw a separator bar in someone's toolbar. I thought, "This is the slickest person in the world," or maybe it was, "Gee, I wonder how he got that separator!" I can't remember which. Either way, they're handy and look cool. To get yours, just Command-Option-click on the little pill-shaped button in the top right of your title bar to bring up the Customize Toolbar dialog (or Control-click on any empty space in the toolbar and choose Customize Toolbar from the contextual menu). Then, in the collection of icons that appears in the dialog, just drag the Separator icon and drop it right where you want it in the toolbar.

   SIDEBAR'S SPACE-SAVING ICON VIEW

If you think the sidebar takes up a little too much room, you can use its icon view (to display just the icons of items in the sidebar, and not their names, which take up most of the space). To get to this space-saving icons-only view, just click-and-drag the gray divider bar (which separates the sidebar from the folder's contents) to the left, covering the names of the sidebar items, until it "snaps" to the icons, leaving just the icons visible (and their names neatly hidden). If after doing this, you're not sure which file is which, just place your cursor over one of these sidebar icons, and its name will pop up. If you decide you want the full names visible again, click on the bar and drag to the right. When you drag past the longest name in the sidebar list, the divider will gently snap into place.

GETTING RID OF THE PREVIEW COLUMN

If you've used Mac OS X's Column view, you know that when you click on a file, you'll get a large preview of that file in a new column called the Preview column. Click on a graphic— you see its preview. Large! This "feature" annoys the heck out of some people (you know who you are), so to turn off this special column, just view a window in Column view, then press Command-J to bring up the Column View options. Turn off the checkbox for Show Preview Column and this wonderful (yet occasionally annoying) Preview column will disappear.

CONTROLLING WHAT SHOWS UP IN YOUR SIDEBAR

By default, a whole bunch of "stuff" shows up in your sidebar, like your hard disks (including any partitions), your iDisk, network volumes, CDs, DVDs, FireWire drives, etc.; plus in the lower section, your Desktop, Home folder, and Applications folders are all there. In fact, there's so much of "their" stuff, there's not much room for "your" stuff. Luckily, you can decide what appears in the sidebar and what doesn't. Just go under the Finder menu and choose Preferences. When the dialog appears, click on the Sidebar icon (up top) and a list of the default sidebar items appears. Uncheck any items you don't want cluttering up your sidebar.

USING "FAVORITES" IN TIGER

If you're used to how previous versions of Mac OS X handled Favorites, you'll have to get used to a whole new flavor, as those who used Panther well know. First, Apple hid the Favorites folder (I think they did this because they want you to use the sidebar for your favorites, rather than the Favorites folder itself). But if you want the Favorites folder back, look inside your Home folder, inside your Library folder, where you'll find a Favorites folder. Drag this folder to the sidebar of any open Finder window. When you do this, the Favorites folder icon will change to the familiar "red heart" icon, and you can put aliases of your most-used folders and files within this Favorites folder. Then you're only one click away, even in Open/Save dialogs.

   OPENING FOLDERS IN NEW WINDOWS

Personally, I really like the way some things worked back in Mac OS 9. In particular, I liked that when I opened a new folder, a new window opened with the contents of that folder. As you've probably noticed, by default Mac OS X doesn't do that: If you double-click on a folder (in Icon or List view), that folder's contents are revealed in your current window. Well, if you're like me, you'd like these folders to open in their own separate window (as in previous versions of the Mac OS). So go under the Finder menu, under Preferences, click on the General icon at the top of the dialog, and choose Always Open Folders in a New Window. Ahhh, that's better!

NEW WINDOWS FOR FOLDERS, PART 2

If you want to make use of Mac OS X's "everything-opens-in-the-same-window" scheme, but occasionally you want to open a folder in its own separate window, just hold the Command key and then double-click on the folder. Hold Option-Command, and you can have the new window open *and* have the old window close automatically.

  NEW WINDOWS FOR FOLDERS, PART 3

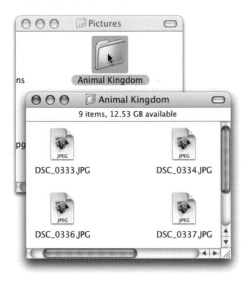

If you're working in a window while in Icon or List view and you want folders to open in their own separate window, just select a folder and press Option-Command-T (the shortcut for Hide Toolbar). This will hide both the toolbar and the sidebar, and by doing so, all folders that you double-click on will now open in their own separate window.

   KNOW YOUR STATUS (ANY TIME, IN ANY WINDOW)

The status bar (the thin little bar that shows how many items are in your window and how much drive space you still have available) was at the top of every Finder window back in Mac OS 9. In earlier versions of Mac OS X (including Jaguar), the status bar was off by default, so you had to turn it on, and then it appeared at the top of your Finder windows. In Tiger you'll find the status bar info displayed at the bottom center of every Finder window by default (well, that's true as long as your toolbar is visible). If that's the case, why is there still a menu command called Show Status Bar? That's because, if you hide the toolbar, it hides the status info at the bottom of the window, so you need the old status bar back. It's still off by default, so to turn on the status bar, first open a window, hide the toolbar (see previous tip), then go under the View menu and choose Show Status Bar. (*Note:* If you don't hide the toolbar first, Show Status Bar will appear "grayed out.")

Old status bar

New "old" status bar

SPEED TIP: FASTER FULL-NAME VIEWING IN LIST VIEW

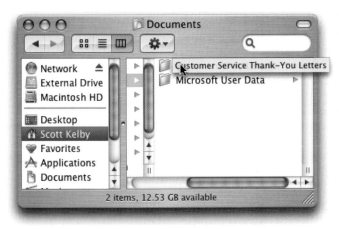

When you're looking for files in either List view or Column view, it's almost certain that some of your files with long names will have some letters (or even full words) cut off from view. Here is a tip that will save you from having to resize your List or Column view columns—just hold your cursor over the file's truncated name for a few seconds and eventually its full name will pop up. So what's the problem? The "few seconds" part. Instead, hold the Option key, then put your cursor over the file's name, and its full name will appear instantly.

   HIDING THE TOOLBAR WHEN YOU DON'T NEED IT

If you don't want the toolbar showing all the time (or at all for that matter), you can hide it by simply clicking on the white pill-shaped button on the top right of the window's title bar (or you can use the keyboard shortcut Command-Option-T). *Note:* This also hides the sidebar.

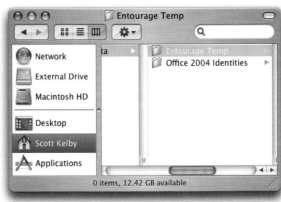

With toolbar

Without toolbar

IN LOVE WITH COLUMN VIEW? MAKE IT A PERMANENT THING

Since Icon view and List view have been around for over a decade, it's not surprising that many long-time Mac users absolutely fall head-over-heels in love with Mac OS X's lovely Column view. If you're one of those lovelorn users, you can request that all new windows automatically open in Column view. Just go under the Finder menu, under Preferences, and click on the checkbox for Open New Windows in Column View. This turns every new window into a moment of unbridled passion that knows no bounds. Well, it does for some people anyway.

HOW TO MAKE THE SIDEBAR WORK LIKE THE DOCK

In this chapter, I show how you can customize the toolbar using the Customize Toolbar command; but you can also customize the sidebar, by adding other icons that make it even more powerful. For example, if you use Photoshop a lot, just open the window where your Photoshop application resides, drag the Photoshop icon right over to the sidebar, and the other icons in the sidebar will slide out of the way. Now you can use this window kind of like you would the Dock—to launch Photoshop, just click on its icon in the sidebar. Plus, like the Dock, you can even drag-and-drop images you want to open right onto the sidebar's Photoshop icon.

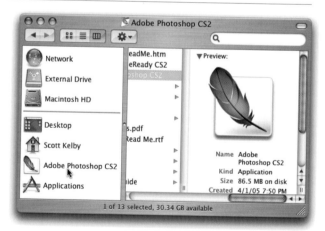

THE ULTIMATE CUSTOMIZE TOOLBAR SHORTCUT

If you want to customize the items in your toolbar (and there's nothing wrong with that), just Command-Option-click the little white pill-shaped button at the top right of your window's title bar, and the Customize Toolbar dialog will appear, right there in your window. Now you can just drag-and-drop icons onto the toolbar.

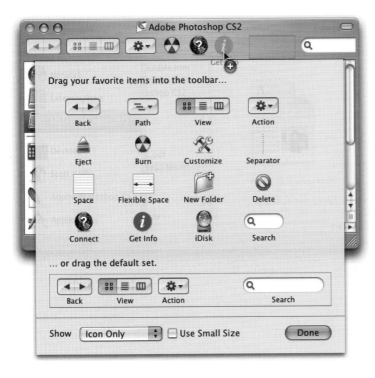

TOO MANY ICONS IN YOUR TOOLBAR? SHRINK 'EM

The toolbar icons are fairly large, taking up considerable space both vertically and horizontally. If you add a few extra icons to the toolbar, the additional icons could wind up being hidden from view. What can you do? Well, you can have the toolbar display just the icons, which shrinks the space between the icons by removing the text. To display the toolbar items by icon, rather than by icon and text, Control-click anywhere within the toolbar and choose Icon Only. If you really want to shrink the toolbar to its bare minimum, try Text Only. For even more space-saving options, try Command-clicking on the white pill-shaped button in the upper right-hand corner of the Finder window. Each time you click, you get a new space-saving look.

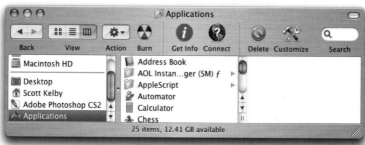

Icon & Text view

Icon view

Text view

FIXING THE WORLD'S WORST KEYBOARD SHORTCUT

Prior to Mac OS X (and for all prior Macintosh history), to create a new folder you'd press Command-N. It was simple. It made sense. It was perfect. Obviously it was too perfect, so when Mac OS X came along, Apple changed the shortcut to Command-Shift-N. I've never gotten over that. But in Tiger, I (you, we) can bring back peace and Command-N harmony. Here's how: Go under the System Preferences, and click on the Keyboard & Mouse icon. When the preferences appear, click the Keyboard Shortcut tab on the far right. Just under the shortcuts window on the left side, there's a plus (+) sign. Click on it and a dialog will drop down. For Application choose Finder. In the Menu Title field, type "New Folder." Click in the Keyboard Shortcut field and press "Command-N," and then click Add. Now, do it all again—click the plus sign, choose Finder as your Application, but for Menu Title type "New Finder Window" and for Keyboard Shortcut enter "Command-Shift-N." Click Add, close the System Preferences, and restart your Mac. From now on, Command-N will create a new folder (hallelujah!) and Command-Shift-N will open the much more seldom-used New Finder Window.

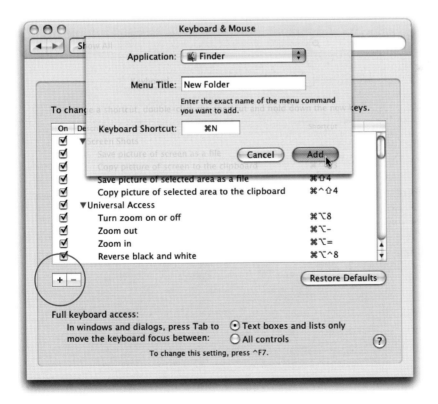

SPEED TIP: CREATING NEW FOLDERS

Okay, so Apple took our beloved "Command-N-creates-a-new-folder" keyboard shortcut from us, but that doesn't keep us from being one click away from a new folder. If you don't want to try the previous tip, try this: Just Command-Option-click on the little white pill-shaped button in the top right of a window's title bar to bring up the Customize Toolbar dialog. Drag the New Folder icon up to your toolbar, and then you're one click away from a new folder anytime you need one.

WHERE DID THAT DOWNLOAD COME FROM?

If you download a file from the Web, you can usually find out exactly where that downloaded file came from (including the exact Web address) by pressing Command-I when you have the file selected. Once the Info dialog appears, click on the right-facing arrow beside More Info to expand that panel, and it will display a Where From header, and to the right of that it will show the exact Web address from which the file was originally downloaded.

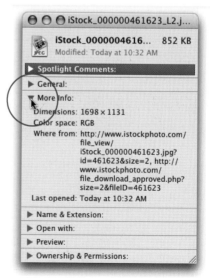

GETTING BACK TO YOUR TOOLBAR DEFAULTS

If you've made a total mess of your toolbar, there's no button for returning the icons to the default set, but getting them back there is fairly easy. First, Command-Option-click on the white pill-shaped button at the top right of your window's title bar to bring up the Customize Toolbar dialog. In the bottom left of the Customize Toolbar dialog, you'll see a set called "the default set." Drag-and-drop it on the toolbar in the top of the Finder window and it will replace the current icons in your toolbar.

   REARRANGING THE HEADERS IN LIST VIEW

Okay, let's say you're in List view and you decide that you want the Size column to appear right after the Name column. You can make it so. Just click directly on the header named Size and drag it horizontally along the bar until it appears right after Name. You can do the same with the other headers—move 'em where you want 'em. There's only one you can't move—the Name header. It's stuck in the first position.

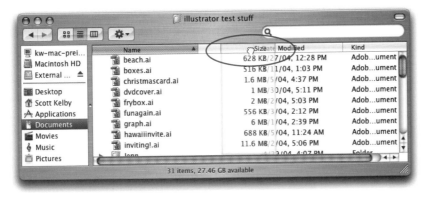

  HOW DO YOU WANT YOUR WINDOWS TO LOOK?

While most of Tiger's settings are done in the System Preferences dialog, you can set up how you want your windows to look by actually moving, stretching, adjusting, and generally setting up a window the way you want it manually, and then closing it. From that point on, all windows will follow the example of that default window. Here's how it's done: Start by pressing Command-N to open a New Finder Window (or if you changed this shortcut, as mentioned in a previous tip, press that shortcut). Now, the rest is up to you—make the window whichever size you'd like (grab the bottom-right corner and drag); leave the sidebar visible (or hide it by double-clicking the little dot on the divider bar); choose Icon, List, or Column view; click the white pill-shaped button in the top-right corner to hide the toolbar (or don't if you want to keep it); and when you're done tweaking things to your personal liking, don't do anything else (don't open any folders or launch a document)—just close the window. That's it—you've set your new window preferences. By the way—you can customize your hard disk's window the same way. (*Note:* If you set it to open List or Icon view, make sure that the Open New Windows in Column View checkbox in the General Finder Preferences is turned off.)

Before customizing

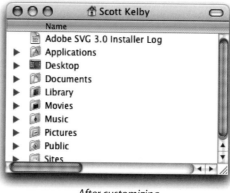

After customizing

STOP THE SCROLLING BLUES

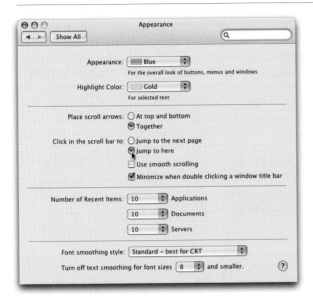

If you don't like sliding the scroll bar up and down in your documents, you can turn on a feature called Jump to Here, which lets you jump to any position in the scroll bar by just clicking on it (rather than using the scroll handles themselves). To turn this on, go under the Apple menu, under System Preferences, and click on the Appearance icon. When the Appearance pane appears, for the setting called Click in the Scroll Bar To, choose Jump to Here.

  ## ANOTHER ANTI-SCROLL BAR TIP

Speaking of hating to use the scroll bars, you can always use the Page Up/Page Down keys on your keyboard to move up and down when you're in List or Icon views. Hey, think of it this way—your hands are already resting on the keyboard—now you don't have to grab the mouse at all. (*Note:* If you have a PowerBook, hold the FN key and then press the Up Arrow key for Page Up and the Down Arrow key for Page Down.)

DON'T LIKE LABELS? TRY COMMENTS INSTEAD

If you're not a big fan of labels (color-coding files and folders by adding a ring of color around their name), you might want to try adding a comment instead. A comment is like your own personal note added to a file or folder. These comments are visible in Finder windows set to List view. To add a comment (your personal note) to a file, just click on the file you want to add a comment to, and then press Command-I. The Info dialog will appear. Click on the right-facing triangle to the left of the words "Spotlight Comments" to reveal a field for entering your personal notes. Just click in this field and start typing. When you're done, close the window. To see your comments when in List view, you first have to change a preference setting to make the Comments column visible. Make sure you're viewing your window in List view, and then press Command-J to bring up the View Options dialog. In the section called Show Columns, turn on the checkbox for Comments. If you want every window in List view to show comments (not just the currently active window), make sure you check the All Windows button at the top of the dialog.

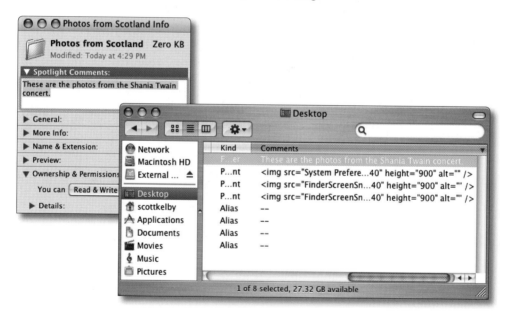

ADDING A PHOTO AS YOUR WINDOW'S BACKGROUND

As long as your Finder window is in Icon view, you can add a photo as its background. You do this by going under the View menu, under Show View Options, and in the Background section (at the bottom of the dialog) choose Picture. Click on the Select button and the standard Open dialog will appear in which you can choose the image you'd like to appear as the background of your window. Click OK and that image will appear. *Note:* This works only when viewing the window in Icon view. If you change to List view, the image will no longer be visible.

   CONTROL WHAT HAPPENS WHEN YOU DOUBLE-CLICK A TITLE BAR

Back in OS 9, you could double-click on a window's title bar, and that window would "roll up," leaving just the window's title bar visible. In OS X, this roll-up feature has been replaced by "minimizing to the Dock," so if you double-click on a window's title bar, it minimizes that window to the Dock. If you want to minimize all your open windows, Option-double-click on any title bar. As cool as this sounds, this "double-click-to-minimize" feature drives some people crazy, because they're constantly minimizing windows when they just meant to move them. If that sounds like you, go to the System Preferences, under Appearance, and turn off Minimize when Double Clicking a Window Title Bar.

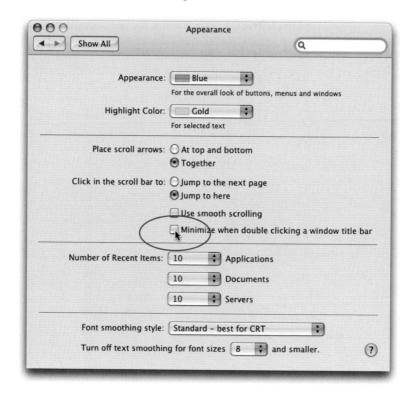

HIDING THE ICONS IN COLUMN VIEW

When you're viewing a Finder window in Column view, you might find it looks cleaner (and less intimidating) if you turn off the tiny little icons that appear before each file's name. To do that, make sure you're viewing a window in Column view, then press Command-J to bring up the View Options. In the View Options dialog, turn off the checkbox for Show Icons, and the little rascals will be hidden from view, leaving you with a cleaner, less cluttered Column view. The downside? With the icons turned off, it's not easy to tell a folder from a hard drive from a file, but it sure is a fun diversion on a boring day. (Actually, this probably should have been in the "Mac OS X Pranks" chapter.)

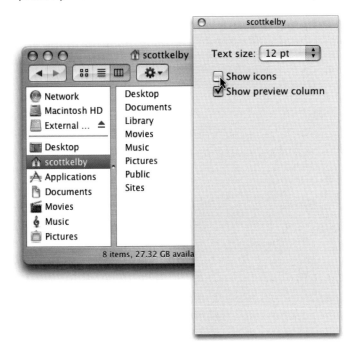

HOW TO TELL IF SNAP TO GRID IS TURNED ON

If you're wondering whether you have
Snap to Grid turned on (found by pressing Command-J) for a particular window
that's in Icon view, just look in the bottom
left-hand corner of the window (just below
the sidebar). If Snap to Grid is turned on
for that particular window, you'll see a
tiny grid icon. If Keep Arranged By Name
is turned on instead, you'll see four tiny
evenly spaced folder icons.

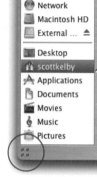

Snap to Grid icon   *Keep Arranged By
Name icon*

HOW TO SEE IF YOU CAN WRITE TO A FOLDER

Mac OS X has a level of security
called "Permissions," and if a
network administrator set up
your Mac, chances are there
are certain folders you're not
allowed to save your files into
(it's that whole "power trip"
thing). So how do you know if
you have permission to write
to a particular folder? In Icon or
List view, where the icons are
pretty large, it's easy—if you
can't write to it, the icon has
a red circle with a dash inside

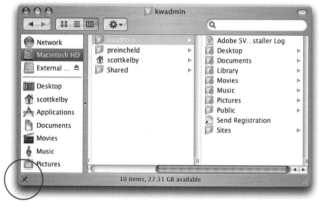

of it. However, when you're looking in Column view, it's not as obvious because the icons
are so small, but if you just click on the folder and then look in the bottom left-hand corner
of the Finder window (just below the sidebar), you'll know. If you see a pencil icon with an
"oh-no-you-don't" line through it, you don't have permission to write to that folder. This is
why so many network administrators one day wind up having an "accident."

BEATING THE ALPHABETICAL TRAP

Want a particular file to appear at the top of your list when sorting in List view by Name? Just type a blank space in front of its name, and it will jump to the top of the list (in the capture shown here, after adding a space before "Winter Report," the document now appears at the top of the alphabetical list instead of the bottom).

   SAVE TIME WHEN CHANGING VIEWS OF MULTIPLE WINDOWS

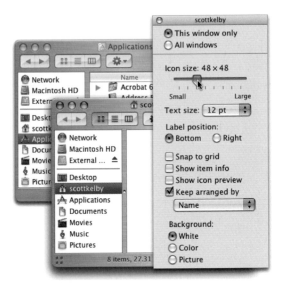

Back in previous versions of the Mac OS, every time you wanted to adjust the View Options for a window, you had to open the View Options dialog. So, if you wanted to adjust 10 windows, you had to open and close View Options 10 times. It was mind-numbing. Now, in Mac OS X, you can leave the View Options dialog open the whole time and adjust as many windows as you want. You can click on the window whose settings you want to see in the View Options, press Command-J to open the dialog, make your changes, close that Finder window (or leave it open), then click on the next window and make changes there—all without ever closing the View Options window. The View Options window always stays in front.

EXPOSÉ SHOW-OFF TRICK #1

Showing off Exposé to a friend or co-worker who uses a PC is more than a blast, it's your duty, because even Windows XP still has nothing like it. But if you really want to be a major hambone, before you press F9 to invoke Exposé, start a QuickTime movie clip, have a DVD playing, or have iTunes playing a song and click on the Visualizer (heck, have all three going at once). When you press F9, the QuickTime clip (DVD, iTunes, etc.) keeps playing even when miniaturized. It's fun to watch their face as it changes from "Cool!" to "Why doesn't Windows have that?"

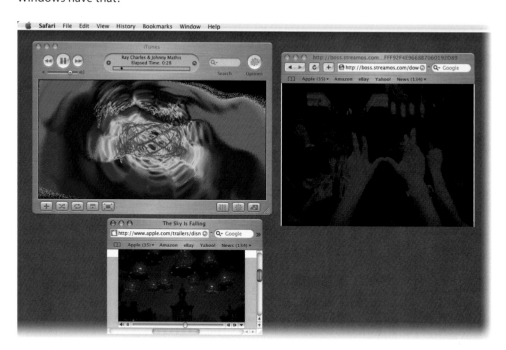

   EXPOSÉ SHOW-OFF TRICK #2

After you show your friends Exposé, give 'em the "instant replay" to really seal the deal— hold the Shift key then press F9, and it gives you a slow-motion version of the Exposé effect, which reminds your friends yet again of how cool you've now become. (By the way, this hold the Shift key slo-mo effect works in other places. Try minimizing a window to the Dock holding the Shift key. Again, totally for show, but "the show must go on!")

USING EXPOSÉ WITHOUT PRESSING A BUTTON

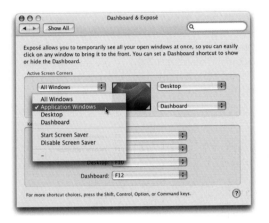

You don't have to use F9, F10, or F11 to invoke Exposé. Instead, many people prefer to simply move their cursor to the corner of their screen to have Exposé "do its thing." So which corner of the screen does which Exposé feat of magic? That's up to you. You set your "hot corners" for each of Exposé's modes by going under the Apple menu, under System Preferences, and choosing Dashboard & Exposé. In the Active Screen Corners section you'll see a small preview of your screen with a pop-up menu beside each corner. Just choose which Exposé mode you want assigned to each corner from these pop-down menus. At the bottom of this preference pane is an area where you can also assign different Exposé keyboard shortcuts (rather than the standard F9, F10, F11 variety).

   ## THE TWO-BUTTON MOUSE EXPOSÉ EXPERIENCE

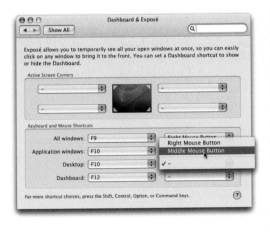

If you're using a two-button mouse, you can access a new world of Exposé functionality that dare not speak its name. For now, my friends, you can use the second mouse button to invoke your favorite Exposé mode. Have you got more than two mouse buttons? Four perhaps? (You decadent American!) Then go under the Apple menu, under System Preferences, and click on Dashboard & Exposé. If your "rich-socialite multi-button mouse" is connected, you'll see a new Mouse section has been added to the Keyboard options for Exposé preferences in Tiger, enabling you to assign various Exposé functions to your various buttons. Just choose your mouse options from the second column of pop-up menus on the right in the Keyboard & Mouse Shortcuts section.

  SWITCHING APPS WITHIN EXPOSÉ

Once you have Exposé invoked (you pressed either F9 or F10), you can toggle through your open applications and Finder windows by pressing the Tab key. Press the Tab key once and the next open application and its miniaturized windows come to the front. Press Tab again, it goes to the next open app. Want the previous app? Press Shift-Tab.

GETTING MORE INFO IN COLUMN VIEW

In Tiger, Apple makes it easy to get more information on your files when you're working in Column view. Now just click on a file while in Column view and a More Info button will appear. Click on this button, and it opens the standard Info dialog, where you can access all the background info on your selected file.

  NARROWING YOUR TOOLBAR SEARCHES

If you use the Search field that appears in the top-right corner of the Finder window's toolbar, you have a little more control over your search than you might think. For example, now when you type in the Search field, you're enabling Spotlight. As soon as you start typing letters, Spotlight begins searching. But if you look in the Finder window, below the title bar, you'll see a gray bar of buttons that potentially speed up your search by letting you narrow (or expand) areas in which you want Spotlight to search.

   ONE-CLICK LONG-FILE-NAME FIX

If you're working in a window set to Column view, you're going to run into this all the time—files with long names have the end of their names cut off from view, because the column isn't wide enough. That doesn't sound like that big of a problem, until you start working with more descriptive file names, and

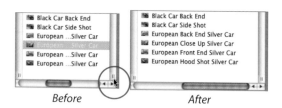

Before   After

you can't see which file is "European Front End Silver Car" and which is "European Back End Silver Car" because everything from "European" to "Silver Car" is cut off. Luckily, there's a quick fix—just double-click on the little tab at the bottom of the vertical column divider bar, and the column will expand just enough so you can see even the longest file name of any file in that column. Option-double-click on the tab, and every column expands to show the longest name in each column. Pretty darn sweet!

   EXPOSÉ BUTTON TIPS

In an earlier tip, I mentioned that you invoke the cool Exposé feature by pressing F9, F10, or F11. But did you know it's how you press those keys that determines how Exposé works? For example, if you press and release the F9 key, Exposé freezes the thumbnails in place, and

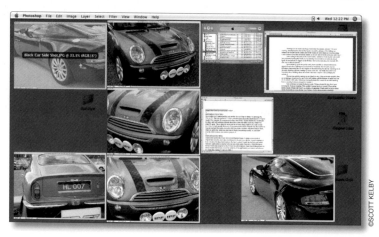

will continue to freeze them there until you either click on a window or press F9 again. This is ideal for when you're not sure which window you want so you need time to look around. However, if you press-and-hold F9, Exposé only stays active as long as you hold the button down (or until you click a window, whichever comes first), which is perfect for when you just want to look at something quickly, or you know exactly which window you want to jump to.

⬤ **EXPOSÉ MOUSE TIPS**

I mentioned earlier that if you have a multi-button mouse, it opens a new world of Exposé functionality, and I also mentioned (in the previous tip) that Exposé responds to how you press the keys that invoke it. So, here's a cool Exposé tip that lets you switch from one application to another with just one click (rather than two). Click whichever mouse button you assigned to the F9 function (All Windows), then keep holding down the mouse button and release it over the window of the application you want to switch to—it's super fast, 'cause it's just one click.

Show Me the Way

NAVIGATING ESSENTIALS

The title of this chapter, "Show Me the
Way," is an obvious tribute to musician

Peter Frampton. I feel that I owe him this tribute

Show Me the Way
navigating essentials

because one day I received an email from a reader

of one of my other books leading me to a website

about Peter Frampton. On the site, Peter names his

favorite movies, books, albums, etc., and among

his favorite books he listed my book Photoshop

Down & Dirty Tricks. *Of course, being a Frampton*

fan myself, I was really tickled, and learning this

has changed my life in immeasurable ways. For

example, if Peter Frampton (who is currently

touring, by the way) is appearing in concert at any

nearby venue, I can just drop by the box office, pay

the admission price, and they'll give me a ticket to

his upcoming performance. Not only that, but if I

go to the local record store and try to buy any Peter

Frampton CD (including his classic "Frampton

Comes Alive" double-album set), they'll let me. No

questions asked. All I have to present is my ID and

credit card. How cool is that?

  ● **MOVING THE SLIDE SHOW CONTROLS**

When you create a slide show—
either from images you selected in a
Finder window (and chose Slideshow
from the Action pop-up menu), or
from the results of a Spotlight search
(by clicking on the Play button)—
once the slideshow is running, the
slide show controller will appear at
the bottom of the screen if you move
your mouse. If you'd like to move the
controller, just click on it and drag it
wherever you'd like it. However, I just
want you to know that your move

only lasts as long as the current slide show. When you start your next slide show, the controller
will be right back at the bottom again. *Note:* Click on the thin vertical lines when you select the
controller—that way you don't accidentally click on a button.

   HOW TO MAKE WIDGETS LAND WHERE YOU WANT 'EM

When you click on a widget in the Widget Bar, that widget appears in the center of your
screen every time. However, if you know where you want your widget to live, just drag it
from the Widget Bar and drop it right where you want it.

Widget automatically centered

Drag-and-drop it where you want it

MAKING ZIP FILES (COMPRESSED FILES) IN ONE CLICK

One of my favorite Mac OS X features is the ability to create ZIP compressed files from within the OS (basically, this shrinks the file size, ideal for files you're going to email—smaller file sizes mean faster file transfers). To create a compressed file, either Control-click on the file and choose Create Archive (which is Apple-speak for "make a compressed ZIP file"). Or you can click on a file, then go to the Action menu (the button that looks like a gear up in the Finder window's toolbar), and choose Create Archive from there. Either way, it quickly creates a new file, with the file extension ".zip." This is the compressed file. You can also compress several different files (like three, for example) into one single archive file—just Command-click (or Shift-click contiguous files) on all the files you want included, then choose Create Archive of X Items from the Action menu. A file will be created named "Archive.zip" (that's it!). By the way, if someone sends you a ZIP file, don't sweat it—just double-click it and Tiger will automatically decompress it.

MOVE ALL YOUR STUFF TO ANOTHER MAC—QUICK!

In the past, if you bought a new Mac, moving all your files, music, photos, and well…everything from your old Mac to your new Mac was quite a production, and I saw it reduce many an NFL lineman to tears. Well, in Tiger, that's all a thing of the past. Now, when it's time to make the "big move," just connect the two Macs with a FireWire cable, then go to your new Mac and look inside the Applications folder, then go to the Utilities folder, where you'll find an application called Migra-

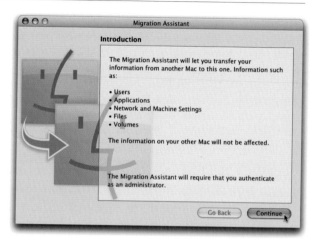

tion Assistant. Double-click on it and since it's an assistant, it will lead you through a series of screens with questions about what you want to do (don't worry, they're pretty simple questions; however, some of the most critical questions are entirely in French. Kidding). That's it—answer the questions and it'll make the move (including copying your settings for things like email, bookmarks, and more).

   ## SEARCHING BY COLOR LABEL

Besides the visual benefits of having certain files tagged with a Color Label, there's a hidden benefit: You can search for files by their color. For example, let's say you misplaced an important file for a project you were working on. You can press Command-F to bring up the Find function, and from the top-left pop-up menu, choose Color Label. Then, click on the color

for the files you labeled in that project, and it will instantly find and display all the files with that color. Searching by color—only Apple is cool enough to come up with a search like this!

CREATING YOUR OWN LABEL NAMES

Don't like the names Apple created for the colors used in the Color Labels feature? Then just create your own by going under the Finder menu and choosing Preferences (or use the keyboard shortcut Command-, [that's the Comma key]). When the dialog appears, click on the Labels tab along the top, and you'll see a field beside each color where you can input custom names. This is great for designating a color for "Hot Projects" or "Back up These Files," or perhaps a project name like "Cross Catalog" or "Vegas Blackjack Table Scam."

HIDDEN COLUMN VIEW NAVIGATION TIP

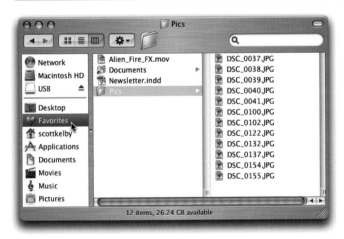

Here's somewhat of a weird problem (and a simple fix): Let's say you have your Favorites folder in your sidebar, and you click on it to get to some of your favorite files. If you're viewing all this in Column view, the first column winds up being the contents of your Favorites. You can't scroll to a column farther back (like to your Library folder, which holds your Favorites folder or to your Home folder, or Users folder, etc.). Well, you can't unless you know this hidden little tip: Just hold the Command key and press the Up Arrow key on your keyboard. Each time you press it, it moves you back farther, so instead of hitting "the wall" when you're in the Favorites column, now you can keep going back as far as you want. *Note:* This works in any viewing mode.

ADDING AUTOMATION THROUGH FOLDER ACTIONS

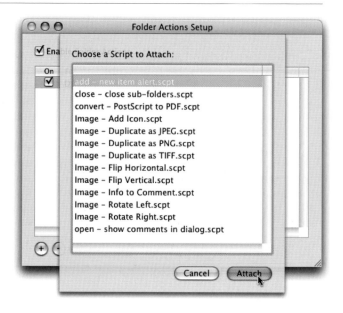

At the office, I'm on a network and I have a Drop Box where my co-workers (freaks that they are) can send me files. However, for a long time, if a freak put something in my Drop Box, I wouldn't know it unless they called or emailed me and told me so. But now anytime one of them drops something in my Drop Box, a message dialog appears that says, "Something freaky is in your Drop Box." This is a simple AppleScript (think of an AppleScript as a built-in automation for your Mac, just like Photoshop actions add automation to Adobe Photoshop). Mac OS X includes some cool sample scripts (actions), or you can download about a bazillion from the Web for free.

To assign a script to a folder, Control-click on that folder and choose Configure Folder Actions from the contextual menu that appears. This brings up the Folder Actions Setup dialog, where you toggle various scripts assigned to folders on and off, or even edit scripts (if you know how to write AppleScripts). Click the plus sign (+) button at the bottom left of the dialog to add your folder to the list (this actually brings up a standard Open dialog showing your folder, so click on your folder in the dialog and click Open). Once you do this, a window will pop down with a list of built-in sample scripts you can assign to this folder, and their names give a cryptic description of what they do. Pick the one that sounds like what you want to do (to replicate my Drop Box warning, choose "add—new item alert .scpt") and click the Attach button (you'll see your newly assigned script appear in the column on the right of the dialog). Now click the Enable Folder Actions checkbox at the top-left corner of the dialog. This is a global on/off switch, so any folder to which you've attached scripts is now "activated."

By the way, once you've applied actions to a folder, you can turn Folder Actions on or off globally by Control-clicking on any folder and choosing Enable Folder Actions or Disable Folder Actions from the contextual menu.

POWER COPY-AND-PASTE

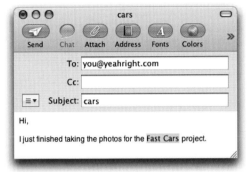

In previous versions of Mac OS X (and Mac OS 9 for that matter), if you clicked on a file, copied it (Command-C), then opened an application (like Mail) and pasted it (Command-V), it would only paste that file's name, which is just this side of worthless. Now, in some applications it pastes the actual file, so you can copy-and-paste a file from a Finder window or the desktop right into your application. Okay, so what if you do want just the name (which happens from time to time)? Just click directly on the selected file's name (to highlight it) and press Command-C to copy it. Now you're copying just the name. It's a Power Pasting thing!

DRAG-AND-DROP DESKTOP PRINTING

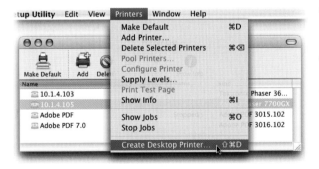

Want the ability to print a document right from your desktop (without opening the application first)? Go under the Apple menu, under System Preferences, and choose Print & Fax. When the preference pane appears, click on the Printer Setup button, and when the Printer Info dialog appears, press Command-L to show the Printer List dialog. Your printer will appear in this dialog. Click on it, then go up under the Printers menu (in the menu bar) and choose Create Desktop Printer. A standard Open/Save dialog will appear asking you where you want to save it (I save mine on the desktop). Click Save and an icon for your printer will appear on the desktop. To print a document, just drag-and-drop it on this icon. Some documents, such as TextEdit files and PDFs, will go straight to the printer. Other files will launch their default application and open the Print dialog.

PRINTING FROM THE DESKTOP (WITHOUT A DESKTOP PRINTER)

Don't want a printer icon cluttering up your desktop, but you still want to print files from the desktop, or a Finder window (kind of greedy, aren't you)? Then try this little trick: Control-click on the file you want to print to bring up a contextual menu. Now just choose Print from the menu. (Or you can click on Other, then use a standard Open dialog to navigate to the Printer Setup Utility—it's inside the Applications folder, within the Utilities folder.) Once you choose it, it will either start printing or take you directly to the default application's Print dialog.

   COPY AND DELETE AT THE SAME TIME

If you're archiving a file to disk (let's say to an external FireWire drive for example), you can drag the icon of the file you want to archive directly to that drive and the Mac will write a copy to that drive. However, your original file still lives on your current hard drive. If you want to have that file

deleted from your drive as soon as it's copied to another drive, just hold the Command key as you drag your icon, and the Mac will do two tasks for you—copy the file to the new drive and delete the original from your drive.

CLEANING UP WINDOWS, ONE ICON AT A TIME

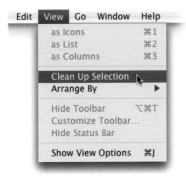

Want to bring some order back to your icons? Just hold the Command key while dragging any icon, and when you release the mouse button, it will automatically snap to an invisible alignment grid, helping, once again, to keep your icons tidy and organized. See, Mac OS X cares. Another way to "clean up," icon-by-icon, is to click on the icon(s) you want aligned, and then choose Clean Up Selection from the View menu.

   HOW TO CHANGE A FILE'S ICON

Just as in previous versions of the Mac OS, if you don't like a file's icon, you can change it. (Check out www.iconfactory.com or www.xicons.com. They both have fantastic selections of photo-quality Mac OS X icons ready to download.) To copy an icon from one file to another, just click on the icon you want to copy and press Command-I to bring up its Info dialog. At the top, click on the tiny icon to the left of the file's name then press Command-C to copy that icon into memory. Then go to the file whose icon you'd like to replace, press Command-I to bring up its Info dialog, click on its existing tiny little icon, then just press Command-V to paste the new icon over the old icon. That's it! Piece of cake. Can of corn. Etc.

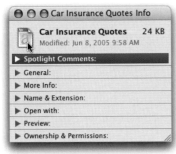

Before

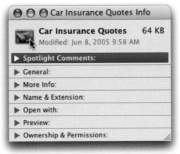

After

 DON'T LIKE YOUR NEW CUSTOM ICON? CHANGE IT BACK

If you've added a custom icon to one of your files and later grow tired of it (custom icons sometimes do get old, just like songs on the radio. You love 'em the first time you hear 'em, but then after hearing it for about the 200th time, the song you once loved is now so…played), then just click on the icon, press Command-I, click on the icon in the top-left corner then press Command-X, and the file's original icon will pop back into place (no radio pun intended).

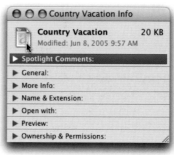

Before   *After*

 SEE YOUR FILE'S HIDDEN INFO

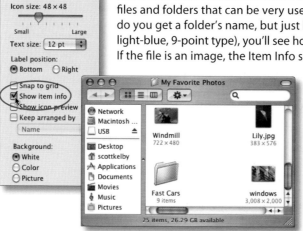

Want more info on your files than the standard Icon view provides (after all, it just gives you the file's name in Icon view)? Then turn on Show Item info. This adds an extra line of information below many files and folders that can be very useful. For example, now not only do you get a folder's name, but just below the name (in unobtrusive light-blue, 9-point type), you'll see how many items are in that folder. If the file is an image, the Item Info shows you how big it is. MP3 files show how long the song is, etc. To turn on Item Info for your current Finder window, press Command-J to bring up its View Options. Then turn on the checkbox for Show Item Info. If you want to show the item info for every window (globally), then choose the All Windows button at the top of the dialog.

EJECTING DISCS FROM THE SIDEBAR

You'll notice when you insert some kind of removable media into your Mac (removable media is geek-speak for CDs, DVDs, FireWire or USB drives, digital camera memory cards, etc.), a micro-icon (I'm not sure that's what they're really called) appears to the right of its name in the sidebar of your Finder window. These are actually buttons, and they're there to save you time and trouble. For example, next to removable drives, that little icon is an Eject button. Click it, and it ejects that drive or CD or whatever (this beats the heck out of dragging the disc down to the Eject icon in the Dock). If you insert a blank CD or DVD, you'll see a little "nuclear" warning sign. This is a Burn icon that lets you burn (write) info to that disc.

INSTANTLY FIND THE ORIGINAL FOR ANY ALIAS

Since an alias is just a copy of the file's icon (not the actual file itself), you may need to find the original at times. To do that, just click on the alias, press Command-R, and the "real" file will appear onscreen in its Finder window.

   CREATING ALIASES WITHOUT THE WORD "ALIAS"

Do you find it as annoying as I do that Mac OS X adds the word "alias" every time you create an alias? (I know, previous versions of the Mac OS did that as well, and it annoyed me there too.) Well, you can bypass the "adding-the-word-alias" uglies altogether by holding the Option and Command keys and clicking-and-dragging the original file outside the Finder window it's currently in (I usually just drag mine to the desktop). This creates an alias without the word "alias" attached.

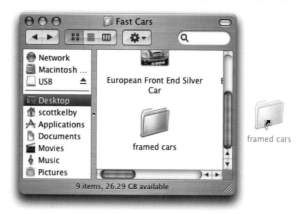

(*Note:* Don't worry, you'll still know it's an alias, because its icon will have a tiny arrow at the bottom left-hand corner.)

   ADDING WORDS TO THE END OF FILE NAMES

In Tiger, if you want to add to an existing file's name (for example, if you had a Photoshop file named "Hawaii Collage" and you wanted to add the words "Summer 2005" to the end), you don't have to be in a certain viewing mode—just click on the icon to highlight it and press Return, then press the Right Arrow key to jump to the end of the existing name. Then all you have to do is type "Summer 2005." Press the Return key again to

lock in your new name. *Note:* To add characters at the beginning of the name, do the same routine—just press the Left Arrow instead.

MOVING ICON NAMES TO THE SIDE: IT'S UNNATURAL

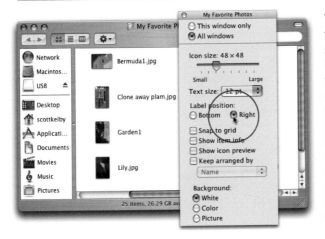

You do not want to mess with this, because an icon's name is supposed to appear beneath the icon. It has been this way since the beginning of Mac-time, and moving the name to the right of the icon, rather than the time-honored tradition of appearing below it, is just plain sick. It's twisted, odd, and unnatural. It's not only weird and perverse—it's perverse *and* weird. Nevertheless, here's how to do it: Just open a Finder window, click on the Icon view button in the toolbar,

then press Command-J to bring up the View Options. Under Label Position choose Right, and the name of each icon will appear to the right of the icon (Yeecch!), and then click on the All Windows checkbox. However, "right is wrong!" Just so you know.

 EJECTING A BLANK DISC

If you've inserted a blank CD or DVD into your Mac, when you look in the Finder window sidebar, you'll see a Burn icon next to your blank disc—not an Eject icon like with other removable media. So how do you eject the disc from there? Just click on the Burn icon. Yes, this brings up the Burn dialog, but on the left side of this dialog is a big ol' Eject button that you can click to eject this blank media.

NAMING SHORTCUTS

If you're naming a number of files with similar names (such as Spain Trip 1, Spain Trip 2, Spain Trip 3, etc.), you can save time by highlighting the words "Spain Trip" and pressing Command-C to copy those words to the Clipboard. Then, when you come to the next icon you want to rename, just press Return to highlight its name, press Command-V to paste in the words "Spain Trip," then press

the Right Arrow key, enter a space, and enter the number for this file (like 4), and so on. You can also copy-and-paste a name from one folder to another, as long as these two identically named folders don't wind up in the same folder. That's a big no-no, and you will be severely disciplined if that should happen (or at least a mean warning dialog will appear).

   STEAL A FILE'S NAME, THEN SAVE RIGHT OVER IT

If you're saving a file, you can use the name of an existing file by just clicking on it in the Save dialog navigation window. Even if the file is grayed out, you can still click on it, and when you do, its name appears as your new file name at the top of the Save dialog. This is a huge timesaver. When you click Save, it will ask you if you want to replace it with the file you're saving. However, if you're saving a different version of a file and all you want to do is add a version number (like "Brochure Inside Cover 2"), you'd just click on the existing file named "Brochure Inside Cover" in the Save dialog, and once the name appears as your new file name, just type a 2.

MENU SPEED TIP

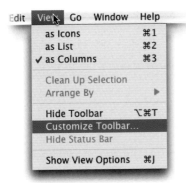

Getting right to the menu item you want fast can save loads of time (since we spend so much time digging around in menus all day). That's why you'll love this tip. The next time you're in a menu, instead of mousing down to the item you want to select, just press the first letter of the command you want and that command becomes selected. For example, to select the Customize Toolbar command, click once on the View menu, press C, and then press Return. That's speed menus, baby! By the way, if there are two commands that start with the same letter, type the first few letters of the command you want.

   FIND THE HIDDEN "GO TO" FIELD

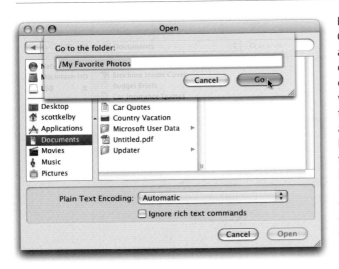

In earlier versions of Mac OS X, there was a Go To field at the bottom of the Open dialog where you could jump directly to the folder you wanted by typing in its location. Well that field no longer appears in the Open dialog, but luckily, it's not gone forever—it's just one simple keystroke away. When you're in the Open dialog, just press the Forward slash key (/) on your keyboard and the Go to the Folder dialog will pop down from the top of the Open dialog, ready for you to type in the path to your folder. *Note:* This doesn't work in all applications, so if typing the slash doesn't bring up the dialog, then just press Command-Shift-G and that'll do the trick.

  SAVE TIME IN THE "GO TO THE FOLDER" DIALOG

Once you've entered a path in the Go to the Folder dialog of a Cocoa app, that last path stays in memory (thanks to an OS auto-complete feature), so if you want to get back to that same folder, don't press the

Forward Slash key (/) when you're in the Open dialog. Instead, press Command-Shift-G, and that way when the Go to the Folder dialog appears, the last path you entered will already be input for you, saving you the trouble.

   SPEED TIP: TAKE OUT THE PAPERS AND THE TRASH

Want to empty the Trash without making a trip up to the Finder menu first? Then just click-and-hold (or Control-click) on the Trash icon in the Dock and choose Empty Trash. Of course, you could also press Command-Shift-Delete when the Finder is active, but how much fun is that? Incidentally, if you want to get something in the Trash in a hurry, just click on it, press Command-Delete, and that file will jump into the Trash lickety-split!

GET INFO'S SECRET SECOND PERSONALITY

While Command-I brings up the regular Info dialog, pressing Command-Option-I brings up a second version with a special hidden feature (you'll know it's the second version because its corners are squared, rather than rounded, and there's no Minimize or Zoom button). This second version stays live when you click on different files—giving you their file info as well (the regular version just deselects when you click on a different file, so you have to press Command-I all over again to get info on that file). This is great for quickly comparing things like file sizes or modified dates, because you can just click from file to file, and the file info is instantly displayed. You can also Command-click multiple files to select them and press Command-I to see separate Info dialogs side-by-side (but if you select more than 10 files, you'll just get the standard Multiple Item Info dialog). Another nice speed benefit of both dialogs is that when you use either keyboard shortcut to open Info, you can use that same shortcut to close it instead of clicking on the red Close button.

Opened using Command-I

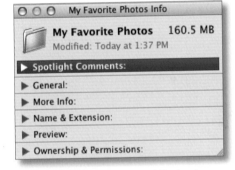

Opened with Command-Option-I

REARRANGE THE MENU EXTRAS

Want to change the order of the Menu Extras along the right side of your menu bar? Just press-and-hold the Command key and drag the icons into the order you want them. It gives you a real feeling of power. Well, a feeling of power over tiny icons anyway.

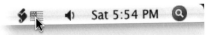

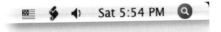

   REMOVE MENU EXTRAS FROM YOUR MENU BAR

To remove a Menu Extra, just hold the Command key and click-and-drag the Extra right off the bar. It doesn't get much easier than that.

Before   *After*

   LOOK INSIDE MULTIPLE FOLDERS AUTOMATICALLY

Need to see what's inside more than one folder while in List view? Do it the fast way—Command-click on all the folders you want to expand, then press Command-Right Arrow. All the folders will expand at once. If the file you're looking for isn't there, just press Command-Left Arrow (you can do that, because your folders are still highlighted) to quickly collapse them all again.

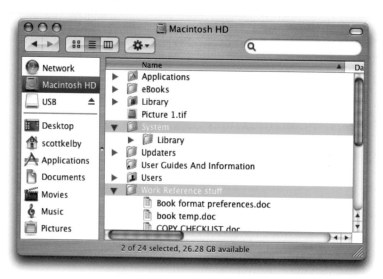

CREATE YOUR OWN KEYBOARD SHORTCUTS

Keyboard shortcuts are such huge timesavers, but sadly, not all Finder commands have
them. But they can, because you can create your own. Here's how: Go under the Apple
menu, to System Preferences, and choose Keyboard & Mouse. When the dialog appears,
click on the Keyboard Shortcuts tab, then click the plus (+) sign at the bottom left of the
dialog. Another dialog will appear. Choose Finder from the Application pop-up menu, and
then type the exact name of the menu command you want to add a shortcut for. Now type
the shortcut you want to use and click the Add button. It's that simple.

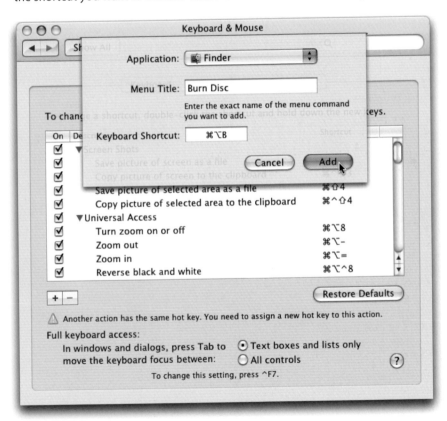

PUT FREQUENTLY USED FILES IN YOUR TOOLBAR

Okay, you know the sidebar is for storing frequently used files and folders, but it can get full pretty fast. If yours gets "packed," try parking some of your most-used files right on the toolbar at the top of your Finder window. Here's how: Click-and-drag the file up to the toolbar. Hold it there

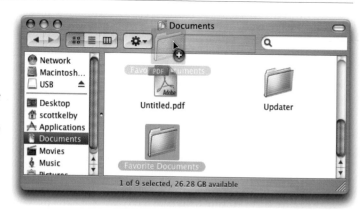

for just a second, and you'll see a thin rectangle appear, letting you know to release the mouse button, and when you do, the file will appear in the toolbar, where it's always just one click away. If you decide to remove it one day, just hold the Command key and drag it off the toolbar.

AUTOMATICALLY ADD FILE EXTENSIONS

Sharing your files with someone using a PC? Make sure you name the file "Don't you wish you had a Mac .txt" or something like that (kidding). Actually, if you're sharing files with a PC, you can ask Mac OS X to auto-matically add the three-letter file extension to your file name every time you save a file. Just go to the Finder menu, choose Preferences,

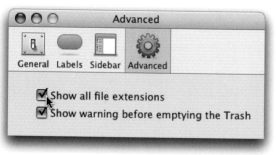

click on the Advanced icon, and select the Show All File Extensions checkbox.

HOW TO BE SELECTIVE WITH EXTENSIONS

In Mac OS X, every file has a three-letter file extension (like PC files do). But by default, Mac OS X hides those three-letter extensions. In the previous tip, I showed you how to make those three-letter extensions visible all the time, but what if you just want to see the three-letter extensions for an individual file or two? If you want to see these extensions (perhaps if you're designing Web graphics and want your files to have the .gif and .jpg file extensions visible), you can do that when you save each file. In the Save dialog, you'll notice a check-box called Hide Extension, which is generally on by default. Just turn that checkbox off, and the appropriate file extension will be added to the file. In some applications, you may see a checkbox for Append File Extension instead; in that case, make sure the checkbox is on to show the extension. *Note:* Some applications may not offer this at all; in that case, just use the previous tip.

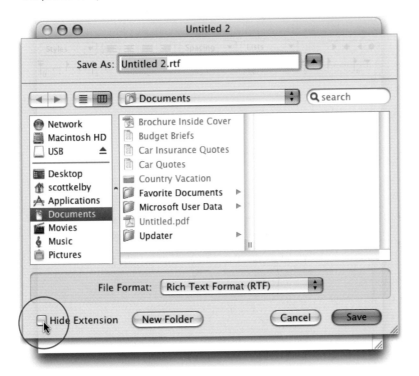

   BECOME THE ULTIMATE MENU MASTER

Want to really speed things up? How about jumping right to the Apple menu without even clicking the mouse? Just press Control-F2, press Return, and the Apple menu pops down (if you're using a PowerBook, press Function-Control-F2). Oh, but there's more! Now that you're in the Apple menu, press the Right Arrow key on your keyboard to move to the other menus (Finder, File, Edit, View, etc.) and the Left Arrow to move back. Once you get to the menu you want, press Return, then use the tip I mentioned earlier: type the first letter of the command you want in the menu and it jumps right there. Now press Return again to choose that command (and you did it all without ever touching the mouse).

   A FASTER WAY TO GET YOUR SYSTEM INFO

If for some reason you run into some serious problems with your Mac (hey, it could happen), you might have to tell Apple tech support, a repair tech, or a Macintosh consultant some technical information about your particular hardware and system software configurations. Luckily, all that information is found by launching Apple's System Profiler. The only bad news is—it's buried deep within your Applications folder, inside your Utilities folder. Here's the tip: There's a quicker way to get to the Apple System Profiler. Just go under the Apple menu and choose About This Mac. When the dialog appears, click on the button at the bottom called More Info and it will launch the Apple System Profiler for you right from there. *Note:* If you need your serial number, just double-click on the Version line below the Apple logo.

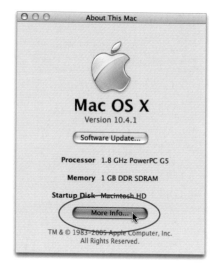

FINDING THE COMBINED SIZE OF MORE THAN ONE DOCUMENT

Let's say you have several files on your desktop, and before you copy them all onto your jump drive, you want to find out their combined size. Here's how it's done: Select all the files for which you want the combined size, then press Command-Option-I, which brings up the Multiple Item Info dialog, complete with a list how many files are selected and their combined size.

  WHICH DISK DID YOU START UP FROM?

If you're one of those people (and you know darn well who you are) who have multiple disks and multiple versions of the OS (like Tiger on one drive, Panther on another, Classic on another), in Tiger you can find out which disk you started up from by going under the Apple menu and choosing About This Mac. When you do this, you'll find a new info field has appeared, which shows you (in no uncertain terms) which disk you started up with.

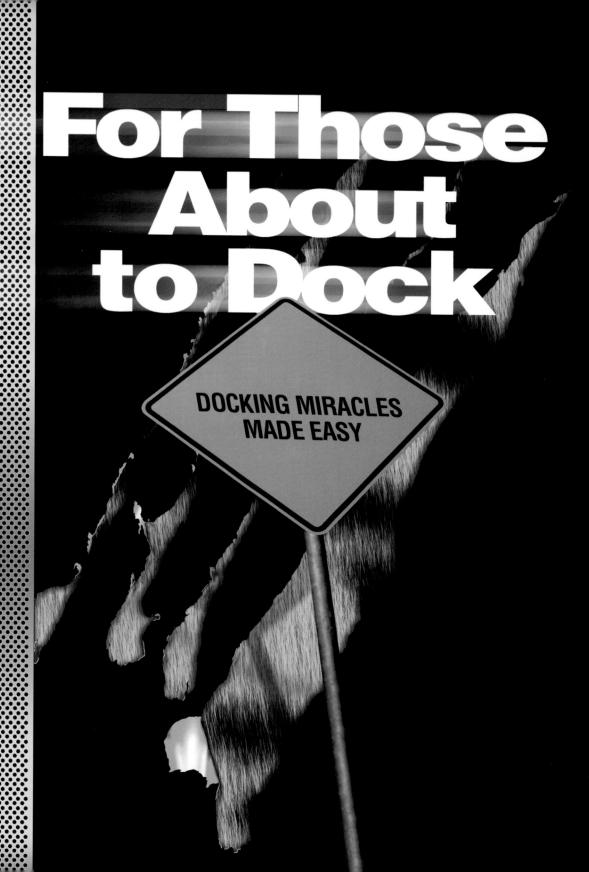

For Those About to Dock

DOCKING MIRACLES
MADE EASY

You have to hand it to Apple: When it comes to application launching and switching, they have created the Venus de

For Those About to Dock!
docking miracles made easy

Milo of application launchers and switchers with Mac OS X's Dock. Okay, that just sounds weird. How about "the crème de la crème" of launchers and application switchers? Nah, it just doesn't sound sexy enough to describe all the really cool things the Dock lets you do. Okay, how about this: "When it comes to doing it, the Dock totally rocks!" Nah, that sounds too "Eminem." Instead, perhaps we should look at the word "Dock" itself. It's clearly a derivative of the popular Latin phrase "One, two, three o-clock, four o-clock, Dock," which, if memory serves me correctly, is inscribed on the torch held high by Lady Liberty in New York Harbor (and Lady Liberty was presented to the United States by French Prime Minister Bill Haley, around five, six, seven o'clock).

   DRAGGING FROM THE DOCK, NOT TO IT

In this chapter, we're always talking about dragging files and folders *to* the Dock, but you can also drag *from* the Dock (out to your desktop or to an open window) by first holding the Command key, then dragging. Want to make an alias of a Dock icon? Just hold Command-Option and drag the docked file to the window you want, and it creates an alias. In fact, most of the things you can do within a window (copying a file, creating an alias, etc.) can be done from the Dock, as long as you start with the Command key.

   THE ONE-CLICK TRICK TO MOVING THE DOCK

Okay, so you're working in a program like Final Cut Pro or iMovie, which takes up every vertical inch of the screen, and when you go to adjust something near the bottom, the Dock keeps popping up. Oh sure, you could move the Dock to where it's anchored on the left or right side of the screen, but that just feels weird. But what if you could move it temporarily to the left or right, and then get it back to the bottom when you close Final Cut Pro, in just one click? Here's how: Hold the Shift key, click directly on the Dock's divider line (on the far right side of the Dock), and drag the Dock to the left or right side of your screen. Bam! It moves over to the side. Then, once you quit Final Cut, just Shift-click on that divider line and slam it back to the bottom (okay, drag it back to the bottom). A draggable Dock—is that cool or what!

FREAKY MOVIE DOCK TRICK

This is one of those "show-off-your-Mac" tricks that really amaze people, but outside of that, I haven't found a real use for it. You start by opening a QuickTime movie, then hit the Play button and watch it for a second or two. Then click the yellow Minimize button on the left side of the title bar to shrink the movie to the Dock (it appears down by the Trash). Here's the cool thing: You'll notice the movie continues to play while in the Dock. You can even hear the audio! Only ants can really enjoy it at this size (in fact, ants love this effect because to them, they're seeing your movie on the "big screen"), but the naked human eye can see the movie too. I've also tested this by putting my clothes back on, and even when not naked, my human eye can still see it. How cool is that?

   ACCESS SYSTEM PREFERENCES DIRECTLY FROM THE DOCK

International
Keyboard & Mouse
Network
Print & Fax
QuickTime
Security
Sharing
Software Update
Sound
Speech
Spotlight
Startup Disk
Universal Access

Remove from Dock
Open at Login
Show In Finder
Show
Quit

Want a quick way to access your System Preferences? (Sure you do.) The next time you have the System Preferences open, don't close or quit; instead press Command-H to hide the preferences. Now, when you want a particular System Preference, just click-and-hold on the System Preferences icon in the Dock for a moment, and a pop-up menu of your System Preferences will appear. Choose the one you want from the list, and that panel then appears onscreen. Very convenient.

   KEEP AN EYE ON THINGS, LIVE FROM THE DOCK

Do you like to know what's going on "under the hood" of your Mac (stuff like your CPU usage, disk activity, memory usage—you know, total geek stuff)? If you do, you can keep an eye on things right from within the Dock using Mac OS X's Activity Monitor. It's found in the Applications folder, under Utilities. Once you've found it, drag it into your Dock, then click on it to launch it. Once it's launched, click-and-hold for a moment on its Dock icon. A menu

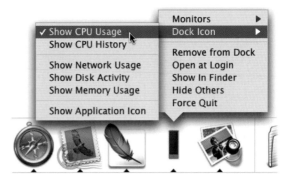

will pop up, and you'll see a Dock Icon menu item. This is where you choose which activity you want to monitor from its live Dock icon. Choose it, and a live graph will appear in the Dock that's updated dynamically as you work.

   THE GIANT APP SWITCHER DOES MORE THAN JUST SWITCH

Holding the Command key, then pressing the Tab key, brings up a giant Dock-like window with huge icons in the center of your screen, where you can cycle through your open apps (using the Tab key, the Arrow keys, or clicking with your mouse). But there's more to it than that—you can quit any currently running app by cycling to it, then pressing the letter Q (don't let go of the Command key; keep holding it while you press the letter Q). Still holding the Command key, press H to hide the highlighted app.

  ● **INSTANT DOCK RESIZE**

If you want to make the Dock larger or smaller, there's a slider in the Dock preference pane, but you don't have to use it. Ever. That's because you can simply put your cursor right over the divider line on the right side of the Dock (the one that separates your apps from your folders and Trash) and your cursor will change to a horizontal bar with two arrows: one facing up and one facing down. When it does that, just click-and-drag your cursor upward to make the Dock bigger and downward to shrink it.

  ● **FOR THOSE WHO DON'T WANT TO "HIDE"**

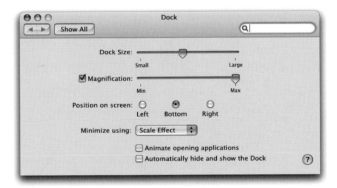

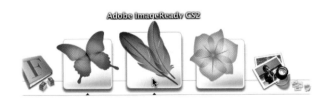

If the Dock seems to be in your way a lot, but you don't like the whole "hiding-the-Dock" thing, try setting the Dock to its smallest size (so you can barely notice it's there at all). Then, go to System Preferences in the Apple menu, click on the Dock icon, and turn on the Magnification checkbox. Ensure the Magnification slider is set to a pretty large size, so when you scroll your mouse over the tiny Dock, the icons will jump up in size so you can see what's what. Now mouse over your Dock and enjoy the enlarged icons.

   YELLOW MINIMIZE BUTTON TOO SMALL? TRY THIS!

Sometimes hitting that tiny middle yellow button (to minimize your current window to the Dock) is tricky, especially if you're using a Titanium PowerBook or Cinema Display set at its native resolution, in which everything is smaller than a gnat's nose. If you'd like something bigger to aim at than that tiny yellow button, go under the Apple menu, under System Preferences, and click on the Appearance icon, and then click on the checkbox for Minimize When Double Clicking a Window Title Bar. Now you can just double-click anywhere on the window's title bar and that window will immediately minimize to the Dock, just as if you had clicked the tiny yellow button. Of course, you could skip the clicking altogether and press Command-M (depending on your application), but that just seems like cheating, doesn't it?

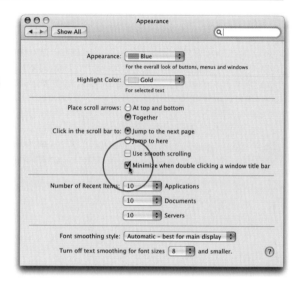

   AUTOMATICALLY HIDING THE DOCK

The smaller your screen, the more important the ability to hide the Dock from view becomes (as you might imagine, this is a very popular feature for Power-Book users). Basically, with this feature active, the Dock hides off screen and only reappears when your cursor moves over the area where the Dock used to be. It kind of "pops up" so you can work in the Dock until you move away, and then it hides again. To turn this Dock feature on, go under the Apple menu, under Dock, and choose Turn Hiding On. If you think you might use this function often, you'll probably want to memorize the Turn Hiding On/Off shortcut, which is Command-Option-D.

ACCIDENTALLY LAUNCHED A PROGRAM? UN-LAUNCH IT

Because it takes only one click to launch a program from the Dock, you're just one click away from launching the wrong application (sadly, I do this all the time—when I mean to click on one application, I accidentally click the Dock icon to the right or left of it). If you do launch a program you wish you hadn't, immediately click-and-hold on its Dock icon and a menu will appear where you can choose Force Quit. This stops the launch dead in its tracks.

   ### KEEPING A RUNNING APP IN THE DOCK AFTER YOU QUIT

If you're running an application and you say to yourself, "You know, I use this app a lot," you can keep its icon in the Dock, so next time it's just one click away. Just Control-click on the app's icon in the Dock and choose Keep In Dock. Of course, there is another way. A cooler way. An "I-don't-need-no-stinkin'-pop-up-menu" way. Just click on the running application's icon, drag it away from the Dock, pause a second, and then drag it right back. It's really not faster, but it makes you look (and feel) less pop-up menu codependent.

   UNLOADING THE DOCK

If you have a few apps running and you like to keep things uncluttered and organized by minimizing document windows to the Dock, it doesn't take long before your Dock gets pretty crowded. If that's the case, here's a tip that might help you bring some welcome space and order back to your Dock: When you're switching from one application to the next, hold the Option key before you click on the new application's icon in the Dock. This hides all of the Dock icons for minimized windows from the application you just left, and helps unclutter the Dock. When you switch back to that application later, its minimized windows reappear in the Dock.

Minimized files docked

Minimized files hidden

   GET RIGHT TO THE FILE YOU WANT

If you've parked a folder full of files in the Dock, you don't have to open the folder to get to a particular file. Instead, just click-and-hold on the folder for a moment, and a pop-up menu of all the files in that folder will appear (that's not the trick). Once that menu is open, on your keyboard just press the first letter(s) of the file you want and that file is instantly highlighted—all you have to do is press Return to open the file.

FOLDERS TO ADD TO YOUR DOCK

Adding folders to the right side of your Dock can be a real timesaver, and two of the most popular folders to add to the Dock are your Home folder and your Applications folder. Another thing you might consider, rather than putting your entire Applications folder on your Dock, is to create a new folder and put in aliases of just the applications and system add-ons (such as the Calculator, etc.) that you really use. Then you can access these by Control-clicking on the folder in the Dock and a pop-up menu will appear that looks a lot like the Apple menu from OS 9.

   FORCE QUITTING FROM THE DOCK

If you're running an application in Mac OS X and for some reason it locks up or crashes (hey, it happens—remember, Apple didn't say applications wouldn't crash in Mac OS X; it said if they did, it wouldn't bring down your whole system), you can easily Force Quit the application by Control-clicking (or clicking-and-holding) on its icon in the Dock, and a pop-up menu will appear. Press the Option key, and you'll see the menu item called Quit change to Force Quit. Click that, and it will force quit the application. Also, if you're a longtime Mac user, you might be afraid to force quit an application, because back in Mac OS 9 (and prior to that), force quitting was an absolute last resort in hopes of saving an open document. If you were lucky enough to get Force Quit to work without locking up the machine (believe me—it was luck—force quitting in Mac OS 9 and earlier usually brought the whole machine down), then all you could really do was restart anyway, but at least you got to save your document. Mac OS X is designed to let you use Force Quit then continue to work, so don't be hesitant to try this feature.

SHORTCUT TO YOUR APPLICATIONS

You probably can't put every application you'll ever use in your Dock, or you'll have one incredibly long microscopic Dock. A popular way around this is to drag your Applications folder to the right of the gray divider bar in the Dock (the left side is for apps only, not folders full of apps). Once your Applications folder is in the Dock, if you click-and-hold (or Control-click) on the folder's icon, a list of the apps inside pops up—then just press the first letter (or first few letters) of the application you want to launch, and once it's highlighted, all you have to do is press Return (or click on it).

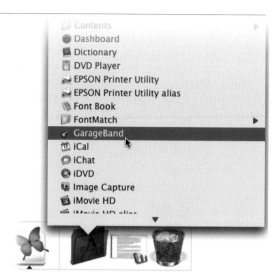

   GETTING RID OF EXTRA WINDOWS WHILE YOU WORK

If you have a few Finder windows open, they can be really distracting when you're working in another application—you always see them floating around in the background. Well, you can hide all those messy windows without ever leaving your current application. Just click-and-hold (or Control-click) on the Finder icon in the Dock and choose Hide from the pop-up menu. All those windows will be instantly hidden from view. Want to hide everything but those windows? Control-Option-click on the Finder icon and choose Hide Others.

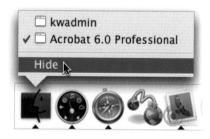

HOW TO CLOSE A FINDER WINDOW IN THE DOCK

If you've minimized a Finder window to the Dock, you can actually close that window without having to maximize it first (saving untold time and keystrokes). Just click-and-hold on the minimized Finder window in the Dock, and choose Close from the pop-up menu. That's it—it's closed, just as if you had maximized it and clicked on the red Close button.

   ## BRINGING HOME LOST SHEEP: FINDING DOCKED ORIGINALS

Okay, so you see the application's (or document's) icon in the Dock, but you have no earthly idea where the app (or doc) really resides on your hard drive. It's there somewhere, but you really don't know where, and that scares you (well, it scares me anyway). To find where the docked application or document really lives, just Control-click (or click-and-hold) on it in the Dock and choose Show In Finder. The window where it lives will immediately appear onscreen.

  STOP THE BOUNCING. I BEG YOU!

When you launch an application, its icon begins to bounce incessantly in the Dock, in a distracting vertical Tigger-like motion, until the app is just about open. I love this feature; but then, I enjoy having my cavities drilled. If you enjoy this animation as much as I do, you can turn it off by going to the Apple menu, under Dock, and choosing Dock Preferences. When

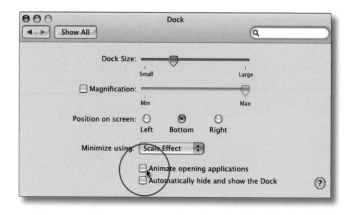

the Dock preference pane appears, turn off the checkbox (it's on by default) for Animate Opening Applications. Turning this off now can save you thousands of dollars in therapy down the road.

   MAKE ONE ACTIVE, AND HIDE THE REST

If you want to make just the application you're working on visible and hide all the other running applications, including any open Finder windows, just hold Command-Option, and then click on the application's icon in the Dock. This is much faster than choosing your application, then going under your application's menu and choosing Hide Others.

FREAKY GENIE EFFECT

There's a little trick you can pull to make the Genie Effect (the little animation that takes place when you minimize a window to the Dock) even freakier (we call it the "freaky genie"). Just hold Shift before you click the Minimize button to hide the window in the Dock and it puts the Genie Effect into a "super slo-mo" mode that looks kinda cool. I say "kinda" because this effect (like the Genie Effect itself) gets old kinda quick, but people who've never seen it before, dig it. At least at first.

   SNAPPING DOCK SIZES

In a previous tip, I showed how you can resize the Dock by clicking-and-dragging on the divider line, but if you hold the Option key first and then start dragging, the Dock will "snap" to some preset sizes. Who chose these preset sizes? Probably Apple's software engineers, but some feel the presets were secretly designated by high-ranking government officials in yet another attempt to exert more "Big-Brotherly" control over our otherwise mundane lives. Personally, I tend to think it was Apple, but hey, that's just me.

   MINIMIZING MULTIPLE WINDOWS AT ONCE

If you have three or four open windows in the same application and want to minimize them all to the Dock at once, just hold the Option key and double-click on the title bar of any one of them, and all open windows will go to the Dock. Be careful when you do this, because if you have 50 open windows, they're all headed to the Dock in a hurry, and there's no real undo for this. Worse yet, you'll eventually have to pull 50 very tiny icons from the Dock one by one (or if you're bright, just close the application, which closes the files in the Dock). So make sure that's really what you want to do before you Option-double-click.

All Word files minimized by Option-double-clicking

   OPEN DOCUMENTS BY DRAGGING THEM TO THE DOCK

Remember how back in Mac OS 9, if you tore the Application menu off and had it floating around your desktop, you could drag-and-drop documents onto an application listed in the menu, and it would endeavor to open them? You can do the same thing now in Mac OS X with the Dock—just drag documents directly to an application icon in the Dock, and if it thinks it might be able to open the document, the icon will highlight, basically telling you "let 'er rip!"

STOP THE ICONS FROM MOVING

In the previous tip, I showed how you can drag a document onto an application's icon in the Dock. But sometimes you may be trying to add the document to a folder in the Dock. When you do this, the Dock thinks you're actually trying to add the document to the Dock itself, rather than dropping it on the folder, so it kindly slides the icons out of the way to make room for your document. That's incredibly polite (for an operating system anyway), but it can also be incredibly annoying if that's not what you're trying to do. If this happens to you, just hold the Command key as you drag and the icons will stay put, enabling you to drop the document into a "non-moving" object.

FULL-SPEED DOCKING BY LOSING THE GENIE!

The Genie Effect that occurs when you send a document to the Dock sure looks cool, but things that look cool generally eat up processing power, and that holds true with the Genie Effect as well (besides, although the Genie Effect looks cool the first couple of times you see it, it doesn't take long before you want to put the genie back in its bottle for good). To turn off the Genie Effect and use the faster Scale Effect, Control-click on the vertical Dock divider bar, and in the resulting pop-up menu, under Minimize Using, choose Scale Effect. This decreases the burden on the system resources and keeps things moving at full speed.

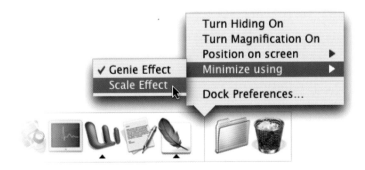

   FORCING A DOCUMENT ON AN APP

Sometimes docked apps don't want to open your
document, even though they may be able to, so
you have to coax (okay, force) them to give it a try.
For example, let's say you created a document in
WordPerfect for Mac a few years back. If you drag

that document to Microsoft Word's icon in the Dock, chances are it won't highlight (which
would be the indication it can open that document). If that happens, just hold Command-
Option, then drag the document's icon to the Word icon in the Dock, and you can force it
to try to open that document.

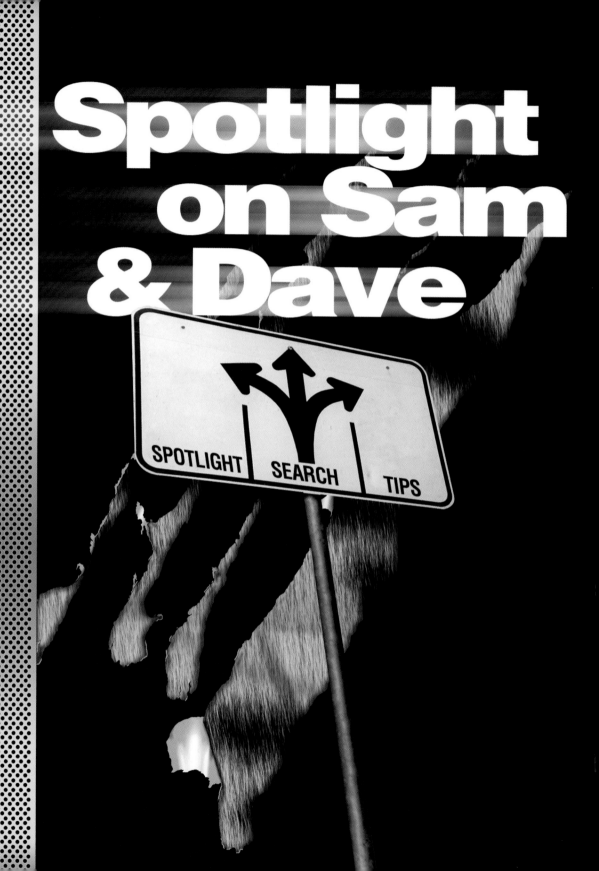

If there was ever a product that richly deserved its own chapter, it's Tiger's amazing Spotlight search feature. That's because

Spotlight on Sam & Dave

spotlight search tips

we spend a ton of our time searching for things on our Macs. Why? Because we don't know where anything is. Ever. Take my car keys for example. You might as well take them, because I generally have no idea where they are. For some reason I can clearly remember undocumented keyboard shortcuts from Mac OS 7.1, but I have no idea where I laid my car keys last night. You know what I need? I need Spotlight outside my Mac, in my regular life. I would just type in "car keys" and it would say "in the kitchen, just to the left of the bowl of fruit," or more likely, "they're still in the ignition." So, how does the name of this chapter "Spotlight on Sam & Dave" fit in? Well, that's the hook from the classic oldie "Sweet Soul Music" from an artist named Arthur Conley. In the song, he "spotlights" other singers, like James Brown and Otis Redding.

   MAKE THE SPOTLIGHT MENU APPEAR WITH COMMAND-F

I absolutely love Spotlight, but there's one thing that drives me crazy—when you press Command-F, you get a Finder Search window rather than the Spotlight menu (which is what I really want). If that's you want (and we both know that secretly it is), you can make it so by going to the System Preferences under the Apple menu and clicking on Spotlight. When the Spotlight Preferences appear, where it says Spotlight Menu Keyboard Shortcut, click once in that field and type Command-F. That's it—the Spotlight menu will now pop down when you press Command-F. Now, doesn't that feel better? The reason I mention this tip at all is in case you want to customize the Spotlight keyboard shortcuts, because it seems like you can only use the built-in shortcuts that appear in the menu, but as you just learned, you can type any shortcut you'd like. (*Note:* You could reverse this so the Spotlight dialog appears—just press the shortcut in the Spotlight Window Keyboard Shortcut field.)

   NARROWING YOUR SEARCH BY GIVING SPOTLIGHT A HINT

If you want to narrow your search right off the bat, you can add a category when you type the term in the Search field. For example, if you're looking for a song named "Vertigo" (by the band U2), there's no sense in having Spotlight bring you a list of email messages from your ear doctor, right? So if you give Spotlight a hint as to what you're looking for, you can get just songs as your Spotlight search results. Here's how: Type "kind:music" (with no space in between or quotations), then add one space and type "Vertigo" (again, you don't need the quotes). So your search will look like this: kind:music Vertigo. Now it will only search songs, and you'll only get song results. Schweet!

ADDING YOUR OWN KEYWORDS TO HELP FIND FILES

Let's say that sometime in the future you want to be able to instantly find all the photos of your kids, regardless of where or when the photos were taken. Well, you can do that by adding your own keyword to any photo that has one (or more) of your kids in the photo. Just click on the image file in an open Finder window, and then press Command-I to open the Info dialog. At the top of the dialog where it says "Spotlight Comments," just click once in the empty field, type the keyword you want to use (for example, "kids" [without the quotes]), and then close the window. Now, when you type "Kids" in the Spotlight Search field, it will find those photos, regardless of what the file name is.

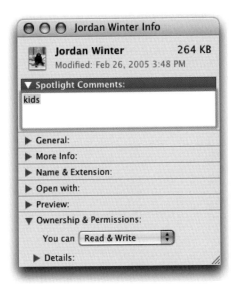 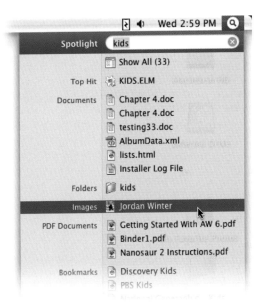

FOCUSING YOUR SEARCHES

By default, Spotlight pretty much searches everything on your Mac, from songs to email, to contacts and system preferences. It's annoyingly thorough (if it were human, it would make a great book editor). Anyway, if there are certain areas you don't need it to search (for example, if you don't want it rummaging through your songs), you can tell it what to search through and what to ignore. You do this by first going to Spotlight's Preferences. Just click on the Spotlight icon in the menu bar, and from the menu choose Spotlight Preferences. When the dialog appears, turn off the checkboxes for the areas you don't want searched.

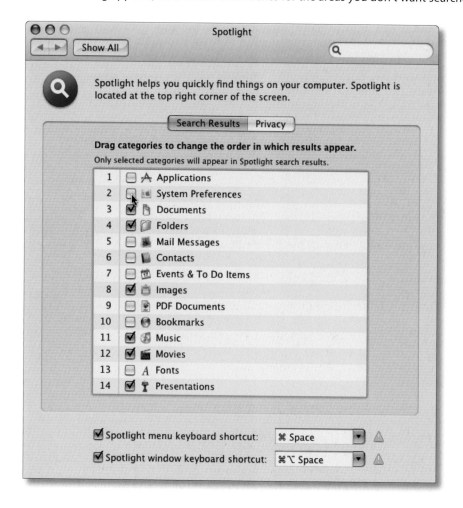

WHAT IF YOU DON'T WANT TO OPEN THE FILE?

The idea behind Spotlight is that it will find the file you want, and then open that file for you, so you can start working on it immediately. But what if you just want to know where the file is, and not necessarily open it? (For example, what if you just want to know where it is, so you can burn a backup copy to a CD?) To do that, once the results appear in the Spotlight menu, just hold the Command key and then click on the file. This will close Spotlight and open the Finder window where your file is. Or if you want Spotlight open, just click on the file and press Command-R, which will open a Finder window with the file selected, leaving the Spotlight dialog open.

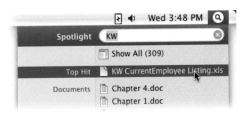 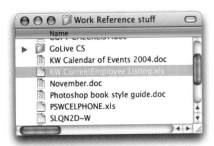

FINDING PEOPLE'S PHONE NUMBERS

Spotlight is great for finding people on your Mac, because it'll search through your email, attachments, bookmarks, Address Book, iCal calendars—you name it. When it comes to finding phone numbers in your Address Book, it totally rocks because once you find the number, you can go to town (so to speak). For example, if you want to call a friend or business associate, rather than launch Address Book, just type their name in Spotlight. When their contact appears, don't launch Address Book. Instead, just click on their name, then press the Right Arrow key on your keyboard to show the info on this contact. Then click directly on their phone number and it will appear so huge on your screen that senior citizens on a passing cruise ship will be able to read it clearly.

FASTER THAN SLIDE SHOW FOR FINDING A PHOTO

By now you've heard that if your search results contain photos, you can see a slide show of those photos (by pressing Enter or clicking on Show All in the Spotlight menu once you've entered a search term, and then in the Spotlight dialog that appears,

you can click on the little Play button to the right of the Images category). The slide show thing is handy, no doubt, but you can also use it to get to a particular photo you want quickly. Here's how: Start the slide show (click the little Play button), and then immediately click the Index Sheet icon in the slide show controls that appear along the bottom of your screen. This tiles thumbnails of all the photos in your slide show onscreen (giving you an Index Sheet view), so you can jump right to the photo you need, saving you the frustration of slowly wading through a slide show when you just want to quickly find one particular photo.

   ### MOVING THAT FOUND PHOTO TO IPHOTO FAST

If you're using the Slideshow (or Index) feature to look at "found" photos, you can instantly add any photo to your iPhoto Library by just moving your mouse (which brings up the Slideshow controls), then click on the Add to iPhoto button (it's just to the left of the [X] close button).

FULL-SCREEN SLIDE SHOW

When you've got a slide show running, you can have your photos fill as much of the screen as possible by pressing the letter F. Press the letter A to fit your photos at regular size onscreen.

Regular size

Full-screen size

GET TO YOUR TOP HIT FAST

If you do a search and notice that
the file it chose as your Top Hit in
the Spotlight menu is actually the file
you were looking for (hey, it could
happen), just press-and-hold the
Command key to jump right to the
Top Hit, then press Return to open
that document (or song, email, etc.),
which closes the Spotlight menu. See,

it even tidies up after you. So basically, just press Command-Return to instantly open the Top
Hit. Easy enough.

WHERE DOES THAT FILE LIVE?

If you found the file you were looking for, and want to know where it
is on your hard disk, just move your
cursor over the result in the Spotlight menu, and in just a second or
two, a tiny dialog will pop up showing the path to that file.

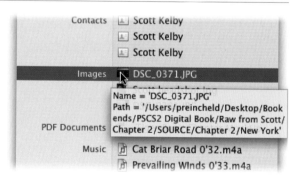

SEARCHING WITHOUT TYPING

Okay, picture this: You're reading an email from an old friend, and he mentions that he saw your friend Alan the other day (of course, this only works if you actually have a friend named Alan, so if you don't, now would be a great time to cultivate a relationship with someone named Alan). So when you see Alan's name, you think: "Didn't he send me some photos?" But rather than going to Spotlight and typing "Alan," just highlight the name Alan within the email, then Control-click and from the contextual menu that appears, choose Search Spotlight. It immediately searches for you, without you ever typing a word.

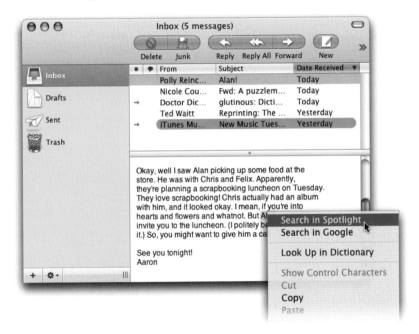

   SEARCH INSIDE YOUR PHOTOSHOP DOCUMENTS

This one's a mind blower. If you've got a layered Photoshop document (saved in PSD format), Spotlight will even search your Type layers to help you find the layered file that has the word you're looking for (as long as you're using Type layers—not rasterized layers, in which case they're not Type layers anymore, so why did I even say that?). For example, here I did a search for the word "Spain," which resulted in Spotlight finding my layered PSD file.

   SEARCHING YOUR SYSTEM PREFERENCES

Can't remember where a particular option is found within the System Preferences? (For example, for some reason I can never remember where to set the date format for my display. No, it's not in Date & Time.) No sweat, because Spotlight also lives right within the System Preferences dialog (in the upper right-hand corner). Just open the System Preferences dialog from the Apple menu, and type the name of the preference setting you're looking for (in my case, I'd type "Format" without the quotes), and then Spotlight

puts a little "spotlight" around the System Preferences that have a control for Format. If there's more than one, it will highlight several icons, but to help you even further, a pop-up search menu will appear with the names of all the "Format" stuff. Click on the one you want in the list (in my case, Date Formats), and it immediately takes you to that preference. That ain't bad, folks.

HOW TO SEARCH WHEN YOU KNOW THE EXACT FILE NAME

If you know the exact name of the file you're searching for, you can do a search just like you did in previous versions of Mac OS X by just putting quotes around your search word(s). So, if you know the name of the file you're looking for is named 2005 Annual Report, you'd search for "2005 Annual Report" with quotes around it as I just I wrote here.

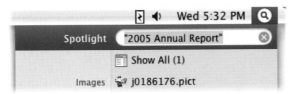

  WHY NOT ALWAYS USE THE SPOTLIGHT DIALOG?

Since the Spotlight menu is so convenient (it's right there in the menu bar no matter which program you're using) and you can just press Command-Spacebar to activate it, so why not always use it instead of the main Spotlight dialog? Well, the main Spotlight dialog has some big advantages: First, you get more than just the top 20 results, so you get a wider range of results from the start. Secondly, you get "rich"

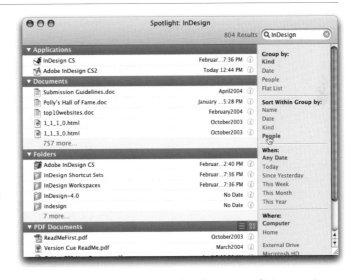

results, meaning if the result is a photo, you can see its thumbnail preview. If it's a movie or audio file, you can play a preview. And thirdly (is that a word—thirdly?), you can refine and re-sort the results in the main Spotlight window, choosing to sort by date, time span, or even just show people. That's why some prefer to only use the main Spotlight dialog for searching, using the shortcut Command-Option-Spacebar.

   CODEC INFO FOR GEEKS

My buddy, DV guru Rod Harlan, went gaga for this one: When you search for a movie, once the results appear, if you go to the Spotlight dialog and click the little "i" icon (while in List view), it expands the amount of info gathered about that file, including the compression Codec used to compress the movie. I know what you're thinking. Who cares? Rod cares. I have no idea why, but he cares. I guess other video guys do too. Freaks.

   OPENING? SAVING? SPOTLIGHT IS THERE

Okay, it's time to save a file, so you choose Save As and the typical Save dialog appears. You want to save your document in a particular folder, but you can't remember exactly where that folder is. No sweat, because Spotlight lives in the Save (and Open) dialog as well (it's everywhere!).

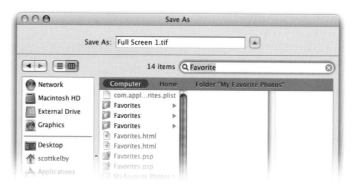

Just type the name of the folder you're looking for in the Spotlight field in the upper right-hand corner of the Save As dialog and all the folders with that name appear in your Save window, so you can get right where you want blindingly fast. Nice.

   SEARCHING BY DATE

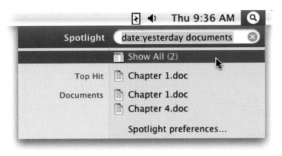

This one's great for those situations where you can't remember the file's name (or even anything close to it), but you know you saved it yesterday. Just type "date:yesterday" (with no space in between or quotations needed), and all the files you created yesterday will appear. You can narrow your search even further if, for example, you not only know you created it yesterday,

but you know it's somewhere in your Documents folder. In that case, you'd type: "date: yesterday documents" (leaving no space as before, but a space between "yesterday" and "documents"—again, no quotations are needed).

   SEARCHING FOR TWO WORDS, NOT A PHRASE

Okay, let's say you want to search for two words individually. For example, you want to search for your name (in my case, Scott), and then you want to search for your last name (Kelby, so I would get all files, email, attachments, etc., from my wife, brother, and son as well). Here's how: First type "Scott" (with no quotations), and then with no space in between type a "pipe," which is what I've always called that vertical line key right above the

Return key on your keyboard (it's really Shift-Backslash), and then type "Kelby." Your search will actually look like this: Scott|Kelby (with no spaces in between or quotations). Now Spotlight will search for every occurrence of "Scott" or "Kelby" but not "Scott Kelby" as a single phrase.

   SEARCHING WITHOUT A PARTICULAR WORD

Let's say you have a bunch
of friends and they're all
named Scott, but you want
to throw a surprise party for
your best friend, Scott Kelby.
So, you need to find all your
Scott contacts so you can
send them invitations, but
you don't want to include
Kelby, because, hey, it's a
surprise. In that case, you'd

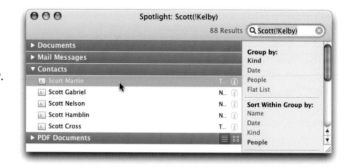

use an exclamation point (or minus sign) as the word "not" (with the exclamation point
directly left of the word you *don't* want searched, with no space in between), and then put
parentheses around that word. So, your search would look like this: "Scott(!Kelby)" (without quotations). That way, it searches for all files with Scott in them, but it will exclude any
contacts with the name Kelby. *Note:* Doing this will limit Spotlight's searches to exclude file
names, folder names, etc.

   SKIP THE TOP 20

If you know that your
search is going to bring
back lots of possible
"hits," you might want to
skip the Spotlight menu's
"Top 20" and go straight
for the Spotlight dialog
instead, so you can start
mining the results right
away. You can jump right
there by pressing Com-
mand-Option-Spacebar.

CHANGING THE ORDER OF THE RESULTS

Let's say you realize that most of the time you find yourself searching for music, movies, and photos (you're a creative type). Well, by default those result categories appear farther down the list (with stuff like Documents and Email and Contacts appearing near the top of the list). And because of that, you've been spending a lot of time scrolling. It doesn't have to be that way. Go to the Spotlight Preferences (found at the bottom of the Spotlight menu), and when it appears, all the categories are listed in the order they will appear. To change their order, just click-and-drag them into the order you want (in this case, you'd drag Music, Movies, and Images to the top).

⬤ ⬤ ⬤ KEEPING ORDER BY COLLAPSING EVERYTHING

When you do a search in the Spotlight dialog, each category displays the top five results. You probably already know that if you want to hide the results for a particular category, you just click directly on the category's name. That's handy, but this tip might be even handier, especially when you get results in lots of different categories, making you scroll down pretty far to see them all. Just Option-click on the top category

and all the other categories immediately collapse. This is great because you can see all the categories at once, so you can now just click once on the category you want see. A great tip for helping you get right to the results you want fast!

⬤ ⬤ ⬤ THAT LITTLE "I" IS HARD TO HIT

I know you know this, but to get more info on a particular search result in the Spotlight dialog, you can click the little "i" (Info) icon that appears to the far right of results that actually have more info (like music, movies, etc.). But that little "i" icon is so small that sometimes hitting it is tricky. So, instead just click on the file you want info on, then press the Right Arrow key on your keyboard to show the info. Press the Left Arrow key to tuck the info back up.

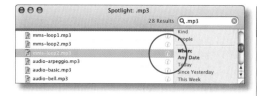 

SEE INFO ON ALL FIVE RESULTS AT ONCE

If you want to see the info on each of the top five results in the Spotlight dialog, just Option-click on any of the little "i" icons in that category (without the file selected). If you've displayed all the results in a particular category by clicking on the "28 more" button (or whatever the number is) at the bottom of the section, you can use this same Option-click trick to see the info displayed on all of the files (it might take a little time scrolling to see them all, but luckily you can use the Up/Down Arrow keys on your keyboard to up and down the list). Just Option-click on the icon again (it'll switch to an arrow icon) to see the normal list without the info.

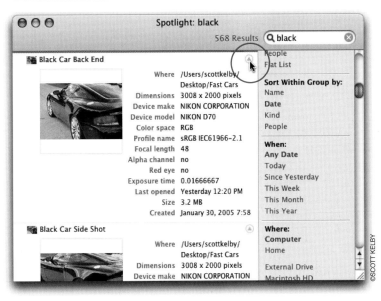

GOT RESULTS? SEE THEM ALL WITH ONE CLICK

The Spotlight menu shows just the top 20 results from your search, but you'll notice that the words "Show All" are always highlighted by default. That's handy, because if you want to quickly see all the results in the Spotlight dialog (rather than the menu), all you have to do is press the Return key. So, to recap: Type a search, and when you see the results you want, just hit Return. Total cake.

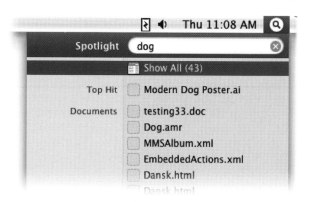

   KEEPING PRYING EYES FROM PRYING

If you don't want other people to be able to search folders on your hard disk (let's say there's a folder where you keep secret stuff, like Steve Jobs' cell number), you can hide that folder by going to the Spotlight Preferences (at the bottom of the Spotlight menu) and clicking on the Privacy tab to the right of the Search Results tab. Now click the little plus (+) button at the bottom left-hand corner to add a folder (or even an entire hard disk) to your Privacy list. You can also drag-and-drop folders, which you want to exclude from Spotlight searches, into this window from your desktop.

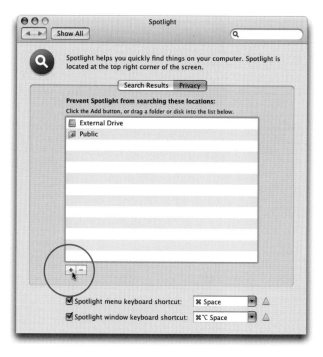

SAVING SPOTLIGHT SEARCHES

Spotlight also lives in your Finder windows (right where the old Search field was in previous versions of Mac OS X), but when you search here, you get a little bonus—savable searches. So, for example, you search for all the email, images, and other junk sent to you by your friend Alan. When you do this in a Finder window, the Finder window updates to show the results right there in your window. Oh, but there's more. Now you'll find a Save button near the top-right side of your window. If you click it, it saves your results in a folder in your sidebar, where you can re-access those files at any time. How cool is that! But this is no ordinary folder, my friend. This is a Smart Folder, which means the next time Alan sends you something (or you mention Alan in a document, email, etc.), it will automatically be added to that Smart Folder. It's live, baby!

CHOOSING WHICH FOLDERS TO SEARCH

When you do a Spotlight search using the Search field that appears at the top-right corner of Finder windows, a row of buttons appears that lists some one-click choices of where you'd like to search. But what if the hard disk or folder you want doesn't appear as one of those buttons? Just click the Others button and a menu will pop down of other folders and drives you can search. This is great for limiting your search to just one folder. To do just that, click on the plus (+) button in the bottom-left corner of this dialog and navigate your way to the folder you want to search. This folder will appear in your Others menu from now on (unless you click on it and click the minus [–] button, of course).

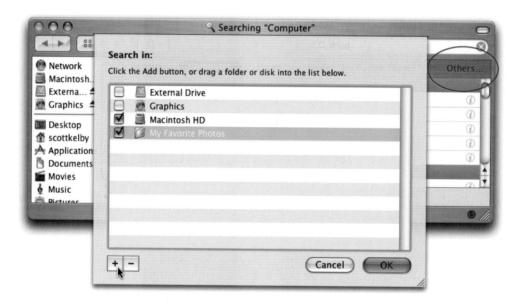

CAN'T REMEMBER THE PASSWORD?

If you can't remember a password for a website (or anything else for that matter), all your passwords are saved in the Keychain Access utility (which probably isn't news to you), but the cool thing is you can do a Spotlight search from right within Keychain to quickly find the password you're looking for. Start by looking inside your Applications folder for the Utilities folder, and inside of that double-click on Keychain Access. When it opens you'll see a Search field in the upper-right corner. Type the name of the site you're looking for, and it will appear. Double-click on the result and an info dialog will appear, and to see your password, turn on the Show Password checkbox.

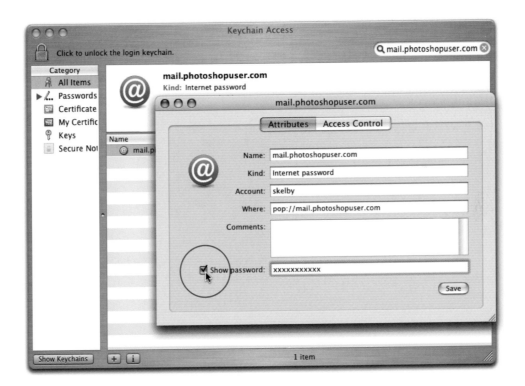

Fly Like an Eagle

MAC OS X SPEED TIPS

If I could show you some Mac OS X *speed tips that would make you more productive at Mac OS X than you ever dreamed*

Fly Like an Eagle
mac os x speed tips

possible, how much would you be willing to pay? 50 bucks? 75 bucks? 100 bucks? Easily. So basically, by paying a list price of about 30 bucks for this book, I figure you're ahead by at least $20 (if you said 50 bucks) and possibly as much as $70 (if you said 100 bucks). Well, if you think about it, only this particular chapter is on speed tips, so in reality, you were willing to pay between $50 and $100 for just the tips in the this chapter, so technically, you should've paid extra for the other chapters. Now granted, they won't all make you faster, so I'm willing to give you a discount—$10 a chapter—so add 10 bucks for each chapter. Now, if you ordered this book from Amazon.com, and got 30% off the list price, you're just flat-out taking advantage of the situation, and I expect you to feel a level of guilt that is commensurate with the value actually received.

   DROPPING TEXT ON THE DOCK FOR FAST RESULTS

Let's say you're reading an article online, and you read a sentence that you want to email to a friend. Don't do the copy-and-paste thing. Instead, just highlight the text and drag-and-drop it right on the Mail icon in the Dock. It will open Mail and put that sentence into a new mail message. This tip also works in other Cocoa applications like TextEdit, Stickies, and Safari. For example, if you're reading a story and want to do a Google search on something you've read, just highlight the next and drag-and-drop it on the Safari icon in the Dock. It will launch Safari and display the Google search results.

  **LEFT-HANDED MAC USERS REJOICE!**

If you're a left-handed Mac user using a two-button mouse, your life is about to get better, because in Tiger for the first time you can switch it so the "Right-click" button is on the left (yippie!). Just go to the System Preferences in the Apple menu and click on the Keyboard & Mouse icon. When the preferences appear, click on the Mouse tab, then choose whichever one of your mouse buttons is the regular click (Right) and which is "Right-click" (which will now be a Left click).

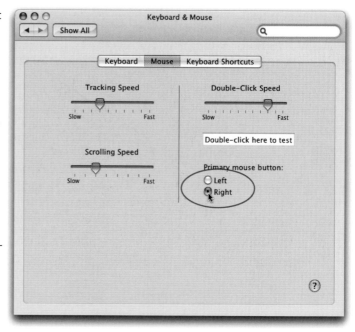

SYSTEM PREFERENCES SUPER-SPEED SHORTCUT

This is a great Tiger tip, because once you learn it, it saves time every day. Back in Panther, you could type the first few letters of a System Preferences icon you were looking for and go directly to that pane. Well, it's a little different in Tiger—now you have options. Open System Preferences from the Apple menu, type the first few letters of the preference you're looking for, and Spotlight will automatically point you in the right direction. A pop-up menu will appear showing the preferences that match the word you entered. Now use the Up and Down Arrow keys on your keyboard to choose your preference from the menu. When you see the preference you want, just press Return to instantly open that pane.

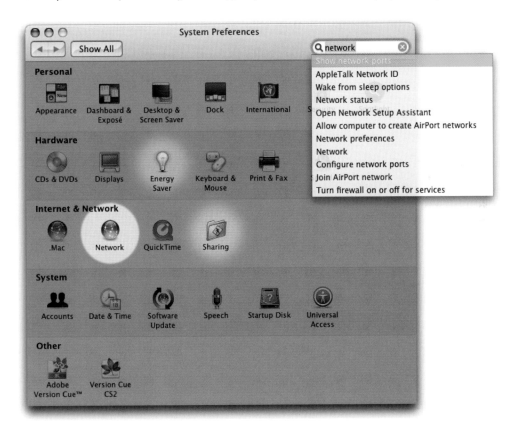

   THE BURN FOLDER ISN'T BURNING ALIASES

When you create a Burn folder in Tiger (which you do by either choosing New Burn Folder from the File menu or from the Action menu [that's the button with a gear icon on it in Finder windows]), if you look inside that folder, you won't see your original files. Instead, you'll see aliases to the originals (you can tell they're aliases because they have a little curved arrow on them). But don't let that throw you—when you do finally

click the Burn button (in the upper right-hand corner of the Burn Folder's window), it actually gets the original files and burns those to disk, so you don't have to worry about having a CD full of aliases pointing to files you no longer have. Why all the aliases in the first place? Because it points to your files (rather than copying them into the folder), which makes burning discs much faster than in previous versions of Mac OS X.

   WILL THE STUFF IN YOUR BURN FOLDER FIT ON YOUR CD?

When you drag items into your Burn Folder for burning to CD (choose New Burn Folder from the File menu), the items in there are just aliases to the real files on your hard disk. Because of this, it doesn't show you how much space all these files take up, so you don't know if they'll actually fit on a 700-MB CD. However, all is not lost. When you click the Burn button (found in the Burn folder itself), a dialog appears that tells you how much storage space you'll need on your CD.

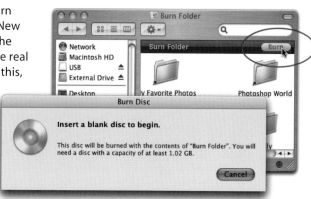

If it's more than 700 MB, hit the Cancel button, then start deleting aliases from the Burn folder until you get below 700 (or whatever the space is on your disc).

IS THAT TASK DONE YET? THE DOCK KNOWS

Let's say you're working in a power-crunching app like Photoshop, and you go to apply a filter to a high-res image, and it's going to take a minute or two to process your command. You're going to get a progress bar so you can see how long the process is going to take, right? Well, thanks to Mac OS X's way-cool Dock, you can switch out of Photoshop to work on something else and the Dock will let you know when the filter is applied. How? Well, when a progress bar appears in Photoshop, the Dock automatically adds a tiny little progress bar to the bottom of the Photoshop icon in the Dock so you can keep an eye on the progress, even when you're doing something else (like checking your mail, shopping online, or writing a letter).

   SUPER SHORTCUT TO HAVING AN APP LOAD AT LOGIN

If you'd like a particular application to open every time you log into (or start up) your Mac, now all you have to do is Control-click (or click-and-hold) on the application's Dock icon and choose Open at Login from the pop-up menu. Now restart your Mac and the application will launch automatically. If you want to hide the application after it automatically launches (so it stays hidden from view until you click on it in the Dock), here's how: Go under the Apple menu (or to the Dock) to System Preferences. In the System Preferences pane, click on the Accounts icon, then in the Accounts pane, click on the Login Items tab. Now click on the Hide checkbox next to the application's name. Close the dialog and your application's set.

   BURNING MULTIPLE TIMES TO THE SAME CD

Generally, when you burn files to a CD once, you're done—you can't burn to that CD again. Unless you use this little trick: First create a new folder and give it a descriptive name (something like "Burn baby burn!" Kidding). Now put the files you want to burn into that folder, then go to the Applications folder and open the Utilities folder. Double-click on Disk Utility. When it comes up, go under the File menu, under New, and choose Disk Image from Folder, and then when the Open dialog appears, find that folder with the stuff you want to burn and click the Image button. A Save dialog appears in which you can leave the name as is or choose a new name (leave the other controls alone), and then click Save. In a few moments, a disk image of your folder's contents will appear in the list on the left side of the Disk Utility dialog. Click on that icon, and then click the Burn button at the top left of the Disk Utility dialog. When you click the Burn button, a dialog will appear asking to insert a disc, do so, and then click once the blue

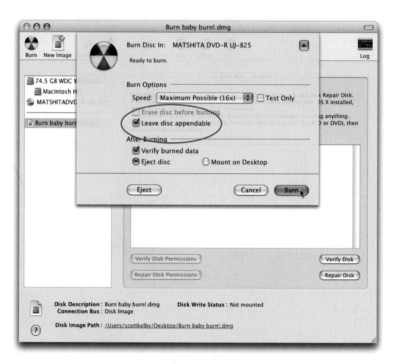

downward-facing triangle on the right side of this dialog to show more options. Click on the checkbox for Leave Disc Appendable, then click the Burn button. Your data will now be written to that CD. To add more files later, just insert that same CD and then you'll use this same process all over again, but when you get to that final Burn dialog, the button won't say "Burn" this time, instead it will say "Append" because you're adding these files to the same disc. By the way, don't forget to remove the files you already burned to this disc from your "Burn baby burn!" folder (and the DMG file it creates) before you make your next disc image.

HOW TO KEEP YOUR RESIZED MOVIES LOOKING CRISP

Images (moving or otherwise) are made of pixels, and images look best at their original size. If you resize them to even multiples (like 150%, 200%, etc.) or shrink them in size (to 30% or 50%), they still look pretty crisp and smooth. However, if you resize them to odd sizes (like 67.7%, 82%, or 129%), these images tend to a look a little jaggy (you Photoshop users know what I mean). Well, in QuickTime 7 you can just grab the corner of the QuickTime Player window and drag it to any size you'd like. So, is there a trick to making the window "snap" to sizes that make your movies look their best when resized (like 50%, 25%, or 200%)? Yup. Just hold the Option key, click on a corner, and start dragging, and as you drag it will snap to those ideal sizes.

 SAVING MUCHO DRIVE SPACE

You know those Apple applications like iCal, Mail, TextEdit, etc. Although you're seeing them in English, each one comes with a foreign language version already installed. That's pretty handy, unless you only read English, in which case those extra languages are just taking up space. A lot of space. Luckily, getting rid of those extra languages is easy—just go to your Applications folder, click an application's icon, then press Command-I to bring up the Info dialog. You'll see a panel for Languages, so click on the little right-facing arrow to show all the languages installed for that application. Click on any language, and then press Command-A to select all languages except English (you'll notice that English is grayed out and cannot be removed if that's your currently selected language). Now just click the Remove button and those extra languages will be moved to the Trash. For example, in Mail it trashed more than 4,000 files from my hard disk, which I clearly didn't need. Not bad for 15 seconds of work. (*Note:* You'll get a scary warning dialog asking if you're sure you want do this, so just be sure and click Continue.)

SAVE TO THE DESKTOP IN A FLASH

When you're in the Save As dialog and you want to save a file to the desktop, just press Command-D and the "Where" pop-up menu will switch to Desktop, so all you have to do is name your file and click OK. Another alternative is saving in the Documents folder (like the OS really wants you to), so get to your Home folder by pressing Command-Shift-H, and Home (which is your user folder) will appear as your destination. Now just click on the Documents folder in the window.

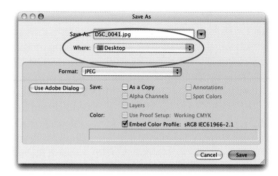

SAVING TIME IN SAVE AS, PART 1

Here's a fairly wild Mac OS X tip for saving a file (this is a great one to show at parties. Well, at least parties where there are lots of Mac-heads). If you're going to save a document and you can see the folder on your drive where you want to save it (it's in a Finder window or on your desktop), in the Save As dialog, expand the Column view by clicking on the blue button with the down-facing triangle next to the Save As field. Then you can actually drag-and-drop the folder that you want to save your document into from the desktop or Finder window to one of the columns in your Save As dialog. This is one of those things you have to try once yourself, but once you do, you'll use it again and again to save time when saving documents.

SPEED NAVIGATING IN SAVE AS, PART 2

Want to speed things up by using the keyboard to get around in the Save As dialog? There's just one thing you have to do first—press the Tab key. That removes the highlighting from the Save As naming field, and changes the focus on the sidebar (notice the blue highlight rectangle around the sidebar shown here). Once the sidebar is highlighted, you can use the Up/Down Arrow keys to move up and down the sidebar. Press Tab again and the Search field is active. Press Tab once more and the Column (or List) view is highlighted, and you can use the Arrow keys on your keyboard to quickly get right where you want to be. When you get there, press the Tab key again to highlight the Save As field so you can name your file, and then hit the Return key to "make it so!" *Note:* If you don't see the sidebar or viewing modes, click on the little blue down-facing arrow button to the right of the Save As field.

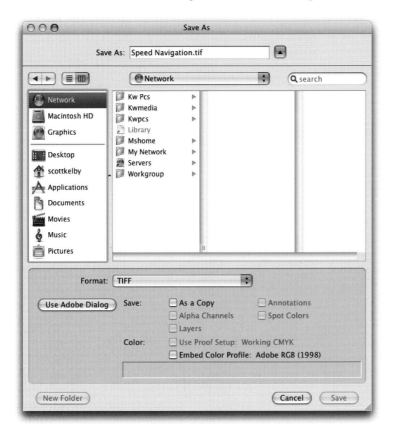

DESKTOP PRINTING? HOW ABOUT "SIDEBAR PRINTING?"

Elsewhere in this book you learn how to create a desktop printer in Tiger (by going to the Printer Setup Utility in the Utilities folder in Applications, pressing Command-L to open the Printer List dialog, clicking on the printer you want as a desktop printer, and then pressing Command-Shift-D). However, once you create a desktop printer, you can really make things convenient by clicking on the desktop printer and pressing Command-T, which adds this desktop printer to your sidebar. Now you can drag-and-drop files from your current window right onto the printer in the sidebar. The mind reels.

NEED THE FIRST AVAILABLE PRINTER?

If you've got a print job on your hands and you need it as soon as possible, but all the printers on your network are often busy, you can pool these printers together so your document will automatically print to the first available printer. Just go to the Printer Setup Utility (in the Applications folder, within the Utilities folder), Command-click on all the printers you want to pool together, then go under the Printers menu and choose Pool Printers. A dialog will open where you can name your pool (the default name is "Printer Pool"), and it shows a list of printers that are in that pool. You can click-and-drag the printers into the order that you want and then click Create, which adds a new printer in your Printer List called Printer Pool. Choose that as your printer, and then when you choose Print, Mac OS X will start looking for the first available printer.

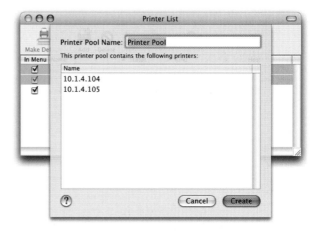

THE CALCULATOR'S HIDDEN POWER

The regular old calculator that comes with Mac OS X is much more than it seems. In fact, it combines two of Dashboard's widgets into one. Not only does it do regular and scientific calculations (which is more than the Calculator widget can do), it also does the same type of conversions that the Unit Converter widget does, including currency conversions using updated exchange rates it pulls from the Internet. To put this baby into action, just open the Calculator (it's in the Applications folder), enter a number, and then choose what you want to convert that number into from the Convert menu in the menu bar. A dialog will pop up where you can choose what you want to convert, and when you click OK, the results are shown in the Calculator's window. So now don't you feel bad about calling the Calculator "old" and "regular"? Oh, wait, that was me. Sorry.

   FIND SPEED TIP: FIND IT AND CLOSE THE RESULTS WINDOW FAST!

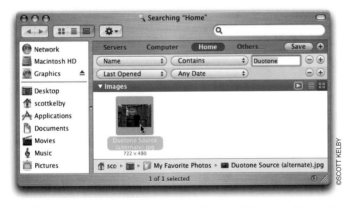

If you use Mac OS X's built-in Find function (Command-F) to find and open a file (instead of the Spotlight dialog), you can save yourself time by having the Find function automatically close the Searching window for you, as soon as your document opens. All you have to do is hold the Option key as you double-click on the file to launch it, and the Searching window will close immediately, saving you from having to close it manually later.

OPENING SIDEBAR ITEMS IN THEIR OWN WINDOW

My buddy Terry White found this cool tip: If you click on an icon in your sidebar, it just opens in the current window, but if you Command-click on an item in the sidebar, it leaves the current window alone, and opens that item in its own separate window. Option-click on a sidebar item, and it closes the old window, while opening a new one. Very handy stuff.

JUMP TO THE FIND FIELD FAST

Want the fastest way in town to jump to the Search field that appears within the Finder window's toolbar? Just press Command-Option-F, and you'll see your cursor blinking in the field, ready for you to type your search term. That's fast, baby!

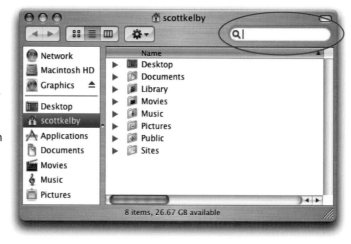

⊖ ⊖ ⊖ CHANGING WHICH APP OPENS WHICH DOC

If you have a file—let's say it's a graphic file in PICT format—by default it will open in Preview, right? And you probably know that you can go into the file's Info dialog and reassign it to open in a different application; but there's an easier way. Just Control-click on the PICT file, select Open With, and choose the app you want to open that particular file (I would choose Photoshop, but hey, that's just me). If you decide you always want that file to open in a different app (such as Photoshop), hold the Option key once the contextual menu is visible, and you'll see that the menu item named Open With changes to Always Open With.

   DESKTOP BACKGROUND QUICK CHANGE

If you change your desktop patterns frequently, you'll love this tip that saves you a trip to the Apple menu. Just Control-click anywhere on your desktop, and a contextual menu will appear. Choose Change Desktop Background and the Desktop & Screen Saver preference pane will appear, ready for you to choose a new background.

   QUICK QUITTING SPEED TIP

You can quickly quit any program without actually going to that program. Hold the Command key and press the Tab key until the program's icon appears highlighted in the Dock-like window that appears in the middle of your screen, and then press the letter Q and it will quit. (Okay, this is kind of cheating: Since you already have Command held down, you don't have to press it again; you're really pressing Command-Q.)

DOCUMENT ALIASES—THE FAST WAY

Want to quickly create an alias for the document or folder you're working on? Just press Command-Option, then click-and-hold on the tiny icon that appears to the left of the document's name in its title bar and drag that little icon to your desktop. (By the way, that "tiny little icon" is technically called the "proxy icon," but that's just so…technical-sounding.)

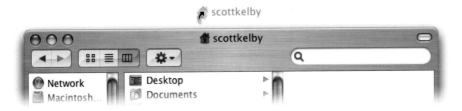

  YOU'RE TWO CLICKS FROM A PHOTO'S EXIF DATA

When you take a photo with a digital camera, the camera embeds info directly into the file, including the make and model of camera, the exposure, shutter speed, and a host of other info (called EXIF data). That info is usually viewed within an application like Photoshop or iPhoto, but now you can view it right from the Finder. Just click on the photo's icon, then press Command-I to bring up the Info dialog. When it appears, click on the right-facing triangle beside the words "More Info" and the basic EXIF data will appear.

   UNLOCK MORE OF YOUR MAC'S POWER!

Wouldn't it be cool if there were extra built-in automation power already on your Mac, and all you had to do was turn it on. Yeah, that'd be cool. Anyway, here's something completely different (just kidding). Actually, you can unlock this automation by just doing a little digging. Start by opening your Applications folder, and then look inside your AppleScript folder (don't worry, you're not going to be doing any scripting—they're already written for you). Now double-click on the AppleScript Utility icon, and in the resulting dialog, turn on the Show Script Menu in Menu Bar checkbox. Close the Utility dialog, and then go to the menu bar and click on the Script icon—a list of all sorts of cool automatic functions are now just a click away.

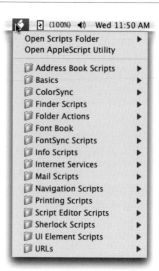

   FTP FILES WITHOUT A THIRD-PARTY PROGRAM

Need to email somebody a file that's larger than his 5-MB email limit? Use FTP, because you can upload huge files with no restriction. You probably already knew that, but did you know that you don't have to buy a third-party FTP client to FTP your files? That's right baby, you can do it right from within Tiger. Here's how: Go to the Finder's Go menu, and choose Connect to Server. When the dialog appears, just type the FTP address where you want the file to go and click Connect. You may either get

directly connected, or depending on whose server you're connecting to, it may ask you for your Name and Password (that keeps people from just jumping on anyone's server and uploading files at random). Once you're "in," you'll see a folder—now you can just drag-and-drop the file you want to transfer into that folder and the transfer will begin.

SPEEDING THINGS UP WITH A TWO-BUTTON MOUSE

Tired of Control-clicking? Maybe it's time to buy a two-button mouse. (What!!!! A Mac with a two-button mouse?) I guess Apple figured at some point we'd get tired of Control-clicking, so in Mac OS X if you connect a two-button USB mouse to your Mac, the second button automatically becomes the "Control-click" function (just like a PC's Right-click). From that point on, every time in this book when it tells you to Control-click (like on application icons in the Dock), instead you can just Right-click.

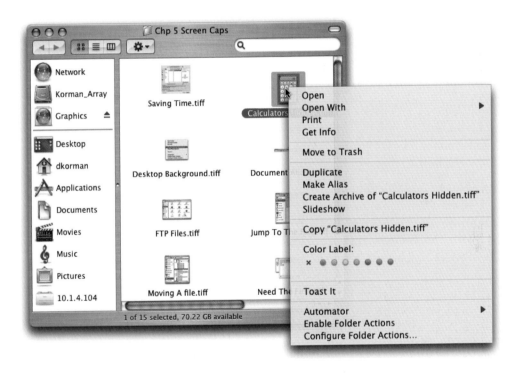

   FOUND MORE THAN ONE? OPEN 'EM ALL AT ONCE!

If you're searching for files using Mac OS X's built-in Find command (Command-F), and it turns up more than one right answer (in other words, you found three files you want to open, rather than just one), you can open all three at once. Just Command-click on the files you want to open (right within the Searching window) and press Command-O; all the files will open, one right after the other.

⬤ ⬤ ⬤ **CREATING YOUR OWN KEYBOARD SHORTCUTS**

One thing that kicks butt in the productivity department is that you can create your own custom keyboard shortcuts. Here's how: Go under the Apple menu to System Preferences, then click on the Keyboard & Mouse icon. In the pane that appears, click on the Keyboard Shortcuts button. Then click the plus (+) sign button at the bottom of the list of existing shortcuts to add your own. The pop-up menu at the top of the dialog that opens lets you choose whether this shortcut works across all applications, or in just an individual app (or just the Finder if you like). In the Menu Title field, enter the EXACT name of the menu item you want a shortcut for, then type the shortcut you want to use and click Add. It's that easy. (*Note:* Make sure the application that you're making the shortcut for isn't open.) Also, you can change existing shortcuts: If you want to use a shortcut that's already in use, you can disable that item (assuming you don't use it much) and use its shortcut for a different command.

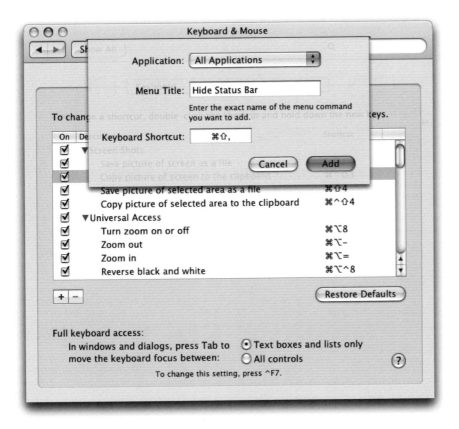

   GET TO SOUND OR DISPLAY PREFERENCES FAST!

Since Apple knows you'll be going to these two fairly often, they gave them shortcuts.
Press Option-Mute (it's the top-left key above the numeric keypad) and the System
Preferences will launch, taking you straight to the Sound preferences. Press Option-F14
(the Brightness key on your keyboard) and the Display preferences will pop up instead.
It doesn't get much faster than that!

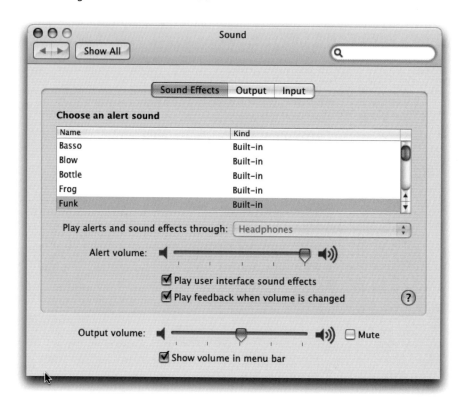

SAVING YOUR UPDATE FILES WHEN YOU UPDATE YOUR MAC

Mac OS X Tiger's Software Update feature is about the world's easiest way to keep your Apple software up-to-date, but when it downloads an update, it immediately installs it and deletes the downloaded file. That's really nice that it cleans up after itself, but what if you wanted to keep a backup of the update file yourself (or what if you wanted to use that downloaded file to update your other Macs)? Well, you can. Here's how: The next time you run Software Update (under the Apple menu), and an item shows up that needs updating, just click on it (or Command-click if there are several updates) to select it, and in the Software Update's Update menu, choose Install and Keep Package. It will download the files and put a disk image of the download on your desktop.

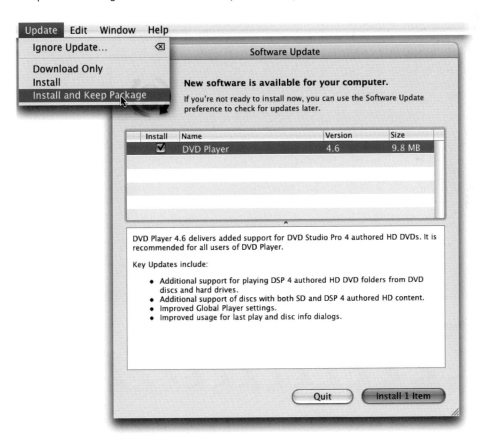

MOVING A FILE OUT OF A FOLDER IN LIST VIEW

Let's say you're in List view, and the file you want is inside a folder you see in the list (hey, this is going pretty good so far). You can expand the folder to get to the file you need, but to get that file out of the folder that it's currently in and place it in the original window, you can drag the icon to the headers. Just drag the icon straight up to the headers below the Finder window's toolbar and your window will highlight to let you know "you're there." Release the mouse button, and your file will appear as a separate item, outside the folder, with the other items in the list.

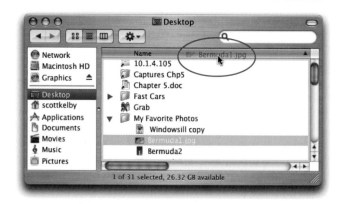

TWO SECONDS TO SLEEP

Want the fastest way to put your Mac right into a deep, sleepy-bear hibernation-like sleep (no whirling fan, no dialogs, no sound—nuthin'—just fast, glorious sleep). Just press Command-Option and then hold the Eject button for about 2 seconds and Zzzzzzzzzzzzz. It doesn't get much faster than that.

FINDING THE RIGHT SPECIAL CHARACTER

Okay, let's say you're in Mail, and you're writing the word "résumé," which used properly should have that little accent over the "é" like I did here. You know it needs an accent, but you have no idea which keyboards combination will create an "e" with an accent above it. Here's a trick for finding any special character: When you're typing, and you need that special character, stop typing and click the Fonts button at the top of the Mail window. When the Font dialog appears, go to the Actions pop-up menu (its icon looks like a gear near the bottom-left corner of the dialog) and choose Characters to bring up the Character Palette. At the bottom-right side of the Character Palette dialog, you'll see a small Search field. Type whatever you need, such as "acute accent" (without the quotes), and in just a moment a menu of different accents will appear. Double-click on the accent you want and the palette will jump to the mark you need. Close by you should see the character you need. Click on it and then click on the Insert button (or Insert with Font button if you're searching in Glyph View) just to the right of the Search field. Now that letter "é" will appear in just the right place in your email message.

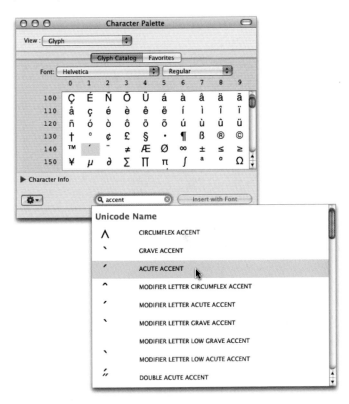

Cool & the Gang

WAY COOL TIPS

I know, I know, it's supposed to be "Kool & the Gang" (with a "K") not "Cool & the Gang" with a "C." Okay, Mr./Ms. Smarty-Pants—

Cool & the Gang
way cool tips

you know so much about the band, which one is Kool? The lead singer? Wrong! That's JT. Kool is actually the bass player—the guy who originally formed the band. Okay, now what was their first million-selling single? "Ladies Night"? "Celebration"? "Too Hot"? "Fresh"? Nice try. It was "Jungle Boogie." Geez, I don't know where you got all this attitude, because apparently aside from spelling their name, you really don't know that much about the band. Now, what does all this have to do with Mac OS X? Plenty. Anyway, here's a "celebration" of tips that were "too hot" to be contained in any other chapters. (I know—they're lame puns, I don't care—I'm using 'em.)

   TURNING YOUR PHOTO INTO A PUZZLE

The default photo for the Tile Game widget in Dashboard is a tiger (big surprise), but you can use any photo you'd like in place of the default tiger image. Here's how: First, you have to open the Tile Game widget by choosing it from the Widget Bar (press Command–+ [Plus Sign] to open the Bar), then click anywhere to close Dashboard (don't close the Tile Game widget, leave it open as you close Dashboard). Now find the photo you want to use, then click, hold, and start dragging it. While you're dragging, with your free hand press the F12 key to bring up Dashboard. When your cursor gets over the Tile Game  widget, just release the mouse and your photo will now appear in the game. However, this only lasts as long as you keep this widget open (not Dashboard—you can open and close it as you like). If you manually close the Tile Game widget, the next time you open it, the tiger photo is back. You knew anything that good wouldn't last.

   RELOADING DASHBOARD WIDGET TRICK

Okay, although this one is more of a trick just for the sheer fun of it (because the onscreen animation is pretty cool), it actually has a practical side as well. Just click on an open widget in Dashboard, then press Command-R on your keyboard and the widget kind of twirls away (for lack of a better term) and then reappears. It looks cool, but beyond that it does actually reload the widget (as if you had just dragged it out from the Widget Bar), which refreshes any data that the widget calls upon. Try it once (although it's nearly impossible to do it just once, because the animation is cool enough that you'll have to do it a few times to get it out of your system). *Note:* Pressing this shortcut too much on one widget could cause Dashboard to crash (I'm being serious here).

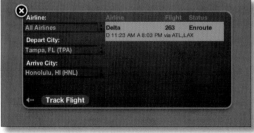

Regular widget

Twisted widget

ITUNES ALBUM ART SCREEN SAVER

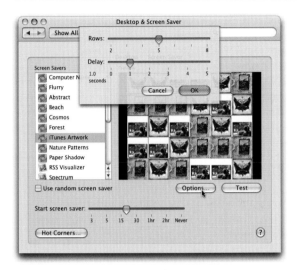

This one I love, and a lot of people (even cool people like yourself) don't know about it. This particular screen saver looks through your album art in iTunes and creates a tiled wall of albums. One by one these tiles flip to reveal other albums. You set it up by going to the System Preferences (under the Apple menu), and clicking on the Desktop & Screen Saver icon. When these preferences appear, click on the Screen Saver tab, then from the list of screen savers on the left side of the preferences panel, click on iTunes Artwork. Click the Options button to set how many rows of albums will be displayed (the less rows you choose, the larger the wall of albums will appear). If you haven't tried this one yet, give it a shot. It'll help you channel your inner musician (whatever that means).

   DON'T KNOW WHAT A WORD MEANS? TIGER DOES

Let's say you're on a webpage and you run across a word you don't understand (for example, let's say you're on Longhorn website and you see a word like "original" or "general"). Just highlight the word in question and then press Command-Control-D (or Control-click on it and choose Look Up in Dictionary). A tiny panel will appear showing the definition (or Control-click and it will launch an electronic version of the Oxford Dictionary, which comes with Mac OS X Tiger). Either way, within seconds the definition will appear onscreen.

   GETTING DEFINITIONS WITHOUT LAUNCHING DICTIONARY

If you're using the Safari Web browser, Text Edit, Stickies, or any Cocoa application, you can have definitions to words appear right within the application (rather than launching the whole Oxford Dictionary application). Here's how: First launch the Dictionary application (it's in your Applications folder), and when it appears, go under the Dictionary menu and choose Preferences. When the Preferences dialog appears, in the Contextual Menu section, choose Open Dictionary Panel. Now when you highlight a word, Control-click on the highlighted word, choose Look Up in Dictionary, and a little panel will pop up right there with the definition. If the page has a number of words you don't understand, you can speed things up by holding Command-Control-D and then move your cursor over any word that you want to know the definition of (by the way, hovering over the phrase "Microsoft innovation" doesn't bring up a definition because that's actually an oxymoron—sorry, I just couldn't help myself).

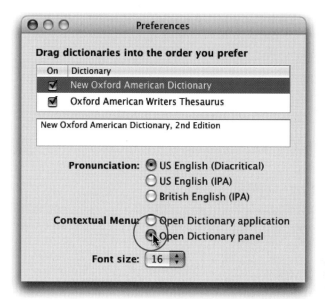

GET NEWS ON YOUR SCREEN SAVER

Dig this: You can set up Tiger's screen saver to display RSS news feeds right onscreen when the screen saver kicks in. Here's how: Go to the System Preferences under the Apple menu and click on the Desktop & Screen Saver icon. When those preferences come up, click on the Screen Saver tab, and there you'll see a list of different screen savers. Click on RSS Visualizer. Click on the Options button to choose which feed you'd like to appear onscreen from the list of approved feeds, then close the System Preferences. Now, the next time your screen saver kicks in, you'll get a live RSS news feed, ensuring that you never have a moment of uninterrupted peace and calm, with some data stream feeding you more input.

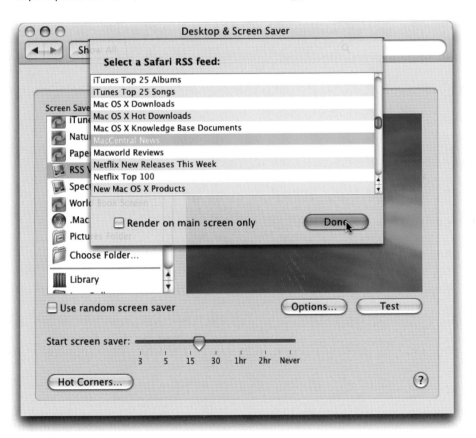

   ADDING YOUR FAVORITE RSS FEED TO YOUR SCREEN SAVER

In the previous tip, I showed how to set up your screen saver to display as RSS feed, but unfortunately you can only choose from the RSS feeds that appear in that dialog. But actually, there is a sneaky way around that, so you can have any RSS feed as your screen saver, instead of just those "chosen few." Here's what you need to do: First, launch Safari and navigate to the site that has the RSS feed you'd like displayed as your screen saver. Now click on the blue RSS feed button that appears on the right side of the address bar to display the feed, then click the Add Bookmark button on the left side of the window. This brings up the Bookmarks dialog, and you'll need to choose Bookmarks Bar and click Add. That's it—now when you go to the Screen Saver tab in the preferences, click on RSS Visualizer, click on the Options button, and the RSS feed you saved will be available as one of the choices. *Note:* If the feed doesn't appear, click on the RSS icon in Safari Preferences (Command-, [Comma key]). It should be set to Automatically Update Articles in Bookmarks Bar.

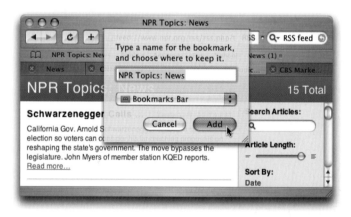

AN EASIER WAY TO RENAME ITEMS IN YOUR SIDEBAR

The sidebar was introduced back in Mac OS X Panther, and it's great for having one-click access to your most-used files, folders, and applications. But there is one thing that was kind of annoying—once something was in the sidebar, you couldn't rename it—you had to go back to the original file, rename that file, and then the new name would be reflected in the sidebar. Seems like an awful lot of work for just a simple rename. But luckily that's changed in Tiger, because now you can just Control-click on any item in the sidebar and a contextual menu will appear that lets you do everything from renaming the sidebar item to running an automation on it. *Note:* Don't rename your Home folder (which likely shows your user name), which can wreak havoc on your Mac.

  GET THE FULL DASHBOARD WEATHER EXPERIENCE

If you've used the Dashboard Weather widget, you've probably already noticed that Apple went to great lengths to design some really cool-looking visuals to let you know in a split second what the weather condition is for the city you're monitoring (including whether it's currently day or night in that city, and it shows the current phase of the moon). But if you live someplace that doesn't get much variation in its weather (for example, I live in Tampa Bay, which means I only see basically sun and thunderstorms), you don't get the full Dashboard weather experience (which includes things like snow, ice, hail, locust plague, etc.). But you don't have to pack up the family and move to Ottawa. Instead, you can have the Weather widget cycle through all its different weather graphics by holding the Option and Command keys, and then just clicking on the Weather widget (avoiding the city's name, as that will launch your Web browser showing more weather details). This takes you to a hypothetical town called "Nowhere," which apparently experiences a new weather phenomenon with every Command-Option-click (much like Seattle).

   GETTING INTERNATIONAL WEATHER

If you want to get the weather for an international city (like Tokyo, Japan), you can just click on the tiny "i" icon that appears in the Dashboard Weather widget when you mouse over its bottom-right corner. Now in the City, State or ZIP Code field, just type the name of the city (in this case "Tokyo"), then press the Return key. A menu with a list of possible matches will appear. Choose Tokyo, Japan, and then press Return again. Now you'll have the current weather for Tokyo. *Note:* The zone you set in your preferences may affect how this works. Also, if you have cookies disabled in Safari, the AccuWeather.com site may not save your default location.

GETTING MORE INFO FROM THE WEATHER WIDGET

Here's one a lot of people miss: If you've got the Weather widget open and you want more information about the weather in the city you're monitoring, just click once directly on the city's name, and it will launch your Web browser, taking you to a page with much more detailed weather information on that city from Accuweather.com.

   REMOVING A WIDGET FROM DASHBOARD PERMANENTLY

If you downloaded a widget, and then decide that you want to get rid of it, you can remove it from Dashboard by going to your Home folder, and looking inside your Library folder. Inside that you'll find a folder named Widgets, which holds all the widgets you've downloaded (from Apple's site and elsewhere). To delete one of those widgets, just click on it and press Command-Delete to send it to the Trash. That's it—it's gone, baby!

USE THE SAME WIDGET MORE THAN ONCE

One of the great yet little-known things about widgets is that you can have more than one of the same widget open at the same time. For example, since I travel a lot, I keep the Weather widget open for my hometown and the next town (or two) that I'm traveling to, so I know how to pack before I head out. To use multiple widgets, just drag them out from the Widget Bar. If you want three, four, or more Weather widgets, just drag them out and configure each one separately.

   DASHBOARD SUPER SLO-MO TRICK

The next time you're ready to close Dashboard (you close it by clicking on anything or anywhere other than a widget), and you're not working on a tight deadline or trying to get ahead in life, try this: Hold the Shift key, then click on something other than a widget. This closes Dashboard using a super slow-motion effect with your widgets slowly zooming toward you. Also, try this "holding-the-Shift-key" trick when closing an individual widget and you get a pretty cool slo-mo effect there as well. Here's another: Try holding Shift when opening or closing the Widget Bar. (I particularly like the way the plus-sign-in-a-circle rotates as the Bar appears. I never noticed it did that at regular speed.) So why did Apple include slo-mo effects in Dashboard? Because they know we just love stupid crap like that.

FROM THE YELLOW PAGES TO YOUR ADDRESS BOOK IN ONE CLICK

If you've looked up a phone number using the Yellow Pages widget in Dashboard, you can instantly add that contact and number to your Address Book by clicking the little plus sign (+) that appears to the immediate left of the company's address.

FASTER WIDGET CLOSING

Want a faster way to close any open widget in Dashboard? Just hold the Option key and move your cursor anywhere over the widget you want to close. The Close button will appear (that little X in the upper left-hand corner), and you can click that X to close the widget.

   PHONE NUMBER WIDGET TRICK

The next time you pull up someone's contact info using the Address Book widget that comes with Mac OS X Tiger's Dashboard, click on his or her phone number. It will now appear in HUGE letters across your screen, as shown here (this also works in the regular Address Book, but for some reason it seems cooler using it in Dashboard).

   SCREEN CAPTURE OF JUST ONE WINDOW

If you want to take a screen capture of just one window, there's a little-known keyboard shortcut you should get to know. Just press Shift-Command-Spacebar-4 (in that order) and your cursor will change into a large camera. Click this camera cursor on the window you want to capture, and it will create a capture of just that window, which will appear on your desktop as Picture 1.

● ● ● ADD ANY PHOTO TO YOUR IPHOTO LIBRARY IN ONE CLICK

If you're on the Web and you see a photo you'd like, with just one click you can add it to your iPhoto Library—just Control-click directly on the photo and in the contextual menu that appears choose Add Image to iPhoto Library.

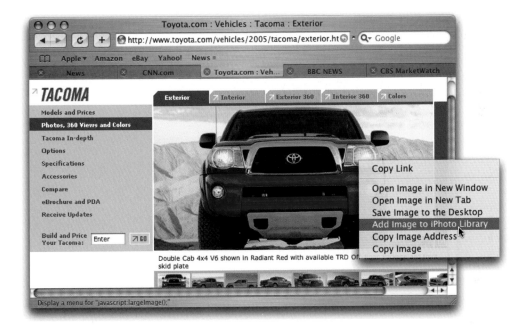

● ● ● DO YOU MISS THE OLD TRASH CAN?

This is one of my favorite tips in the whole book, because I'm a longtime Mac user and darn it, I admit it—I miss having the Trash at the bottom-right corner of my screen. If you miss it there too, here's how to get your own (even though there are four steps, it's absolutely simple to do):

STEP ONE: Go to your desktop and create a new folder by pressing Shift-Command-N. Make an alias of this new folder by pressing Command-L, then name this alias folder "Trash" (you can now delete the original folder—you don't need it anymore).

STEP TWO: Click on the alias folder and press Command-I to bring up its Info dialog. Click on the Select New Original button under the General pane, and then the Select New Original dialog will appear. Press Shift-Command-G to bring up the Go to the Folder dialog. Type in this: /users/yournamehere /.trash (of course, don't type "yourname-here," instead enter your user name there. If you don't know what it is, look inside your Mac's Users folder and see what the Home icon is named). Click the Go button and it takes you to the invisible Trash file on your drive. Now, click the Choose button to make that folder become an alias of your Trash. You're almost there.

STEP THREE: Click on the Trash icon in the Dock to open its window. Then press Command-I to open the Trash's Info dialog, click on the tiny Trash can icon, then press Command-C to copy the Trash icon.

STEP FOUR: Go back to your Trash folder on your desktop, click on it, press Command-I to bring up its Info dialog, click on its tiny folder icon in the top-left corner, then press Command-V to paste the Trash icon over the folder icon. All that's left to do now is drag your new Trash alias down to the bottom right-hand corner of your screen, and you've done it!

FROM EPS TO PDF IN NO TIME FLAT

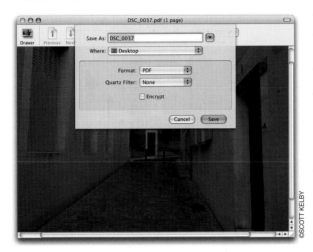

This trick is pretty much just for graphic designers who work with EPS images from applications like Adobe Illustrator, CorelDraw for Mac, Freehand, and Photoshop. If you want to convert your EPS image instantly into a PDF (ideal for emailing), just drag it onto Apple's Preview application icon in your Dock (or in your Applications folder) and OS X automatically converts your PostScript file to a PDF on the fly. When you choose Save from the File menu, it will save as a PDF.

   ## TWEAKING YOUR VIDEO IN QUICKTIME PRO

If you have Apple's QuickTime Pro installed (rather than just the standard QuickTime Player), you have more video-tweaking controls than you might have thought. Open a movie, then press Command-K, and a host of Video Controls will appear at the bottom of your QuickTime screen, including controls for Brightness, Color, Tint, and Contrast. To increase any of these values, just click right on the horizontal bar and drag. To move to the next setting, click the tiny gray up/down arrows to the right of the adjustment's name. When you're done, save your movie and your changes are saved right along with it.

APPLYING FILTERS TO YOUR PHOTOS

You can edit the tonal
values in your photos by
applying filters to them
at the printing stage.
To do this, just open a
photo in Preview (or any
Cocoa app like TextEdit),
and choose Print from
the File menu. In the
Print dialog, click on the
pop-up menu for Quartz
Filter and a list of tonal
filters will appear, which
you can apply by choos-
ing them from the list.

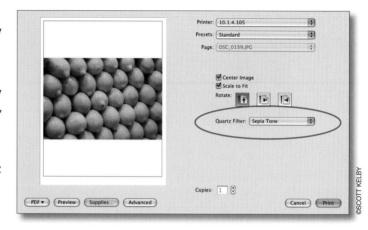

But how do you know how these filters will really look when applied to your photo? Just
check out the large preview window on the left.

THE TRICK FOR GETTING TO YOUR FAVORITES

Although Apple no longer lists Favorites in Open/Save
dialogs, and the Command-T shortcut no longer adds
files to the Favorites folder, your Favorites folder is still
around (it's in your Home folder, in your Library folder,
but I recommend dragging it to your sidebar). But
here's a trick that helps make using the old Favorites
folder easier. Go under the Finder menu and choose
Preferences. Click on the General icon, and for New
Finder Windows Open, choose Other from the pop-up
menu, then navigate to your Library folder (inside your
Home folder) and click on Favorites. By doing this, if
you press Command-N, it now opens your Favorites
folder, rather than a new Finder window, and you can
then Command-Option-drag items into your Favorites
folder (which makes an alias of them, just like the old
Favorites folder).

HOW TO MAKE ONE PRINTER YOUR DEFAULT PRINTER

In previous versions of Mac OS X, your default printer was whichever printer you used last. This kinda stunk, because if you used the same printer most every day, but changed to a different printer to print even just one document, the next time you'd go to print, that's the printer you got. Well, now you can designate one printer to always be your default printer, and even if you switch to another printer temporarily, the next time you come back, your default printer will be right there waiting for you. To assign a printer as your default, go under the Apple menu and choose System Preferences. Click on the Print & Fax icon, then click on the Selected Printer in the Print Dialog pop-up menu near the bottom of the dialog. Click on the printer you want as your default (just be sure not to choose Last Printer Used) and close the Print & Fax options. That's it!

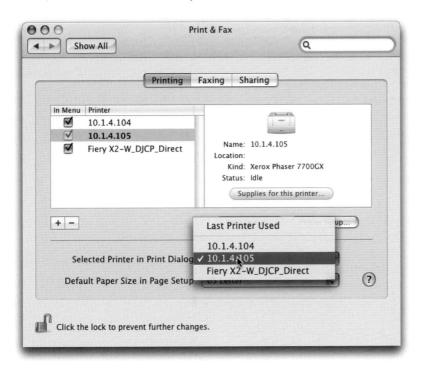

   LET TIGER TYPE IT FOR YOU

If you're typing a long word (like existentialism or existentialisms), and you're feeling particularly lazy that day, rather than typing all the letters yourself, just type the first few letters then press the Escape key on your keyboard. A list of your most likely choices will appear— just scroll down to the one you want and click on it. This works in applications like Apple's TextEdit, Stickies, etc.

   MAKING WEB PHOTOS OPEN IN PHOTOSHOP

If you download any photos from the Web, chances are they're compressed JPEG files, and if you double-click on them, by default they open in Apple's Preview application. If, like me, you'd prefer that all JPEG images open in Adobe Photoshop, here's what do to: Download a photo from the Web, click on it, and press Command-I to bring up its Info dialog. Click the right-facing gray arrow to the left of the words "Open With" to expand this pane. From the Open With pop-up menu, look for Adobe Photoshop. If you don't see it, just choose Other, and then navigate to it. After you've chosen Photoshop, click the Change All button in the Open With pane. From now on, all JPEG photos will open in Photoshop rather than Preview. Cool, eh?

OPENING THE CD TRAY BY MAGIC (ON OLDER MACHINES)

If you're running Mac OS X on an older machine (by older, I mean it's not one of the newer units that have an Eject button for popping out your CD tray on the keyboard), you may not be out of luck—try holding down the F12 key for a few seconds (which invokes the Eject CD command), and your keyboard tray should pop out. I say it "should" pop out, because I haven't tried it on every machine with every keyboard, so instead, let's say "I hope it will pop out," or "I feel pretty good about it popping out," or perhaps even "I bet it pops out."

QUICK SET: WARNING BEEP SOUND

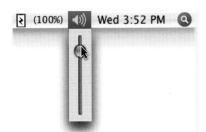

Here's a hidden little tip right from the desktop for changing the volume of your alert beep. The pop-down Volume control (a Menu Extra on the top right of your menu bar) controls the overall system volume; but if you hold the Option key, the pop-down slider now controls the volume of just your system's alert "beep."

   A FASTER ROUTE TO THE WIDGET BAR

Want to peruse your collection of Dashboard widgets? Rather than clicking on that big plus sign (+) button in the lower left-hand corner of your screen, next time try pressing Command–+ (Plus Sign key) and the Widget Bar will pop right up. You can use the same shortcut to hide the bar once it's visible.

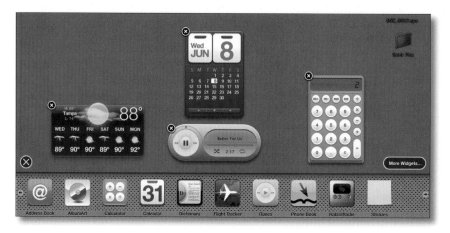

   DON'T FEEL LIKE OPENING PHOTOSHOP?

If you need to take a quick look at a Photoshop file, but don't feel like launching Photoshop, just drag the image's icon to the Preview application icon in the Dock (or in your Applications folder), and Preview will open the Photoshop file. If the Photoshop file is layered, it will display as a flattened image.

   BUILT-IN TEXT STYLE SHEETS

If you have formatted some type (let's say it's in the font Times New Roman, at 18 point, and it's both bold and italic) in a Cocoa app like TextEdit or Stickies, and you want to apply those same type attributes to another block of text that has completely different font formatting (let's say the other text is Helvetica 12-point regular), try this: Highlight some of the text that has the formatting you want and press Command-Option-C. Then, highlight the text that you'd like to have these attributes (the Helvetica 12-point), and press Command-Option-V. The highlighted text will take on your originally copied font attributes (Times New Roman, 18-point, bold, and italic)—kind of like a style sheet in QuarkXPress, InDesign, or PageMaker.

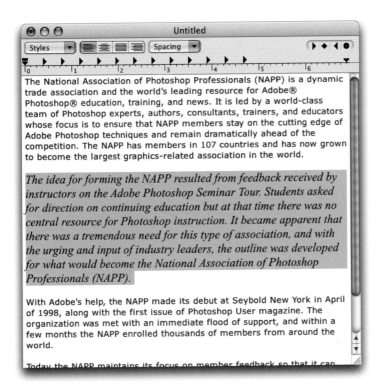

   REMOVING THE DASHBOARD ICON FROM THE DOCK

If you find that you're always using the F12 key on your keyboard to bring up Dashboard, there's not much reason to keep its icon down in your Dock, just taking up space. However, you can't just drag Dashboard off the Dock like other applications. Instead, you have to click-and-hold (or Control-click) on the Dashboard icon in the Dock and choose Remove From Dock from the pop-up menu that appears. If you remove Dashboard

from the Dock, there are two ways to get it back: The hard way: If you're pretty comfortable with the Terminal application, you can execute a "Kill" command to actually quit Dashboard, then you'll need to go to the Applications folder and double-click on the Dashboard icon to restart it, which will put the icon back in the Dock. The easy way: You can drag the Dashboard icon from the Applications folder down to the Dock like you can with other apps.

   SHERLOCK: DASHBOARD'S UGLY COUSIN

If for some reason you don't like Dashboard (hey, I've heard of a few people who, for whatever reason [they're just plain cranky] don't like it), you can get most of Dashboard's built-in functionality from a surprising place. Believe it or not, a lot of the built-in Internet-activated features are available in Sherlock (it's in your Applications folder). When you open

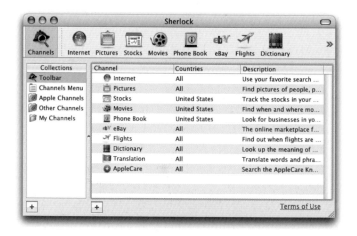

it, you'll notice that Sherlock does a lot of the same things that some of the most popular Dashboard widgets do, like tracking your flights, looking up things in Yellow Pages online, translating foreign languages, plus it's got a dictionary and thesaurus, and it even tracks your stocks.

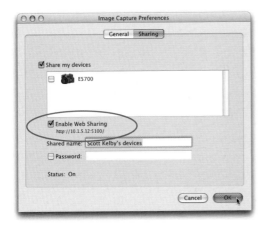  

CREATE YOUR OWN WEB CAM

Want your own Web cam (of course you don't, but play along with me, will ya, cause this is actually kinda cool)? So plug in your digital video camera to your Mac's FireWire port, then aim it at something (your dog, your front door, anything but your driveway, etc.), then go to your Applications folder and open Image Capture. Open the Preferences dialog (it's found under the Image Capture menu) and click on the Sharing tab. Turn on the checkbox for Share My Devices, and you should see your digital camera listed there (if not, check the connection). Now, turn on the checkbox for Enable Web Sharing. (*Note:* Right below that checkbox a URL will appear [something like http://10.1.5.12:5100/]. That URL is where you will send friends to see your live broadcast on the Web.) Click OK and your Web browser will launch, taking you to that URL I mentioned earlier (if it doesn't, launch your browser and enter the URL). Once it opens, click on the Remote Monitor tab at the top of the window and you'll see a preview of what your camera is seeing. That's it—you're on the air (at least until the FCC finds out. Kidding!). Here's an extra tip: You can also use a regular digital still camera, and you can set how often (in seconds) it takes a photo and broadcasts it in the Remote Monitor tab.

GO DIRECTLY FROM YOUR VIDEO CAMERA INTO QUICKTIME

There's a very cool feature that snuck into QuickTime Pro 7 that has kind of flown below the radar so far. It's the ability to record directly from your digital video camera (or a microphone) right into a QuickTime file, without having to go through iMovie, Final Cut Pro, or any other third-party application. Just connect your digital video camera (or even your iSight camera), launch the QuickTime Pro Player, then from the File menu choose New Movie Recording. A QuickTime window will open showing you a preview of what your camera is seeing. Now just click the round red record button at the bottom of the QuickTime window and it starts recording. Click

the Stop button when you're done, and you've got an instant QuickTime movie. It works the same way for recording audio using your Mac's built-in microphone (provided of course that your Mac actually does have a built-in mic), but instead of choosing New Movie Recording, you'll choose New Audio Recording. *Note:* You have to upgrade from the standard QuickTime to QuickTime Pro to have access to this feature.

   PAUSING YOUR DIRECT-TO-QUICKTIME RECORDING

If you're using the previous tip, here's another little tip you'll want to know: When you're recording video or audio clips, and you need to pause for a moment, just hold down the Option key and the Stop button changes into a Pause button. When you're ready to record again, just release the Option key and click the red Record button.

DON'T LEAVE FULL SCREEN MODE TO ADJUST YOUR VIDEO

If you're accustomed to using the QuickTime Player, you're probably used to leaving Full Screen mode any time you need to change the volume, rewind, fast forward, etc. But with Tiger (and QuickTime 7 Pro), you can now make those adjustments while you're still in Full Screen thanks to the onscreen controls that will appear if you just move your mouse. By default, this controller only stays visible for about 2 seconds after you stop moving your mouse, but you can make it hang around longer if you'd like—just go under the QuickTime menu and choose Preferences. When the dialog appears, click the Full Screen icon, and then from the Hide After menu, choose the amount of time you want the controller to stick around. If you want the controller to stay visible all the time, choose Never from the Hide After menu.

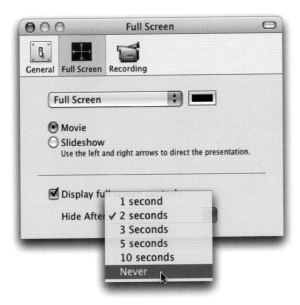

  THE SECRET SCREEN CAPTURE SHORTCUT

Okay, you probably already know the ol' Command-Shift-3 shortcut for taking a screen capture of your entire screen, and you may even know about Command-Shift-4, which gives you a crosshair cursor so you can choose which area of the screen you want to capture. But perhaps the coolest, most-secret hidden capture shortcut is Control-Command-Shift-3 (or 4), which, instead of creating a file on your desktop, copies the capture into your Clipboard memory, so you can paste it where you want. (I use this to paste screen captures right into Photoshop.)

   SENDING TEXT MESSAGES VIA BLUETOOTH

If your Mac has Bluetooth, and you've got a paired Bluetooth cellular phone nearby, you can send text messages using your Mac's keyboard (rather than those miniature keys on your cell phone's number pad). Just go to the Address Book application, and find the person you want to send your text message to. You see the word "Mobile" that appears before their cell number? Click-and-hold directly on that and from the contextual menu that appears, choose Send SMS Message. Now it's time to start typin', enter their number, and hit send, and it will use your phone to send

the message. *Note*: This may not work on all Bluetooth-enabled phones, as it depends on the make and model of your cell phone, and whether the phone receiving the message can accept SMS messages.

GETTING PHOTOS INTO YOUR PHONE

Okay, so you've created some cool background patterns for your phone using Photoshop, and you've got some photos of your spouse and kids, and you want the photos to get into your phone too. Well, Tiger can help. Actually, Tiger can do more than help—it can do it (as long as your phone is Bluetooth enabled). Go to your Applications folder, look inside the Utilities folder, and there you'll find an application called Bluetooth File Exchange. Open this application, go to the File menu, choose Send File (or choose this option by clicking on the Bluetooth icon in the far-right side of the menu bar), and it will ask you to navigate to the photo (or file) you want to upload to your phone. Find your file and click Send to get to the Send File dialog. Now, I'm assuming if you have a Bluetooth-enabled phone, you've already paired it with your Mac (so you can transfer your Address Book and iCal calendar into your phone), but if you haven't paired them yet, go to your phone's Bluetooth section and make your phone "Discoverable," then on your Mac, click the Search button in the bottom-left corner of the Send File dialog (as shown in the second capture). This searches for your phone, and when it discovers it, your phone will be added to the list. Now just click the Send button to upload the photo to your phone wirelessly. Pretty slick, eh?

KEEPING YOUR PRIVATE DATA PRIVATE

If you have sensitive information on your computer, you're probably most vulnerable to "peekers" when your computer is up and running (like at the office), but if you step away for a moment to grab a Starbucks Peppermint Mocha Frappuccino (or maybe you just go to the bathroom. Either way, for a few minutes it's "open season" for anyone with a curious mind). If that's a concern, you can keep those prying eyes away by going under the Apple menu, choosing System Preferences, and clicking on the Security icon. When the FileVault preference pane appears, turn on the checkbox for Require Password to Wake This Computer from Sleep or Screen Saver. Of course, before you do this, make darn sure you know your password.

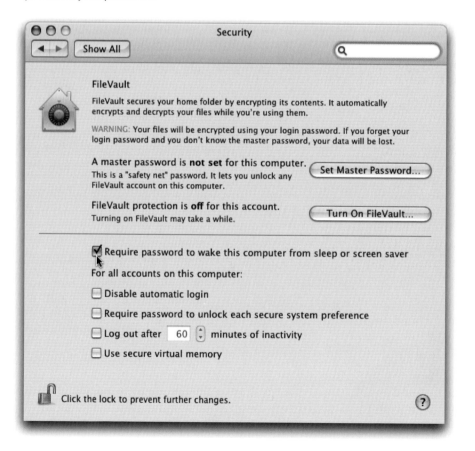

CHANGING YOUR DEFAULT DESKTOP PICTURE

The ubiquitous blue desktop background that is the default for Mac OS X is named "Aqua Blue.jpg" and it's found in the main Library folder (in your Home folder), in the folder called Desktop Pictures. (*Note:* You could always Control-click on your desktop and choose a new photo from the Desktop options, but let's imagine you have some time to yourself and want to create your own default desktop background.) Drag this image into Photoshop, erase the blue background, and create the image you want for your desktop background (or drag an existing file into this document). Then, replace the "Aqua Blue.jpg" file in your Desktop Pictures folder with this new Photoshopped file. *Another Note:* This one might be a good trick to pull on a co-worker because it'll take them a while to figure out how the default changed, but if you do, be sure to create a backup copy of Aqua Blue.jpg *before* you make changes to it.

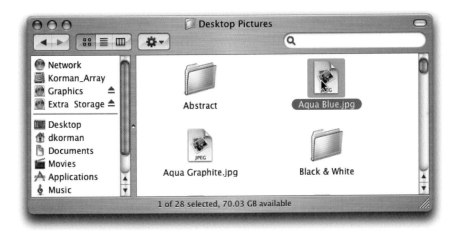

   GET THE MEGA CURSOR

If the standard-size cursors seem a bit too small for you, now you can make that cursor huge. Just go under the System Preferences (in the Apple menu), click on Universal Access, then click on the Mouse tab, and when that panel appears, near the bottom of the panel you'll see a slider for Cursor Size. Just drag the slider to the right, and as you do you'll see the new size. This is great to use when you're doing presentations projected onto a big screen, so people don't lose track of the cursor while you're working.

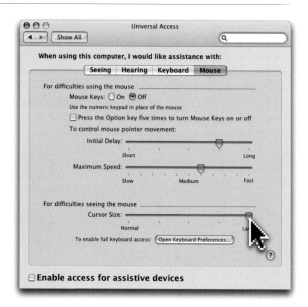

   DISABLING THE CAPS LOCK KEY

For some people, this tip alone will be worth the price of the book (and frankly, I love those people). You can completely disable the Caps Lock key on your keyboard by going to the System Preferences (in the Apple menu), then clicking on Keyboard & Mouse icon. When the preferences appear, click on the Keyboard tab. At the bottom of the Keyboard preferences is a button named Modifier Keys. Click on that button, and the first pop-up menu is for the Caps Lock key. From its pop-up menu, just choose No Action, click OK, and that's it. Life is good.

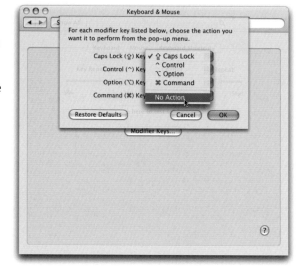

THE SILENCE OF THE BEEPS

If you have a keyboard that has volume controls right on the keyboard (like most PowerBooks), then you're probably used to hearing a little "confirmation" beep each time you press one of these volume controls. If those little beeps get on your nerves (who needs more things beeping at them?), then just hold the Shift key and this will silence the beeps as you press the volume keys. If you want to turn these sounds off permanently, go under the Apple menu, under System Preferences, then choose Sound (or press-and-hold Option as you press a sound key to open the Sound options). Click on the Sound Effects tab, then uncheck Play Feedback When Volume Is Changed.

   IF I COULD TURN BACK TIME

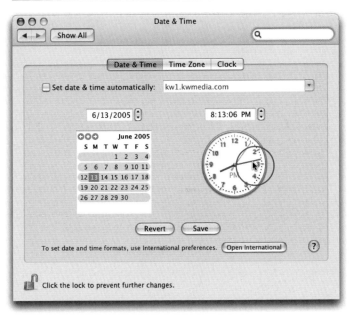

This tip is just for fun, because honestly, it's not tremendously practical, but it looks pretty cool. The next time you're changing the time, using your System Preferences (found under the Apple menu) Date & Time pane, and one of your friends or co-workers is watching you, try this: Turn off the Set Date & Time Automatically checkbox, and then instead of typing in the desired time, just grab an hour or minute hand on the preview clock and move it to set your time. Again, it serves no real purpose, but every time I set my clock like this with someone looking, they're always amazed by it. Unless they're Swiss, of course.

   GETTING FONTS TO LOOK THEIR BEST ON YOUR SCREEN

Mac OS X already does a special brand of font smoothing (a form of anti-aliasing) to make your fonts look crisp and clean onscreen. However, you can tweak how it "smooths" your fonts to give you the best possible look depending on which type of monitor (flat panel, CRT, etc.) you're using with your Mac. To choose which style of font smoothing works best for your monitor, go under the Apple menu, under System Preferences, and click on the Appearance icon. In the Appearance options, in the bottom section, choose the type of font smoothing that matches the type of monitor you're using from the Font Smoothing Style pop-up menu.

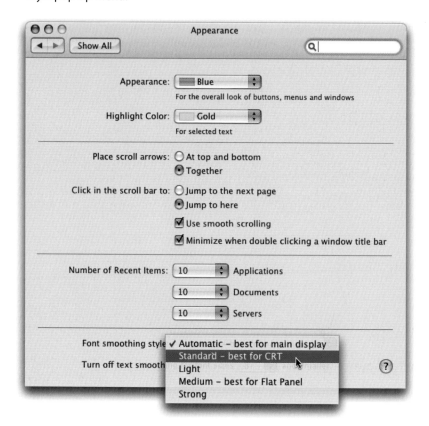

COLORSYNC SHOWOFF TRICK

I'm sure there's an important reason for this feature; I just can't figure out what it is. But it sure looks cool, and therefore it's a perfect tool for showing off to your PC friends (which may be the real reason it's in the Mac OS in the first place). Here's how it works—look inside your Applications folder, inside your Utilities folder, and double-click on ColorSync Utility. When the ColorSync panel appears, click on the Profiles icon, then click the gray triangle beside System to display a list of profiles. Click on Generic RGB Profile and to the right a Lab Plot color graphic will appear. Here's the show-off part—it's a 3D object—click your cursor right on it, drag upward, and the object will rotate around in 3D. Totally cool. Totally useless. I love it!

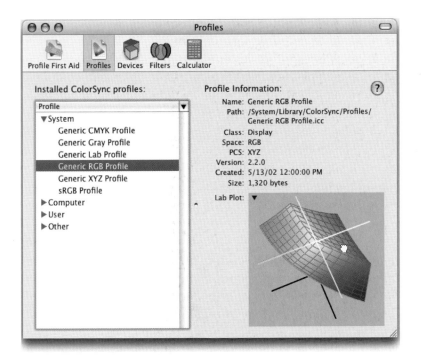

GETTING A SUPER-SMALL FONT PANEL

If you don't need all the typographic features of Apple's Font panel (the Font panel that appears in Cocoa apps like TextEdit), you can use a much smaller version. Just click-and-drag the bottom-right corner of the regular Font panel and it will automatically reconfigure itself into a much smaller one-row panel, with just three pop-up menus (rather than windows), giving you access to the most-used Font panel functions. When you think about it, it's pretty amazing that the Font panel can morph into an entirely different scheme (from scrollable windows into pop-up menus) on the fly. Even if you don't use the Font panel, it's worth trying it once just to see this amazing technology at work.

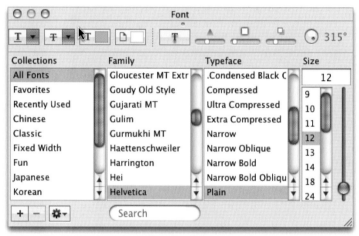

Regular dialog

Same dialog, super small

USING YOUR PHOTOS AS DESKTOP PATTERNS

©SCOTT KELBY

You're not stuck using Apple's default sets of desktop backgrounds, because now you can use any photo in your hard disk as a desktop pattern. Just Control-click anywhere on your desktop background and choose Change Desktop Background from the contextual menu that appears. In the Desktop preferences panel, near the bottom of the left column (where all the default sets of photos are), click on iPhoto Library folder (or click Choose Folder to navigate to a folder of images). The photos in your iPhoto Library (or folder) will now appear in the main window, and you can click on any one to instantly become your desktop background.

 **FONT BOOK: COMPARING FONTS SIDE-BY-SIDE**

If you're trying to make a decision on which font to choose, and it's down to just a few choices, here's a great way to do some side-by-side comparisons. In the Font panel, double-click on the first font you want to compare. This brings up a preview of the font in its own separate floating window. Then double-click on the next font, and its preview appears in another floating window, so you can position them side-by-side and see which you like better. You can open as many different font preview windows as you need to help you find just the right font. Also, once the floating preview window is open, you can choose different font weights and variations from the pop-up menu at the top of the window.

   FONT BOOK: FINDING ALL YOUR BOLD FONTS FAST

If you've ever been working on a project, and you know you need a bold font for the headline, but you're not exactly sure which bold font you should use, this tip is for you. Just type Bold into the Search field in the top-right corner of the Font Book dialog. This instantly gives you a list of every font that has a bold variant, and once you click in the Font panel, you can use the Up/Down Arrow keys on your keyboard to get a

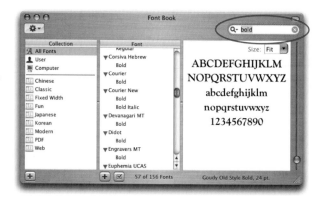

quick look at how each bold font looks. Of course, this isn't just for bold fonts, you could search for all italic fonts, or script fonts, or bold and italic…you get the idea.

   FONT BOOK: CREATING YOUR OWN CUSTOM PREVIEW TEXT

By default, the Font Panel preview text shows "ABCDEFGHI-JKLMNO…etc.," and although seeing your fonts previewed like this can be helpful, it pales in comparison to seeing the font previewed using your own text from the project you're working on. Here's how to make that happen: Go to the font you want, then press Command-3 (the shortcut for Custom Preview). Now you can type in your own text over the highlighted copy in the preview window.

Even cooler: You can copy-and-paste text right from your project (from InDesign or QuarkXPress) straight into the Custom Preview panel. Nice!

FONT BOOK: FONT FIELD SIZING TIP

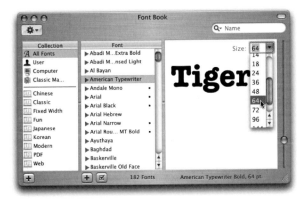

If you want to see your font in various sizes, you could use the slider on the far right side of the preview window, but it moves so quickly and so freely (it's not stopping at the common sizes used in page-layout applications) that you find yourself using the Size pop-up menu more. If you do, here's a tip on how to speed things up a bit: To choose your size quickly, just click in the Size field, then use the Up/Down arrow keys on your keyboard to quickly jump to the size you want. Here's where it might throw you—unlike the slider, the font doesn't change size as you change sizes in the list, so what you have to do is click on the highlighted size in the menu and your font will resize to your chosen value.

FONT BOOK: FIXING FONT PROBLEMS

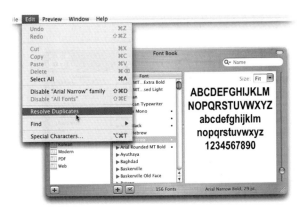

If there's one thing that messes with an application's (or a system's) head, it's font conflicts (duplicate copies of the same fonts installed on your hard drive). Thankfully, Font Book kicks this problem in the butt. If Font Book detects a duplicate font, it puts a little bullet point in front of the font's name. Then, it's up to you to choose which version you really want to keep open (you shouldn't have both open). Click on the version you want, then go under Font Book's Edit menu and choose Resolve Duplicates, and it will automatically turn off the duplicate, leaving you free and clear to enjoy a single-font family life.

   FONT BOOK: SEE ONLY THE FONTS YOU WANT TO SEE

If you're like most people, you probably use only a handful of fonts on a daily basis—your favorite, workhorse, use-all-the-time fonts. But even though you use only a few, you still have this long list of fonts, including a bunch Apple throws in (many of which I still, to this day, have never used). Wouldn't it be wonderful to have a font list of just the fonts you use, and not all the other filler fonts? It's easy. Just go to Font Book, click on the All Fonts category in the Collection panel, then Command-click on every font you don't use (you'll probably click on most of them). Then click the Disable button (it looks like a box with a checkmark in it) at the bottom of the center panel. A dialog will tell you that you've turned off multiple fonts. Click Disable and your font list just got much shorter. (*Note:* You didn't delete the fonts, you just turned them off from view.)

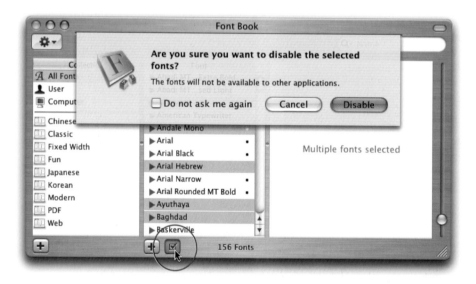

FONT BOOK: GET THE INSIDE SCOOP ON YOUR FONT

Believe it or not, Font Book knows more than it's letting on about your fonts. To find out the full inside info on a particular font, just press Command-I. This spills the beans about that font, including the name of the foundry that created it, when it was created, the font type (Postscript, Truetype, etc.), and more.

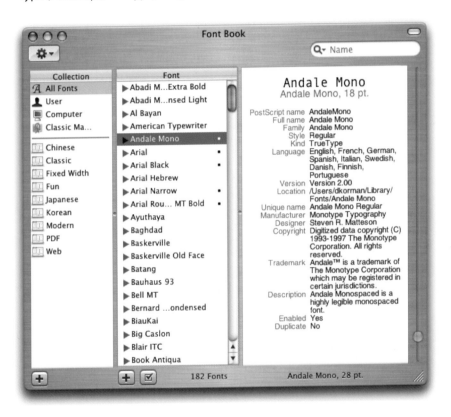

Cheap Trick

MAC OS X PRANKS

Although this is one of the shortest chapters in the book, it may be the most: (a) fun, (b) cruel, or (c) a delightful combination

Cheap Trick
mac os x pranks

of the two. (The difference between "fun" and "cruel" is the difference between "reading the pranks" and "perpetrating them.") The original outline for this book didn't have a "pranks" chapter at all, but as I was writing tips for the other chapters, I'd sometimes think, "Boy, if you didn't know about this, and somebody who did know it wanted to mess with you, they could pretty much bring your Mac life crashing down around you." I imagined this could create a new brand of Mac heroes— people who would pull these pranks in secret on the machines of unsuspecting co-workers, then show up later to offer to "take a look at the problem," and with a few clicks, fix it—winning the respect and admiration of the victim and other office co-workers. I feel pretty safe in sharing these pranks, because I know you're not the type of person to use or abuse these little gems. Right? Right? Hello...

   IF THEY PLAY MUSIC CDS, THIS WILL BE MUSIC TO YOUR EARS

Annoyance Factor 6: If you know a friend or co-worker listens to music CDs on their Mac, this is going to be music to your ears. Currently when they insert a music CD, by default it opens iTunes so they can play it. Makes sense. But that seems so routine. Wouldn't it be more fun if, instead of launching iTunes when they inserted a music CD, the Mac would quickly go to the Web, download the latest U.S. weather map, and then launch Preview and display this map? No music. Just a map. If they pop it out and try again, they get another map. And another and another. It's map mania! Here's how it's done: Go to the System Preferences under the Apple menu, and click on CDs & DVDs. When those preferences appear, from the pop-up menu where it says "When you insert a music CD," choose Run Script. Then, in the resulting dialog, navigate to the Applications folder, click on the AppleScript folder, and inside of that click on Example Scripts. Then click on the URLs folder where you can finally click on Download Weather Map.scpt and click the Choose button. Of course, this is just a start. Tomorrow, try a different script. Maybe a printing script or a mail script. The mind reels.

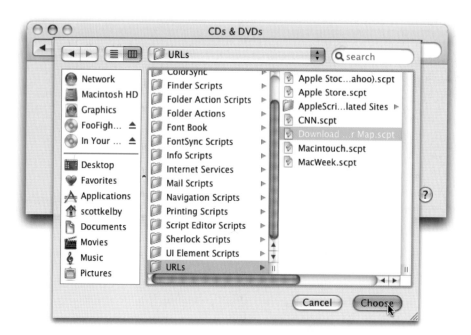

TURN THEIR MAC INTO AN ASYLUM

Annoyance Factor 7: Imagine how annoying it would be if everything your friend (co-worker, evil nemesis, etc.) did was spoken aloud by a person who's clearly one sleeve short of a straight-jacket? Now make it happen: Go under the System Preferences in the Apple menu and choose Universal Access. First, at the top of the panel in the VoiceOver section, click the On button. Next, click on the button named Open VoiceOver Utility. When this separate dialog opens, click on the Voices tab, and from the Default Voice pop-up menu, change the default from Fred to Deranged. Want to make it a little eerier? Lower the Pitch to around 20. Then close this window, close the System Preferences, and call Nurse Ratched, because it's time to pass out the "happy pills." If they've been using the Mac for a while, they may go straight to the Speech preferences to see if Speakable Items is turned on, but it won't be. By the way, if they're working late and you want to freak them out, lower the lights, then do this same trick, but instead of Deranged, try Whisper and set the master volume to 100%. If you try this one, better keep a mop nearby.

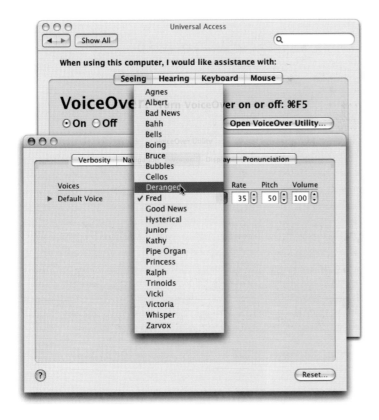

  CHANGING THE LANGUAGE FOR THEIR KEYBOARD

Annoyance Factor 6:
This one can be as subtle or as infuriating as you'd like. For example, changing a U.S. keyboard to a U.K. keyboard is subtle. In fact, they might not even notice it that much until they go to type in a # symbol (which is Shift-3) and they get a British pound sign (£) instead. What throws them is that the # symbol is right there printed on their keyboard (right above the number 3), yet every time they press Shift-3, they get the British pound sign. Again, this is subtle,

and the pound sign does give them a hint. Or you can go for something a bit more disconcerting, like changing the keyboard layout to Hungarian, which works fine until they type the letter Y, because it types the letter Z (and vice versa). Also, it really starts to get fun when they use any punctuation whatsoever. To start this international keyboard fest, go to the System Preferences under the Apple menu and choose International. Click on the Input Menu tab, and now simply click the checkbox beside one of the installed foreign keyboard layouts from the long list of languages. In the Input Source Options section, turn on the option that says "Use one input source in all documents." Then, before you close the System Preferences, turn off the checkbox for Show Input Menu in Menubar at the bottom of the dialog, or they'll see up in their menu bar that you've changed the keyboard, and then just walk away...

CREATE A TERRIFYING FAKE DIALOG

Annoyance Factor 7: Picture this: Your co-worker comes back from lunch, double-clicks on the folder that holds the project she's been working on for three weeks, and a dialog appears telling her: "Alert: There was a fatal read/write system IO error and the contents of this folder are permanently damaged and cannot be restored." Sound like fun? It's easy to pull off, because the ability to create your own custom message that appears when a folder is opened is built right into Tiger. Here's how it works: First, click on the folder and then press Command-I to bring up the Info dialog. Then, click on the triangle next to Spotlight Comments. In the field write a scary-sounding warning (feel free to use the one here or make up your own. Messages mentioning how a virus has attacked the folder also work nicely). Collapse the Spotlight Comments pane by clicking on the arrow again, then close the Info dialog. Now, Control-click on the folder, and from the contextual menu choose Configure Folder Actions. In the Folder Actions Setup dialog, click the plus sign (+) button in the bottom left-hand corner of the dialog. A standard Open dialog will appear; navigate your way to the person's folder and click Open. When you do this, a window will pop down prompting you to Choose a Script to Attach. Choose the script "open—show comments in dialog.scpt" and click the Attach button. One last thing: Turn on the Enable Folder Actions checkbox at the top of the Folder Actions Setup dialog (if it's not already on), then close the dialog, sit back, and let the fun begin. By the way, I might add one more line to the Spotlight Comments field if you want this prank to last a little longer. Add "Choosing Open Comments will delete this folder—Choosing Clear Comments will perform a Secure Empty Trash as well." It adds a nice touch, dontchathink?

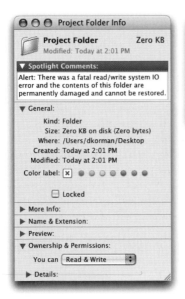

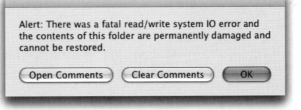

   HIDING, WELL…EVERYTHING!

Annoyance Factor 6: This is a great trick to pull on people who keep lots of stuff on their desktops. First, hide all open windows, then press Command-Shift-3 to take a screen shot of their entire desktop. Go to the System Preferences under the Apple menu and choose Desktop & Screen Saver. Click on the Desktop tab, then drag your screen capture into the preview well at the top left of the pane to make the screen capture their desktop. Close the System Preferences. Next, create a folder on their desktop and drag everything on the desktop into that folder and drag this folder into their Home folder (for safekeeping). Then, go under the Finder menu, under Preferences, and click on the General icon. Where it says Show These Items on the Desktop, uncheck Hard Disks, CDs, DVDs, and iPods, and Connected Servers. Now go under the Apple menu, under Dock, and choose Turn Hiding On. When they return, they can't click on anything (except the menu bar)—all the icons, folders, hard disks, etc., appear frozen because they're seeing the desktop capture. Even if they figure out that it's a desktop pattern, when they remove it, their drives are still missing and the Dock is still hidden. This is one sweet prank.

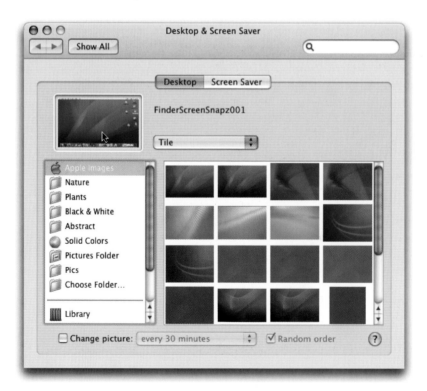

LOCKING THEM OUT OF THEIR OWN MACHINE

Annoyance Factor 5: This is a good one to pull on someone who is a single user (they're not sharing their machine with other users); thus they're not used to logging in each day with a user name. Go under the System Preferences in the Apple menu, click on the Desktop & Screen Saver icon, click on the Screen Saver tab, and slide the Start Screen Saver slider to, say, 3 minutes. Now (this is the key to the whole thing), click on the Show All button, go to the Security preference pane and check the box next to Require Password to Wake This Computer from Sleep or Screen Saver. Now, every time their computer sits idle for 3 minutes, it will require them to enter their user password—if they can even remember what it is. Ahh, it's the simple things in life.

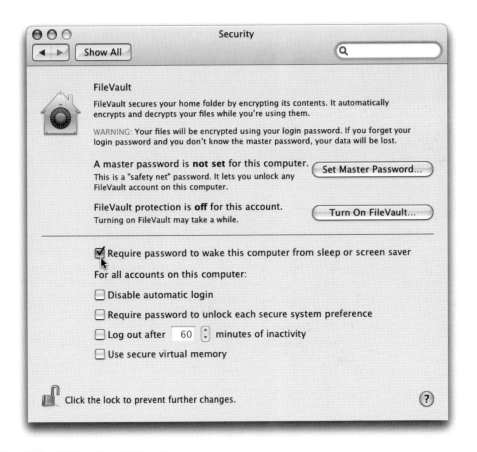

   UNCOLOR THEIR WORLD

Annoyance Factor 4–7: This has a variable amount of annoyance—from mild to strong—because you have options. Start by going under the Apple menu, choose System Preferences, click the Universal Access icon, and then click on the Seeing tab. Click the large Switch to White-on-Black, which gives their entire computer the "negative" look. Perhaps even better is the button to the right of that: Use Grayscale, which removes all color from everything. Very effective, as shown here and Universal Access is the last place they'll look—they'll spend hours looking in Display preferences and/or ColorSync.

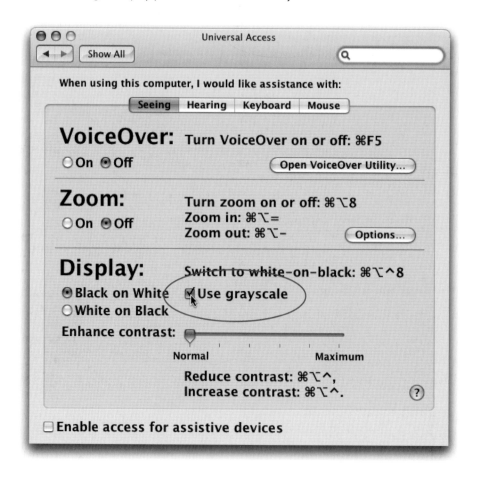

JAMMING THE DOCK

Annoyance Factor 8: This is just one of those things that make people crazy, because without getting your hands dirty, there's really no quick way to undo the damage, and it takes a long time and a lot of clicking to get things back to the way they were. Start by looking through the victim's hard drive until you find a folder with lots of items from one application (for example, any folder with 50 or more files qualifies, but think, "the more, the merrier!"). Shift-click to select files in groups of 10, and then drag them to the Dock. Repeat this with as many files as you like, until your victim has countless items in the Dock. Not only will this make their Dock microscopic in size, but there's only one way (short of some serious under-the-hood system tweaks) to get these items back out of the Dock—dragging them out one by one. A full reinstall is probably faster. This is something you should probably save for your last day at your current job, for obvious reasons.

   THE CASE OF THE MISSING HARD DISK

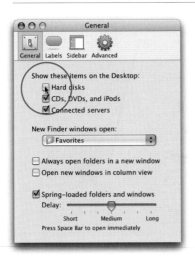

Annoyance Factor 7: It's the simple things in life that make it worth living. Like removing someone's hard disk icon from the desktop. To do this, go to the Finder menu, under Preferences, click on the General icon, and under Show These Items on the Desktop, uncheck the box for Hard Disks. The next time they start up, their hard drive won't appear on their desktop, and their subsequent freak-out will begin.

  ● ● ● **TAKING AWAY THEIR PRIVILEGES**

Annoyance Factor 2–8 *(depending on whether or not they're on a network):*
This is a great prank to play on a single user who's not connected to a network, because they won't have any experience with setting folder privileges. Go to their Documents folder (found under their Home folder), click on it, and press Command-I to bring up the Info dialog. Click on the right-facing gray triangle to the left of Ownership & Permissions, then click on the triangle next to Details. From the first Access pop-up menu (under Owner), choose Read Only, and then click on the Apply to Enclosed Items button. This makes the contents of their Documents folder (where documents are saved by default) pretty much locked. They can't drag files into it, they can't delete files within it, they can't even save an open document into their own Documents folder (how ironic is that?). They can basically only read files within it, and that's about it. When they try to do most anything else, they'll get a nasty warning dialog informing them that they don't have privileges to do what they're trying to do. People seem to really get annoyed with that. If you're in a really bad mood, maybe set the Owner/Access permissions to No Access or Write Only.

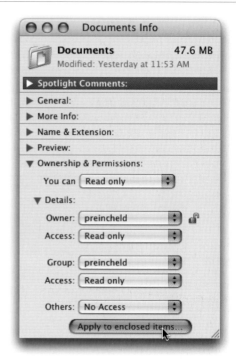

UNEXPLAINED LAUNCH MYSTERIES

Annoyance Factor 6: If you know which applications your victim uses most, the fun is about to begin. Click on a document from one of those applications. For example, let's say that they use TextEdit quite a bit. Look on their drive for a TextEdit file. Click on one of those documents, and then press Command-I to bring up the file's info. In the Info dialog, click on the right-facing gray triangle to the left of Open With to reveal the Open With pane. When that pane appears, click on the pop-up menu and you'll see a list of applications that you can use to open the TextEdit file. Choose a different application than Text-Edit. Try something like Adobe Illustrator CS2 (if you've got it), or if not, you can try something as tame as Safari (which comes with OS X). Then, click on the Change All button, and finally, close the window. The next time they double-click a TextEdit file, it won't launch TextEdit—instead it will launch Illustrator (or Safari). Annoying? You bet. Try changing any Photoshop files to open in Preview or, worse yet, have them open in Graphic Converter. There's just no limit to the fun.

  SHIFT-BEEP. OPTION-BEEP. COMMAND-BEEP. BEEP-BEEP!

Annoyance Factor 7: Would it drive you crazy if suddenly every time you pressed Shift, Option, Command, or Control it would make an annoying typewriter sound and then giant icons (that represent those modifier keys) appeared on the upper-right side of your desktop? Sure it would. Wouldn't it be funny if that suddenly happened to a friend's or co-worker's machine? Sure it would. Go under the System Preferences under the Apple menu, click on the Universal Access icon, click on the Keyboard tab, and turn on Sticky Keys. Will they know where to go to turn the sound and giant icons off? I doubt it. One of two things will happen: (1) They learn to live with it, or (2) they'll do a reinstall.

Universal Access

Show All

When using this computer, I would like assistance with:

Seeing | Hearing | **Keyboard** | Mouse

For difficulties pressing more than one key at a time

Sticky Keys: ◉ On ○ Off
Treats a sequence of modifier keys as a key combination.
☐ Press the Shift key five times to turn Sticky Keys on or off
☑ Beep when a modifier key is set
☑ Display pressed keys on screen

For difficulties with initial or repeated keystrokes

Slow Keys: ○ On ◉ Off
Puts a delay between when a key is pressed and when it is accepted.
☑ Use click key sounds

Acceptance Delay:
Long   Short

Key repeat delay can be set or turned off in Keyboard preferences: (Set Key Repeat...)

(?)

☐ **Enable access for assistive devices**

APPLICATION ICON MADNESS

Annoyance Factor 9: Imagine if you clicked on an application and instead of launching the application, it just opened an empty Finder window. This would get mighty frustrating, wouldn't it? This type of thing would basically bring a person's work to a halt, wouldn't it? Sound good? Here's what to do:

STEP ONE: Press Command-Shift-N to create a new blank folder on the desktop and name it "Gotcha!"

STEP TWO: Go to their Applications folder, open a folder for one of their major applications (something like Photoshop), and click on the Adobe Photoshop CS2 application icon. Press Command-I, and when the Info dialog opens, click on the icon in the top left-hand corner and press Command-C to copy the Photoshop application icon.

STEP THREE: Now drag just the Adobe Photoshop CS2 application icon into your Gotcha! folder.

STEP FOUR: Go back to their Applications folder and open their Photoshop folder. Press Command-Shift-N to create a new blank folder within the Photoshop application folder.

STEP FIVE: Click on the new folder and press Command-I. When the Info dialog opens, click on the folder icon and press Command-V to paste the Photoshop application icon onto this blank folder. Rename this folder "Adobe Photoshop CS2."

STEP SIX: Then, go to the Dock and remove the Photoshop icon (if it's there). Repeat this process for the rest of their major apps, and every time they launch an app, all they'll get is an empty Finder window. Once they're in tears, you can lead them to the Gotcha! folder—for a small fee.

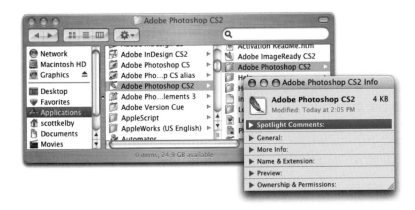

   MAKE THEIR APPLICATION FONTS LOOK BITMAPPED

Annoyance Factor 4: I gave this one a fairly low annoyance factor, because some people won't really notice it, but some people (like designers) will and it will irk them just a little every single day. Not enough to reinstall, not enough to call the IT department, but just enough to make them cringe on a daily basis. Go to the System Preferences under the Apple menu and click on the Appearance icon. When the panel appears, where it says "Turn off text smoothing for font sizes," change the size to 12 from the pop-up menu. What this does is remove the anti-aliasing from any small text that appears within their application's palettes and other dialogs. For example, in Adobe InDesign, it makes any text in places like the Character palette look really bitmapped and awful. It's still readable, but it's painful to look at. Again and again, day after day, week after week, month after…well, you get the idea. In fact, this one is so subtle, it's just plain mean. Or bold mean, or italic mean.

BLOWING OUT THEIR SCREEN

Annoyance Factor 8: This has such a high annoyance factor because it makes the victim's computer just about unusable, and the fix, while absolutely simple, is found in an unlikely place. Plus, this is just so darn simple to set up, you almost can't deny yourself. Open the System Preferences from the Apple menu and click on the Universal Access icon. Now, just drag the Enhance Contrast slider all the way to right (to Maximum) and close the System Preferences dialog. Doing this pretty much blows out their screen, and removes the anti-aliasing, making it unusable for pretty much anything. While you're there, you might even want to turn on the Use Grayscale checkbox, just for good measure. Hopefully, they have a friend who can bail them out.

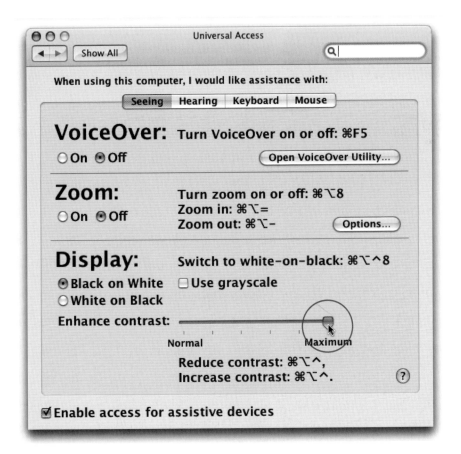

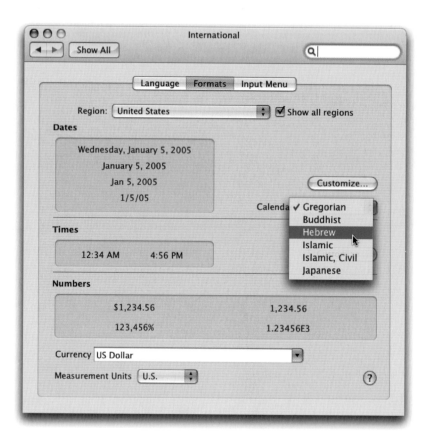

GIVE THEIR CALENDAR SOME INTERNATIONAL FLAIR

Annoyance Factor 3: This is a good one to start you on your road to Mac mayhem, because it's a pretty low-intensity prank. It's so low-level that it may not reveal itself immediately to your mark, but when it comes around, it's pretty sweet. Go to the System Preferences under the Apple menu and click on the International icon. When the options appear, click on the Formats tab, and on the right side of the dialog, you'll see the Calendar pop-up menu (I know this is a weird place to keep calendar format preferences, and that's half the fun of it). By default, it's set to use the Gregorian calendar format we're used to, but it doesn't have to be that way, so try one of the other formats, like Hebrew, Japanese, or Buddhist (you'll see a preview right there in the preferences dialog). Also, click on the Customize button in the Dates section and change the Show format to Full. Then close the System Preferences and just smile—their world will soon start to unravel.

TURN THEIR WORLD UPSIDE DOWN

Annoyance Factor 8: What would you do if you turned on your PowerBook one day and the entire screen was sideways, with the menu bar on the far left side of your screen, and everything else was turned sideways? Your hard disk, icons, everything—kind of like picking up your monitor and turning it on its side? Well, as it turns out, this hidden feature of Mac OS X Tiger adds a wonderful new prank opportunity. Now, chances are likely that you'll have no actual use for this feature in your everyday life, but turning a friend's or co-worker's screen on its side may become something you'll start doing quite often. Here's how it's done: Go to the System Preferences under the Apple menu (or in the Dock), press-and-hold the Option key, then click on Displays. When the Display preferences appear, you'll see a Rotate pop-up menu. So basically, choose the direction you want the screen to go (90°, 180°, or 270°). Try 180° if you want to turn their world upside down. This works with most PowerBooks, and I can tell you from personal experience that trying to get it set back to Standard using a track-pad can be surprisingly challenging.

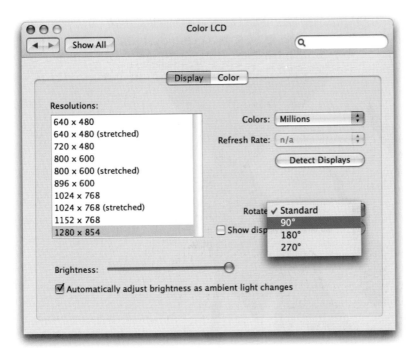

She Drives Me Crazy

HOW TO STOP ANNOYING THINGS

Mac OS X is an amazing operating system. Yet, it can also be an annoying operating system. So, depending on what you're

She Drives Me Crazy
how to stop annoying things

doing with it—it's either annoyingly amazing or amazingly annoying. Okay, I'm not really being fair, because in reality it's not the operating system itself that's annoying; it's things in the operating system—aspects of it (if you will) that are annoying. This chapter is about how to quickly make some of the most egregious annoyances go away. But make no mistake about it—Mac OS X isn't the first Apple operating system to include wildly annoying features. Remember Balloon Help—Apple's attempt at coming up with a better form of onscreen help, which could only have been devised by the Prince of Darkness himself (not Darth Vader—El Diablo!)? There's a hint, just a hint, of that type of stuff in Mac OS X, but this chapter will help you exorcise those demons fast!

  THE WORKAROUND FOR REAL MULTIPLE-USER ACCESS

If you have multiple users sharing the same Mac (and with Mac OS X's fast user switching, it's a breeze), you're going to run into a snag when you share files among users. If you've created a file and you want the other user (or users) on your Mac to be able to open and view this file—no problem—just put it in the Shared folder (found in the Users folder). However, they don't have permission to edit or delete this original file (it's built that way by default). But what if you *want* them to be able to edit and delete? Or what if you're the only person using your Mac, but you've set up multiple users so your Mac is configured differently for different tasks—you can only edit or delete your own files in the Shared folder. So how do you get around this? Just attach an external drive (like a FireWire or USB drive), then when it mounts on your desktop, click on it, then press Command-I to bring up the Info dialog. Go to the Ownership and Permissions panel and choose Ignore Ownership on This Volume. Now, anything you put on this external drive will be available to all users. Also, if you don't want to use an external drive, you can do the same thing by partitioning your startup drive, using Apple's Disk Utility.

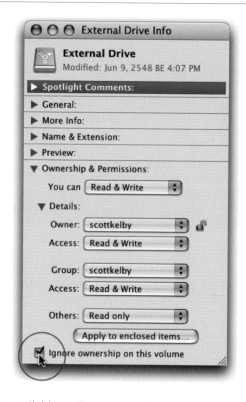

HOW TO STOP THE QUICKTIME PLAYER BLUES

Apple does listen sometimes because the QuickTime Player no longer automatically checks for updates when you launch it. If you don't believe me, go to the System Preferences in the Apple menu, under QuickTime, and click on the Update tab. Notice how the Check for Updates Automatically checkbox is deselected by default? Amazing, eh? Well, something that's still annoying is called the "Content Guide," and if you like pop-up windows and banner ads, you'll love this. If you launch the QuickTime Player while you have an Internet connection, before you can do anything else, it goes to the Web, downloads a little advertising clip (usually for a new album or movie), and plays it in your QuickTime Player. The good news is that you can turn this annoying "ad feed" off. Just launch the QuickTime Player, then go under the QuickTime menu, under Preferences, and in the General section turn off the Show Content Guide Automatically. Ahhhh, now isn't that better?

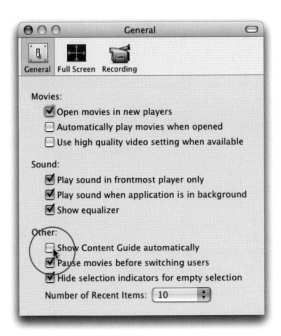

   STOPPING THE SOFTWARE AUTO-UPDATING MENACE

The idea is great—whenever Apple releases even the tiniest update to your system software or any of the iApps, a window pops up to tell you that it's been released, and it even offers to download the software for you. The problem? It always, always opens at the wrong time: when you're on deadline, when you're 5 minutes from leaving the office—really, any time you don't want it to pop up—it pops up. Personally, I'd rather decide to update at my leisure (once a week or so) rather than when my system feels it needs a fix. To turn off this Auto-Updating menace, go under the Apple menu to System Preferences. Click on the Software Update icon, and under the Update Software tab, make sure to turn off the Check for Updates checkbox. Or you can choose to be interrupted at the wrong time only once a month (from the pop-up menu). Either way, "another one bites the dust!"

STOP ASKING ME WHAT TO DO!

There's a feature in Mac OS X that's both a blessing and a curse (it's a blessing if it does what you want, but otherwise…). For example, when you insert a blank CD it brings up a dialog asking what you want to do with it. Chances are, you do the same thing over and over (prepare it for burning, launch Toast, launch iTunes, etc.), but it keeps asking you, again and again, every time you insert a CD. It's just this side of maddening. You can change Mac OS X's list of "When you insert this, I'm opening that…" by going under the Apple menu, under System Preferences, and choosing CDs & DVDs. There you'll find a plain-English list of pop-up menus that lets you stop opening any applications that you don't want, and you can choose which apps, if any, you do want opened. Most importantly, Mac OS X will stop asking you what to do.

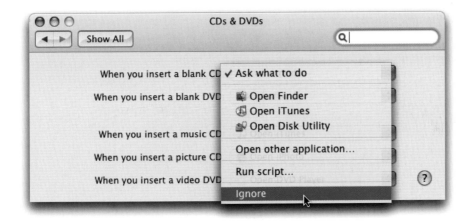

   IT WON'T LET ME ERASE A DISK!

In previous versions of Mac OS, when you wanted to erase a disk, you just went under the Special menu and chose Erase Disk. But in Mac OS X, there's no Special menu (Apple might counter that all the menus are special—they're not). Now to erase a disk, you have to launch Disk Utility (inside your Utilities folder, which is in your Applications on your hard drive). When you launch Disk Utility, just click on the tab for Erase and you're there!

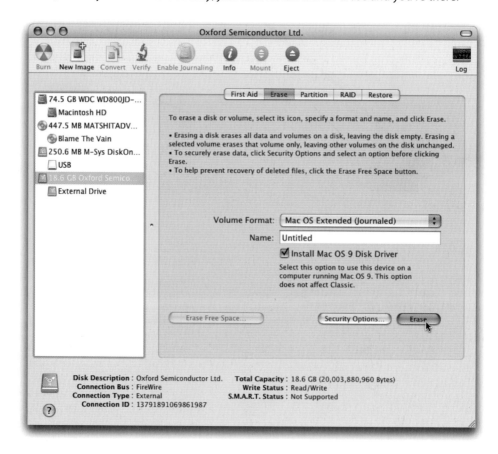

HOW TO STOP MAGNIFYING YOUR DOCK

This may be a very embarrassing subject for some of you, so I'll try to handle it with the utmost sensitivity. If you have a very small Dock (and you know who you are), the Magnification feature is almost a necessity. However, if you leave your Dock icons at their default size (which many people do), magnification can be wildly annoying, and because the icons are so large to begin with, magnification is totally unnecessary. When my wife first saw large Dock icons being magnified even more, the first thing she said was, "Is there a way to turn that awful thing off?" There is: Control-click on the Dock's vertical divider bar (on the far right side of the dock) and from the pop-up menu that appears choose Turn Magnification Off.

TURNING OFF THE "EMPTY TRASH" WARNING

There's nothing like executing a simple command and having the OS ask: "Are you sure you want to do this?" By default, every time you go to empty the Trash, it asks this annoying question (and it has for years upon years). Disabling the Empty Trash Warning is a little different in Mac OS X than it was in previous versions. Now you go under the Finder menu, under Preferences, and click on the Advanced icon. Then deselect the checkbox for Show Warning Before Emptying the Trash.

STOP CLASSIC FROM LAUNCHING WITHOUT PERMISSION

If you're just making the migration from Mac OS 9 to Mac OS X, one day you'll be doing a search for a file you created last year. You'll find it, then double-click on it, and since it was created in a Classic application on your old machine, it will boot Mac OS X's Classic mode and launch your old Mac OS 9 application. My bet is that you don't want to open that application in Classic (unless you absolutely have to). That's why you might want to have your Mac ask you if you really want to start Classic. To turn on this helpful warning, go under System Preferences in the Apple menu, click on the Classic icon, click on the Start/Stop button, and then choose Warn Before Starting Classic.

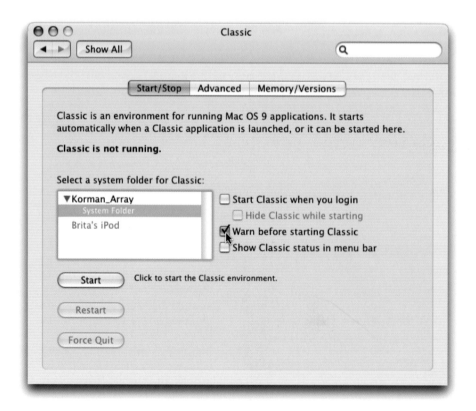

DISABLING SCREEN SAVER HOT CORNERS

Does your screen saver keep turning on when you rest your cursor in one of the corners of your screen? Well, this used to drive me crazy. (I say used to, because I used this tip to fix it.) What's happening is that one of your corners has been designated as a "hot corner" (at least as far as Mac OS X's Screen Saver is concerned), and whenever your cursor winds up there for more than a second or two, it starts Mac OS X's built-in Screen Saver. To make this "hot corner" stuff go away, go to the System Preferences in the Apple menu and click on the Desktop & Screen Saver icon. When its pane appears, click on the Screen Saver tab, then click on the Hot Corners button to bring up the Hot Corners panel. When it appears, you'll see four pop-up menus, each representing one corner of your screen. If one or more of these pop-up menus says Start Screen Saver, that indicates a hot corner. To turn off a hot corner, click on the pop-up menu and choose " — " to make that corner go "cold." The full screen is now yours to enjoy uninterrupted.

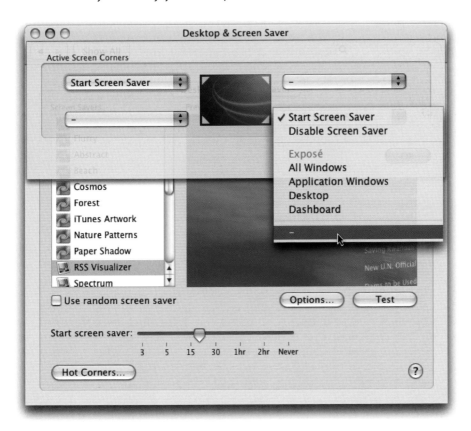

 PUTTING THE GENIE BACK IN THE BOTTLE

Certainly the Genie Effect (which is that genie-like special effect that occurs by default when you minimize a window to the Dock) would be a nominee for the "Mac OS X Annoying Hall of Fame." Luckily, putting this genie back in its bottle is easy—just go under the Apple menu, under System Preferences, and when the dialog appears, click on the Dock icon. In the Dock preference pane, in the pop-up menu for Minimize Using, choose Scale Effect rather than Genie Effect, and that should put a cork in it (so to speak).

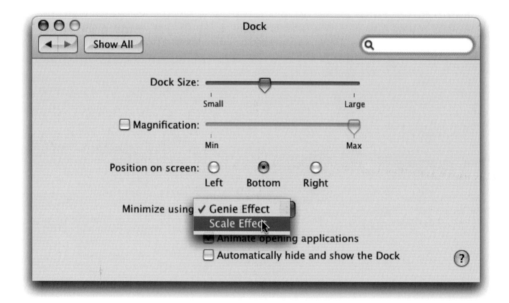

STOP ASKING ME FOR MY PASSWORD

Are you like me? No. Then how about this: Are you like me in the sense that you're the only person that works on your Mac? Maybe it's your Mac at home, and not a single soul but you uses your machine (meaning, of course, your spouse, your kids, and the cat all have their own Macs). Then you don't need an administrator to tell you what you can and can't add to your own single, solitary machine, right? It's just you. And you're a good person. Then when you install Mac OS X, and it asks you for an administrator password, don't put one in. Leave it blank, and that way, you'll never have to remember your password. Oh sure, it'll try to tell you that you may have a security problem (the cat might try to sneak a virus onto your machine), but if you're the only one who will ever install a program on that machine, wouldn't you love to just click the OK button when the annoying password dialog pops up the next time you want to install a program?

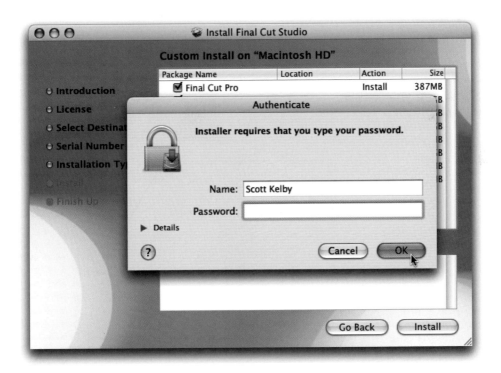

HIDING THE ANNOYING MICROPHONE DISC THINGY

When you open an application that supports Mac OS X's built-in
Speech control (like Chess for instance), it brings up what I call "the
incredibly annoying round microphone thingy." It floats around,
taking up space, and if you're not using Speech control (which most
of us aren't), it's just plain annoying. If you are actually using Speech
control, it's still annoying (necessary perhaps, but still annoying). To
get it out of sight, double-click on the top half of it (avoiding the bottom because of a
built-in pop-up menu), and it will tuck itself into the Dock while you work.

 SLEEP LESS—WORK MORE

Have you plugged your
PowerBook or iBook into
an A/C outlet, but it's still
going to sleep on you
every 5 or 10 minutes?
Honestly, that drives me
nuts, and if you're like me,
once you plug in, you'll
want to go to the System
Preferences (in the Apple
menu) and click on the
Energy Saver icon. When
its pane appears, click
on the Sleep tab (if you
don't see the tab, click on
the Show Details button
on the bottom right),
and then drag the top
slider over to a reason-
able amount of time (like

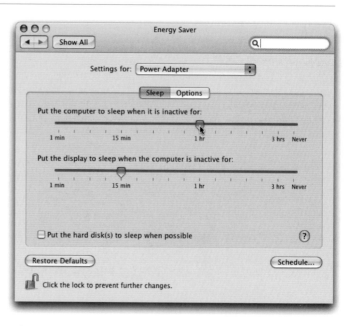

30 minutes or more). That way, if you do call it a night and forget to put your PowerBook to
sleep, eventually Energy Saver will kick in.

HOW TO STOP AN APPLICATION FROM LAUNCHING

If you've accidentally launched an application that you didn't want to launch (this can happen quite frequently, especially if you're drunk), you can stop that launch dead in its tracks by pressing Command-Option-Shift-Escape. (Just in case you were wondering, we used Adobe InDesign to lay out this book, and their splash screen looks so cool, I thought I'd show it here.)

   ## SHUTTING DOWN WITHOUT THE WARNING

When you choose Shut Down from the Apple menu, a dialog appears asking if you really want to shut down. Yes, it's annoying. To make the bad dialog go away, just hold the Option key before you choose Shut Down, and it will just shut down (without insulting your intelligence by asking you if what you chose is really what you want to do).

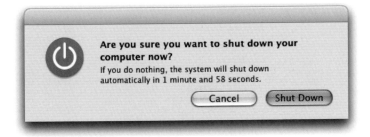

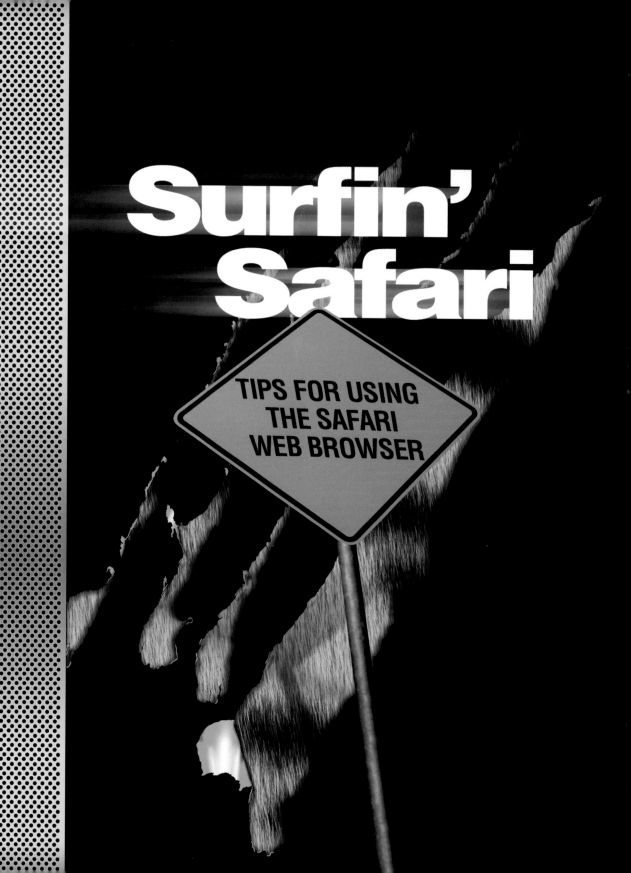

So how does Safari wind up getting its own separate chapter? Well, there are a number of reasons, none of them sound. First, the

Surfin' Safari
tips for using the safari web browser

Safari browser is one application that we use a lot. And by a lot I mean "a whole bunch." It is our access to the Web, and by Web I mean Internet, and by Internet I mean Information Super Highway, which is perhaps the corniest phrase ever conceived to describe the Internet, with the possible exception of Cyberspace. Politicians use these terms, because they don't actually use the Internet, but their staffers and interns do. Anyway, you (me, we, us, them, they) wind up using Safari a lot, but it got its own chapter because I had so many Safari tips that if I included those tips in another chapter it would be just too many tips. It would be "tip overload" (or as the politicians refer to it "Tipformation Super Overload"). By the way, it was Al Gore who invented the Safari browser. That's right, Al Gore. Not that Al Gore. The other Al Gore.

  BUILT-IN TIP FINDER

You can uncover a number of cool little tips from right within Safari itself by looking at the very bottom left-hand corner of the Safari window (if you don't see it there, choose Show Status Bar from the View menu). When you put your cursor over a link on a webpage, before you even click the link, it shows you what will happen when you do click it. For example, if you put your cursor over a link to

my website, in the Status Bar it would say "Go to http://www.scottkelby.com." Now, here's where it gets fun: Hold a modifier key (Command, Option, Shift, Control, etc.) and then take a look down there. As you hold each key, the status bar changes to show you what will happen next. For example, if you hold the Command key and move over the link, it would say something like "Open http://www.scottkelby.com in a new tab," so you now know that holding the Command key and clicking a link does just that—it opens that site in a new tab. I won't spoil the rest for you, but try it yourself by moving over a link and pressing Control, Option, Command-Shift, Command-Option, Command-Shift-Option, etc., and a number of cool little tips will be revealed.

   HIGHLIGHT THE ADDRESS BAR FAST

Want to enter a new address? Don't drag your cursor over the old address—that's way too slow. Instead, just press Command-L and the URL address field will highlight, ready for you to type the new address.

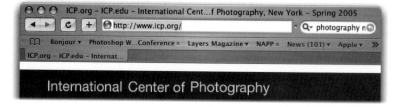

IMPORTING YOUR INTERNET EXPLORER BOOKMARKS

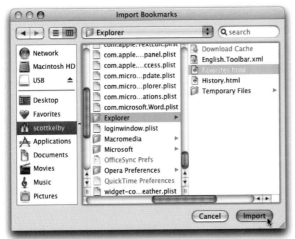

If you've finally given up on Micro-soft Internet Explorer (which is a good idea since they've stopped developing it for the Mac), in Tiger you can easily import your Internet Explorer bookmarks (also called Favorites) right into Safari by go-ing under Safari's File menu and choosing Import Bookmarks. Now navigate your way to your Internet Explorer folder by clicking on your Home folder, going to your Library, under Preferences, and choosing Explorer. Click on the Favorites .html file in the Explorer folder, and then click the Import button.

The bookmarks will appear grouped in a folder in the Bookmarks dialog, and the name field will be highlighted, ready for you to name your new set.

  ## HIDING YOUR TRACKS

Let's say that you've been visiting some sites that you don't want other people to know about (like Microsoft.com, PreparationH.com, etc.). If that's the case, you prob-ably want to hide any tracks that might lead others to learn of your whereabouts. Just choosing Clear History from the History menu isn't enough. Heck, these days your average middle-school student could trace you back to those sites in about 5 minutes. If you really want to hide your tracks, go under the Safari menu and choose Reset Safari. This brings up a warning dialog that says, in essence, choosing this is the next best thing to a clean reinstall of your browser. It basically "cleans house," so don't click it unless you're on the run from the CIA (or a crafty middle-school student).

TURN ON THE TABS, BABY!

This isn't actually a tip, but so few Safari users I run into realize it's there, I had to include it, because for many people this will forever change the way they get their info on the Web. It's called Tabbed Browsing and what it does is let you put a folder of sites you visit daily (like news sites, Apple news sites,

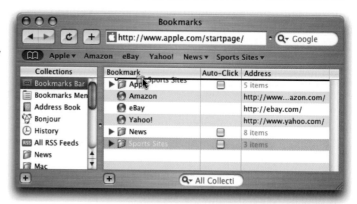

graphics sites, sports sites, etc.) up on the Bookmarks Bar. If you Command-click on that folder, it loads every single site in that folder, and puts each one on its own separate tab just under the Bookmarks Bar. It loads the first site in the list first, so while you're reading that page, all the others are loading (in order). So when you click on the second page, it's already loaded (unless you have a really slow Internet connection, of course). While you're looking at the second site, the rest are all still loading. It makes you feel as if you're browsing at hyper speed, and if you try it once, you'll be hooked!

You turn on Tabbed Browsing by going under the Safari menu, under Preferences, and clicking on the Tabs icon, then turning on Enable Tabbed Browsing. Close Preferences. Next click on the Show All Bookmarks icon in the Bookmarks Bar to bring up all your book-marked sites. Press Command-Shift-N to add a new Bookmarks folder, and you'll see a new folder appear in the Collections list on the left side of the Safari window. Give this folder a name (for our example, we'll name it "Sports Sites"). Then click on the collection named Bookmarks Menu to reveal all the bookmarks saved in your pop-down menu. Drag your favorite sports websites from this list into the Bookmarks Bar, and then into the Sports Sites folder in the left column (mine has ESPN, CNNsi, and the Buccaneers' homepage).

Once you have all your sports sites in that folder, click on the Bookmarks Bar collection at the top of the Collections list to reveal its contents. Now, just click-and-drag your folder into the main window and position it where you want it (to load first, second, etc.). That's it—you've got your first tab. Repeat this process for as many folders as you want (or as can fit in your browser's Bookmarks Bar), and you're in business. Again, try this once and you'll be hooked on it forever.

ONE-CLICK TABBING

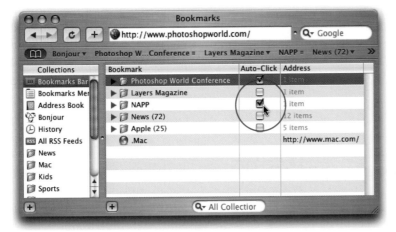

By default, you have to Command-click to load a particular folder of sites for Tabbed Browsing (see previous tip), but if you find you're loading full folders of sites (rather than just one individual site within the folder), you can change how Safari lets you click. That way, just a simple click loads the folder for Tabbed Browsing, and if you want just one particular site in the folder to load, *then* you Command-click that site from the folder's pop-up menu in the Bookmarks Bar. Surprisingly, this isn't found under Safari's Preferences; instead, click on the Show All Bookmarks icon up in the Bookmarks Bar and then under Collections, click on the Bookmarks Bar to bring up a list of the sites and folders. To make any folder a one-click load, click on the Auto-Click checkbox, and now all the sites in that folder will load with just one click.

   HOW TO STOP MULTIPLE TABS FROM LOADING

I love Tabbed Browsing. In fact, once you've used Tabbed Browsing, it's hard to live without it, but there's one thing about it that drives me nuts, and that's when I load a folder of sites by accident (which I do almost daily). It usually happens when I'm getting ready to dig down into a folder and just choose one site from the list, and I either forget to hold the Command key, or I just click on it accidentally while trying to get somewhere else. If that happens to you (and if you use Tabbed Browsing, my guess is it does at least once in a while), hit Safari's Back button and it will stop loading those tabs, as if nothin' ever happened.

JUMPING FROM TAB TO TAB WHEN USING TABBED BROWSING

Tabbed Browsing is about the coolest single thing in Safari, and jumping quickly from one tab to the next may well be second. To get from tab to tab in a flash after you've clicked on a tab, just press Command-Shift-Right Arrow to move right, and press…do I really need to mention how to move left? Didn't think so.

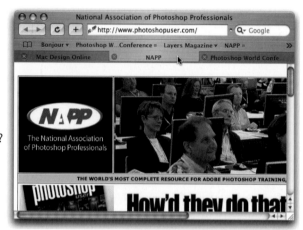

   ## SUPER-FAST WAY TO EMAIL A URL

If you run across a cool website and want to email that site to a friend, probably the fastest way is to press Command-Shift-I. This opens Mail, and inserts the Web URL into the body of your email. Now all you have to do is type the recipient's name, enter "Check this site out" in the Subject line, and click Send. Then all you have to worry about is their spam blocker stopping your email from getting through with such a generic subject in the title. Really don't want it to get there? Add the word "Viagra" some-where in the title too. (*Note:* If you want

a super-slow way, highlight the website's name, go under the Safari menu, under Services, under Mail, and choose Send Selection—it basically does the same thing.)

EMAILING WEBPAGES

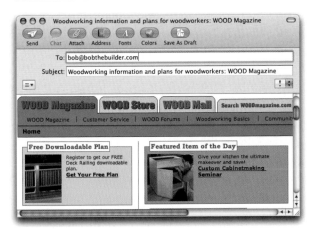

If you run across a webpage you want to share with a friend, don't send them a link to it—send them the page itself. Just press Command-I and a dialog will appear, asking for the email address of whom you want to send this webpage to. Just enter his or her email address, along with your text message, and click Send, and it will send the contents of that page (complete with graphics, formatting, links, etc.) to your friend. He'll be able to see that page right within his email application.

  OPENING GOOGLE RESULTS IN A SEPARATE WINDOW

By default, when you do a Web search using Safari's built-in Google Search field, the results of your search replace what was currently in your browser window. That's okay unless you're using that search to look up something relating to the page that you were on (which seems to happen, at least to me, more often than not). Here's a way around that: Once you enter your search term in the Google Search field, instead of hitting Return (or Enter), press Command-Return, and the Google results will open in their own separate window. (*Note:* If you have Tabbed Browsing turned on, it will open the results in a separate tab.)

   A KEYBOARD SHORTCUT EXTRAVAGANZA

As you might expect, there are dozens of keyboard shortcuts for Safari,
and I could include them all in this
book; but I don't have to, because
believe it or not, they're already
on your hard drive (they're pretty
much buried, so don't feel bad if
you haven't run across them yet). To
find this exhaustive list, go to your
Applications folder, Control-click on
the Safari icon, and choose Show
Package Contents from the contextual menu. This brings up a folder
named Contents. Look inside for a

folder named Resources, then look in the Resources folder for a folder named English.lproj.
Now look inside that folder (I told you it was buried) for a folder named SafariHelp, and then
inside that folder open "pg2." There you'll find a file named "shcts.html." Double-click this file
to see a pretty darn complete list of Safari's keyboard shortcuts.

   TYPING URLS THE FAST WAY

Before you can type a new URL (Web address) in the address bar, you have to get rid of
the one currently in the address field. Of course, you could drag your cursor over the old
address to highlight it, and if you're charging by the hour, I highly recommend doing it
that way. However, if you want the fastest one-click method in town, just click on the little
Apple icon (or custom site icon) that appears immediately before the address in that field.
This instantly highlights the field, and you can type your new URL over the old URL lickety-
split (whatever that means. I heard some guy at the General Store say that once).

FINDING YOUR DIGITAL BREADCRUMBS

Like any browser, Safari keeps track of where you've been, page by page. If you want to hop quickly back to a page where you've been recently, just click-and-hold on the Back button in Safari's toolbar. The sites you visited will appear in a contextual menu. If you've hopped back, and want to jump ahead, click-and-hold on the Next button. (I didn't really have to tell you that Next button trick, did I?)

USING GOOGLE'S SEARCH TERM MEMORY

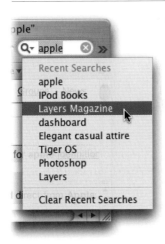

When you're using the Google Search field in Safari's toolbar, Safari keeps track of your last 10 searches, just in case you want to re-search using one of those same terms. To access one of your previous search terms, just click on the Magnifying Glass icon within the Google Search field and a pop-up menu of recent terms will appear.

   SEARCHING JUST YOUR BOOKMARKS

If you're trying to search for a particular bookmark, you'll want to know this trick: First, click on the Show All Bookmarks icon in the top-left corner of the Bookmarks Bar. Doing this makes the Collections column visible on the left side of Safari, but more importantly, it adds a Search field at the bottom center of the Safari window. When you type search terms in this field, it searches just within your bookmarks, so you get super-fast results.

   A FASTER BOOKMARKS MENU

If you thought adding your favorite sites to Safari's Bookmarks Bar sped things up, wait till you hear this tip: Once your favorite sites are added, you can have even faster access to those sites than clicking on them. Instead, press Command-1 to load the first site in the Bookmarks Bar. Press Command-2, Command-3, Command-4, and so on to instantly load the sites in order. *Note:* Sadly, this trick only works with individual sites added to your Bookmarks Bar—it doesn't work with folders on the bar.

MAKING ONLINE ARTICLES EASIER TO READ

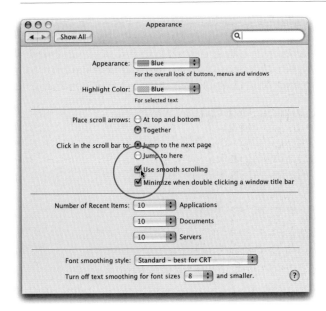

This is a great tip for people who read a lot of articles online, because when you're reading these articles and you come to the bottom of the page, using the scroll bars is a pain and pressing Page Down usually moves too far. However, you can set up Safari to better accommodate reading articles using Smooth Scrolling. To turn it on, go under the Apple menu, under System Preferences, and choose Appearance. Click on the Use Smooth Scrolling checkbox, and then when you hit the Page Down button, it moves line by line, rather than page by page.

   READING RSS FEEDS OUTSIDE OF SAFARI

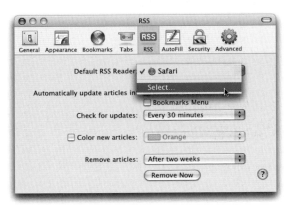

Although Safari does a nice job of letting you read RSS feeds without leaving Safari, if you prefer to use your favorite RSS reader to read RSS feeds, just make a quick trip to Safari's Preferences (found under the Safari menu) and click on the RSS tab. When the RSS pane appears, from the Default RSS Reader pop-up menu at the top of the dialog, choose Select to change the default RSS reader to whichever program you prefer. Navigate to your reader and close Preferences. Now when you click on the RSS icon in Safari's address field, it will open that feed in your preferred reader.

  PUTTING YOUR BOOKMARKS ON THE WEB

If you decide to share your Safari bookmarks with the world by posting them to the Web, it's easy: Just go under Safari's File menu and choose Export Bookmarks. Enter a name in the resulting dialog and click Save. This creates an HTML file that can be uploaded directly to the Web, and your bookmarks will be separated in their various categories, and all the links will be live. This ability to export your bookmarks is also handy if you decide to use another Web browser, rather than Safari (shudder to think). Just export the bookmarks in Safari, and import them into your new browser (knowing all the while that you might feel a little bit guilty for turning your back on Safari like that).

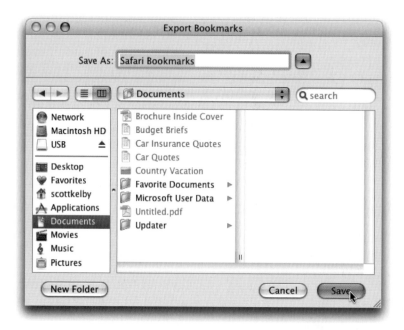

CAPTURE THAT WEBPAGE

I'm sure this has probably happened to you: You find a website with some great information, so you bookmark it, but a few weeks later when you go back to that bookmark,
the page you saved has been changed, and that info is long gone. Well, you can protect
against that with Safari by saving that page as a Web archive. When you save as a Web
archive, not only is the text on the page saved, but the entire page—just as you saw it
(including the full layout, graphics, you name it)—is saved right along with it, so when
you open the archive, even years later, the page will look exactly as you remember it. To
save a page as a Web archive, just go under Safari's File menu and choose Save As. When
the Save dialog appears, at the bottom (if it's not already chosen) choose Web Archive
as the Format and click the Save button. To open a Web archive later, just drag-and-drop
the saved file directly on Safari's icon in the Dock.

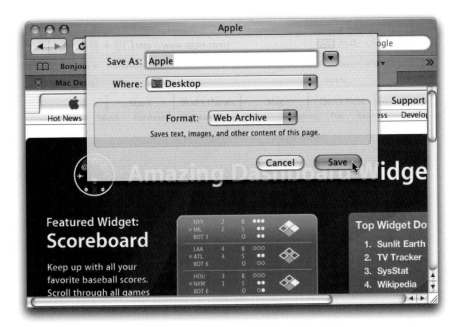

SECRET BROWSING SECRETS

When you're on the Web, certain websites collect information about you and your browsing habits, and if you buy products online, they keep even more information than that. If you'd prefer to remain anonymous (especially if you're using a computer that is shared by other people), you'll want to know about Private Browsing. You turn on Private Browsing by going under the Safari menu and choosing Private Browsing. That's it (now you can secretly go to Microsoft's or Dell's website without your Mac buddies finding out).

 OPENING THAT ORIGINAL PAGE AS A TAB

If you're using Tabbed Browsing (and I hope you are, as it's one of the most compelling things about Safari), here's a great tip to keep you from unnecessarily reloading a page you've already been to. Let's say, for example, that you're visiting a site, and you click on a link that takes you to a different site. If you click the Back button, it reloads that page that you were just at. Instead, try this—hold the Command key

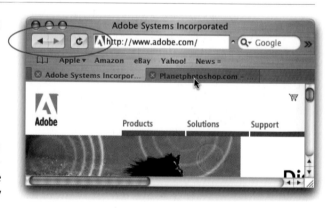

and click the Back button. This opens the original page in a separate tab, without reloading the whole thing from scratch. Need I say that you can do this with the Next button as well? Okay, I didn't think so.

KEEPING YOUR KIDS FROM UNSAVORY SITES

If you're concerned about your children accessing sites that are inappropriate, you can help make sure that doesn't happen by turning on the Parental Controls. When you do this, your kids can only visit sites that you have bookmarked in advance for them (they can't visit or bookmark sites on their own). These Safari Parental Controls are actually turned on by going to the System Preferences (under the Apple menu), clicking on the Accounts icon, and then clicking on your kid's account. Once the account preferences appear, click on the Parental Controls tab, and then turn on the checkbox beside Safari. Now, close the Accounts dialog, choose Log Out from the Apple menu, and then log in as your child. Launch Safari, go to the websites that you feel are appropriate, and bookmark them by clicking on the plus (+) sign button in the toolbar (it will ask you for your Administrator's password when you do this). Then, log out and log back in again as yourself. That's it—the only sites your child will be able to visit are the ones you bookmarked. If he or she tries to access any other site, it'll be locked, and Safari will direct your child back to the site last you approved.

  SEARCHING THROUGH YOUR HISTORY

If you want to quickly find a site you've visited recently, just click on the Show All Bookmarks icon on the left side of the Bookmarks Bar, and then go to the bottom of the Bookmarks dialog where you'll find a Search field. To limit this search to just the visited sites in your History, click on the word "History" in the Collections list on the left side of Safari's window. Now enter the name of the site you're searching for and the results will appear. You can search your Bookmarks folders the same way—just click on a folder in the list on the left.

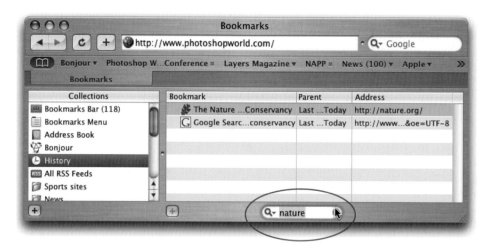

HOW TO REMOVE JUST ONE SITE FROM YOUR HISTORY

If you'd like to remove one or more sites from your History, but you don't want to choose Clear History from the History menu (which deletes the trail to all the recent sites you've visited), try this: click on the Show All Bookmarks icon in the top left of the Bookmarks Bar, then click on the History folder in the Collections list on the left side of the Bookmarks dialog. Now you can expand any day, including today, by clicking on the little gray arrow next to the day, and then when you locate the site you want removed, just click on it and press the Delete key.

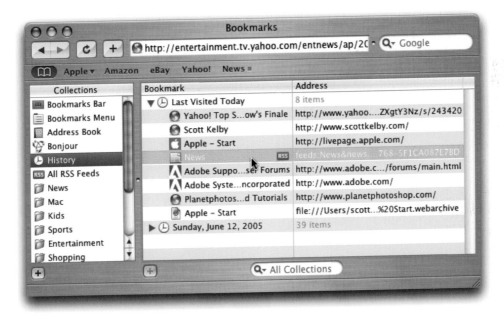

You've Got Mail

TIPS FOR USING MAIL

All right, you're probably thinking "Hey,

that's not a song or a movie, that's the

AOL greeting when you have mail in your inbox,

You've Got Mail
tips for using mail

right?" Well, it actually was a movie based on AOL's

email greeting, and it starred Tom Hanks and Meg

Ryan. It actually was a pretty decent movie, but

it was clearly not the Sleepless in Seattle, Part 2

they hoped it would be. The problem was that it

wasn't shot in Seattle, and that's what Sleepless

in Seattle *was really about. It wasn't about Tom*

and Meg, it was about Microsoft (as all things

ultimately are). The whole love story was just a

subterfuge for what was really going on—which

was a thinly veiled marketing campaign by

Microsoft designed to draw potential Microsoft

employees to the Seattle area. See, it's all so simple

when you break it down. Anyway, what does all

this have to do with Apple's Mail application?

Well, I was hoping we wouldn't get to that. Hey,

how about that Tom Hanks, though, he's some

actor. Did you see him in Apollo 13?

   INSTANT SLIDE SHOW WHEN SOMEONE SENDS YOU PHOTOS

When someone emails you some photos, you can instantly see a full-screen slide show of those emailed images from right within Mail. When you click on the message to read it, to the immediate right of the word "Attachments" in your email message you'll find two buttons. The first button, Save, lets you just save the photos to your hard disk, but if you click the next button over (Slideshow), you'll start a full-screen slide show of those attached photos without having to save them first. To stop the slide show at any time, press the Escape key on your keyboard. To have a list of slide show controls appear at the bottom of your screen, just move your mouse (the technical term for this is actually "jiggling your mouse"). Once the slide show is running, if you want the photos to appear larger onscreen, press the letter F on your keyboard. To return to regular size, press the letter A.

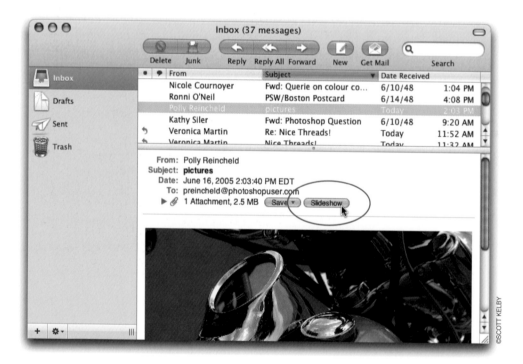

GETTING EMAILED PHOTOS INTO IPHOTO FAST

If you've received some photos, you don't have to save them to your hard disk, and then import them into iPhoto manually—that takes too long. Instead try this: When the photos arrive in your email, within the email message itself click-and-hold on the Save button. From the pop-up menu select Add to iPhoto. This will instantly open the iPhoto application and import your selected photo. Amazing!

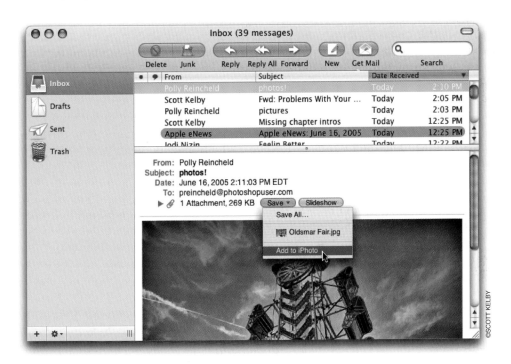

  CREATING SMART MAILBOXES FROM SEARCHES

If you're just dipping your toe into the world of Smart Mailboxes, try this: In Mail's Search field, search for all the mail from a particular person (or company). For example, you could do a search for all incoming mail from eBay. Enter "eBay" in the Search field, choose From in the bar below the toolbar, and then when the results appear, you'll find a Save button in the upper-right corner of your results in the main window. Click on it, and a Smart Mailbox dialog will appear, and Mail's pretty much filled out all the Smart Mailbox criteria for you—so just enter a name and click OK. Now you'll have a new Smart Mailbox that contains all the email you've received from eBay, and from now on, any new email from eBay will also appear in that Smart Mailbox. Basically, you just created a Smart Mailbox from your search. Not bad, matey! (Said in my best pirate voice.)

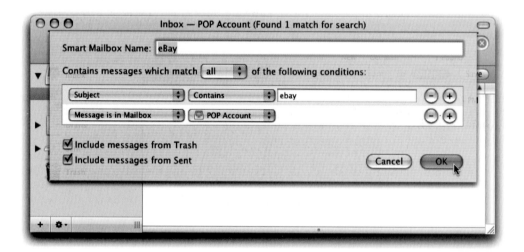

SMART MAILBOX IDEA #1: MAIL OLDER THAN ONE YEAR

If you've got email that's more than a year old just clogging up your Inbox (and taking up valuable space), you can use a Smart Mailbox to help you do some fast email house cleaning. Just Control-click on the email account (or your Inbox if you don't have multiple accounts) that you want to clean up, and then choose New Smart Mailbox from the contextual menu. When the Smart Mailbox dialog appears, from the first criteria pop-up menu on the left, choose Date Received. From the next pop-up menu over, choose "is before the date," and in the final field, type a date that is approximately one year before today. Click OK and all your email that is one year old (or older) will appear in that Smart Mailbox. To delete that old email, just click on the Smart Mailbox, press Command-A to select all the email, then press the Delete key on your keyboard. Now, the nice thing is that tomorrow more one-year-old email will appear in that Smart Mailbox (thanks to its live updating), and the next day, and the next day, and so on, so your mailbox never has more than one year of archived messages. So, about once a month, click on that Smart Mailbox and easily delete all the old email.

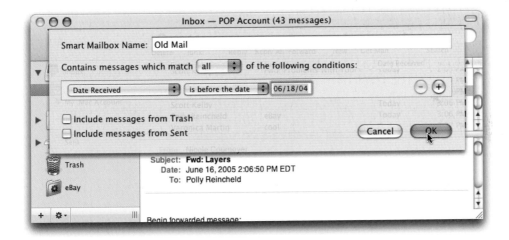

 SMART MAILBOX IDEA #2: MAIL FROM YOUR BOSS

This is just a good idea aimed at increasing your job security. First, click on an email message from your boss, then create a new Smart Mailbox (as shown in the previous tip). By default, the first field will be set to From, the second field will be set to Contains, and in the third field your boss's email address will already be there. Just click OK, then remember to check this Smart Mailbox several times a day to make sure your boss's message doesn't get lost in the flood of spam that comes your way. This wouldn't be a bad idea for messages from your spouse either. Last week my wife emailed me a Hallmark card and I missed it because it went straight into my Junk folder as Mail thought it was spam. Had I had that Smart Mailbox, I would have spotted it, and sidestepped a potentially life-threatening situation. (*Note:* You could also create a Smart Mailbox for just email from your co-workers—just click the plus [+] sign button after your enter the first co-worker's email address, then add their addresses one by one until they're all in the same Smart Mailbox.)

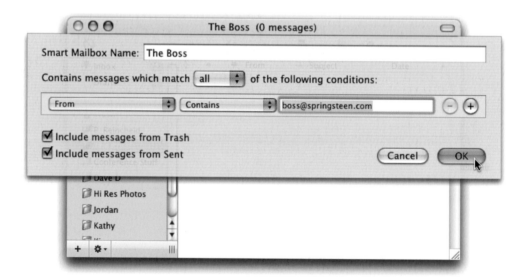

KillerTips

 ⬤ ⬤ ⬤ **SMART MAILBOX IDEA #3: UNREAD MAIL**

A lot of users (myself included) have more than one email account. For example, I've got a public email address that's posted on several websites that is the recipient of floods of spam, then a private address I only give my friends, and another address I only use for shopping online. So, if you have multiple email accounts, you can make your life easier by creating a new Smart Mailbox for all your unread mail. That way, no matter which account the mail comes into, you'll be able to see all your new unread mail in just one nice, neat Smart Mailbox. Here's how: Choose New Smart Mailbox from the Actions pop-up menu in the bottom-left corner of the Mail window. When the Smart Mailbox dialog appears, from the first pop-up menu choose Message Is Unread. That's it—that's the only choice you have to make—now click OK and all your unread mail will be just one click away. As you read a message, it removes itself from the Smart Mailbox. This thing's not smart. It's brilliant!

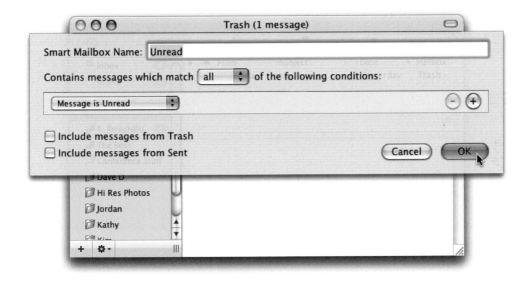

   SMART MAILBOX IDEA #4: MAIL WITH ATTACHMENTS

If you get a lot of photos or text documents sent your way, this is a good way to get right to all email with attachments. A nice thing about this one is that it helps you quickly find files with large attachments, making it easy to delete ones that are clogging your Inbox. Just click on the Actions pop-up menu in the bottom-left corner of the Mail window and choose New Smart Mailbox. When the options appear, in the first pop-up menu choose Contains Attachments, and then click OK (no further choices needed). You'll have a Smart Mailbox with nothing but attachments. And although you could sort all your mail with attachments by clicking on the Attachment header at the top of the main Mail window, by using a Smart Mailbox it updates live every day. It's handier than you'd think.

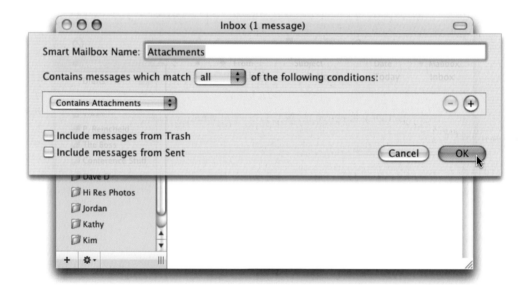

CUSTOMIZING YOUR NEW MESSAGE TOOLBAR

Besides being able to customize Mail's toolbar, you can also customize the toolbar in the New Message window, and to do that you only have to make one little move—first click the New button to create a new message, then go under the View menu and choose Customize Toolbar. Normally, this would open the standard Customize Toolbar dialog for Mail, but because you have a New Message window open, it opens a different dialog that allows you to customize the toolbar for new messages only. To add a tool to the bar, just click-and-drag it right up to the New Message toolbar. To remove a tool—just drag it off the bar.

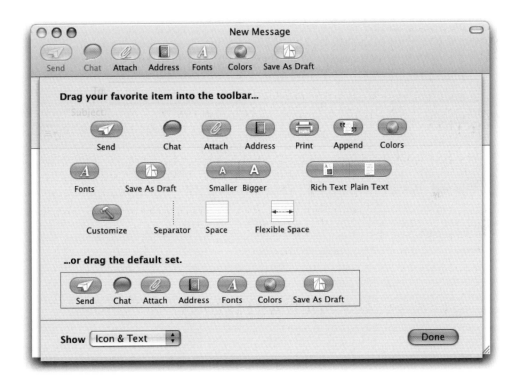

RESIZING PHOTOS FOR EMAILING

Have you ever noticed how freaked out relatives get when you email them high-res photos from your 6- or 8-meg digital camera? For example, Grandma Esther in Minnesota may not have Photoshop CS2, and so dealing with that 26-MB, 41"-wide photo you shot with your 8-meg camera might put a strain on her system (as well as her heart, and you know how Grandma Esther gets when she hasn't had her medication). That's why you might want to reduce the size of those photos you're about to email, but you don't have to launch Photoshop either, because you can do the resizing right within Mail. After you attach a photo to your email message (you can just drag-and-drop the image into the New Message window), take a look in the bottom-right corner of your email message window, and you'll see a pop-up menu where you can choose the Image Size you'd like to send. As soon as you choose a size (other than Actual Size), the image is immediately scaled down right within the email message window so you can see the exact size of the photo you're sending.

CAN'T GET ONLINE? CALL THE DOCTOR!

If you're having a hard time making a connection to the Internet to get your email, maybe the Doctor can help. Go under the Window menu and choose Connection Doctor, and the MD (Mac Doctor) will use some powerful medicine to try and cure your Internet aches and pains (yes, that was a string of lame doctor puns. I'm not proud of it, but I did it, and I'm man enough to own up to it).

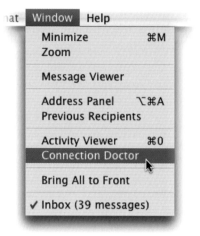

UNCOVERING THE PRIORITY POP-UP MENU

In Mac OS X Tiger, Mail now lets you apply a priority to your email that can be seen by your recipient. You can assign priorities by going under the Message menu, under Mark, and choosing your priority level. But wouldn't it be more convenient to have those priority choices available from right within your Mail message window? You betcha! Here's how it's done. First, click on the New button to create a blank outgoing email message. Then, click on the little rectangular button to the left of the Subject field (or Account pop-up menu if you have multiple accounts) and choose Customize from the pop-up menu. This makes a number of once-hidden fields and options appear. Look all the way to the right, and you'll see an icon with an exclamation point in the bottom-right corner of the dialog. Click on the checkbox to the left of that icon, then click the OK button. From now on, a Priority pop-up menu will be available anytime you create a new message. Nice.

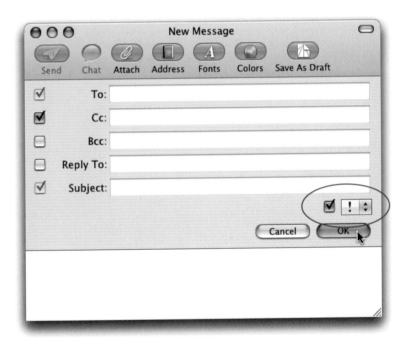

   AVOIDING APPLE'S "ACCOUNT SETUP ASSISTANT"

Every time you create a new Mail account, Apple has a step-by-step wizard that walks you through the process. That's great if you're brand new to Mac OS X, but if you've been using the Mac for a while, and you pretty much know the info you need to add to set up a new Mail account, you can bypass the somewhat annoying wizard by going to Mail's Preferences (found under the Mail menu). In the Accounts section, start by holding down the Option key, then click on the plus (+) sign button on the bottom-left corner of the Preferences dialog. This instantly gives you a new account with the fields ready for you to complete, without the help of the annoying assistant.

GETTING THE INSIDE SCOOP ON YOUR MAIL ACCOUNTS

Here's one of those tips that was really hidden beneath the surface—did you know that you could view a dialog full of details about a selected Mail account, including a summary of the account? It's true—you just have to know how to get there. You can either Control-click on the Mail account (in the list of accounts below the Inbox on the left side of the Mail window) or click on an account and press Command-I. Either way, this brings up the Account Info dialog for that account. If you click on the Mailbox Behaviors tab, you can even adjust how that particular mailbox handles certain email situations.

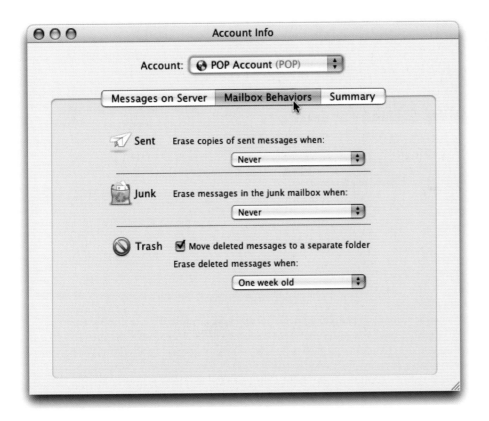

  WEB LINKS: UNCOVER WHERE THEY'RE GOING BEFORE YOU CLICK

More often than not, email
is sent in HTML format
(meaning, it looks like a
webpage, rather than just
text). At times, these HTML
pages will have a Web link
built right into them, but
you can't always see where

they're going to send you, because the underlined link just says something like "Click
Here," or "Learn More," etc. Well, if you're concerned that the link might lead you somewhere you don't want to go, just take your cursor and put it over that "Click Here" link in
your message window, and in just a second or two, you'll be able to view the full URL.

   FINDING OUT WHAT MAIL IS DOING RIGHT NOW

Okay, so you're
downloading
your email, and
the little status
circle beside
your email
account keeps
spinning and
spinning. You're
wondering if a

huge email attachment is being downloaded. You're wondering if it's doing anything at
all. You're wondering why my explanation is taking so long. You get the picture. The sad
truth is that you don't know what Mail is doing. You don't know, I don't know. I'm not sure
Apple even knows. It's a mystery wrapped in a riddle. Okay, Apple does know, and actually
you can too by pressing Command-0 (that's zero, not O). This brings up the Activity Viewer,
which shows you exactly what (if anything) Mail is doing. So if, for example, it's downloading a huge email attachment, you'll be able to tell. Now you can breathe a sigh of relief. It
doesn't make the download go faster, but it does have a surprisingly calming effect simply
to know what's going on.

CONTROLLING YOUR MAIL SEARCH

If you're searching for a particular piece of mail (aren't we all? I'm still searching for that one from Publishers Clearing House), you can either expand or narrow your search by choosing search options. These appear right under Mail's toolbar as soon as you start typing in the Mail's Search field. To focus your search to only the From field, To field, or the Entire Message (as I did here), just select the corresponding button.

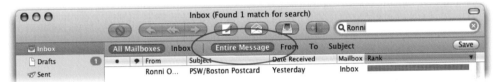

 ## CHECK THE SPELLING JUST WHEN YOU'RE DONE

If you need a little help with your spelling (as I do, just ask the platoon of editors who check my spelling), by default Mail checks your spelling as you go (underlining mis-spelled words in red), but if you find that underlining obtrusive, you can change it so it just checks the spelling once—when you hit Send. You do that by going to Mail's Preferences (found under the Mail menu), and when the Preferences panel appears, click on the Composing icon. In the Composing dialog you'll see a pop-up menu for checking your spelling. The default is set to check spell-

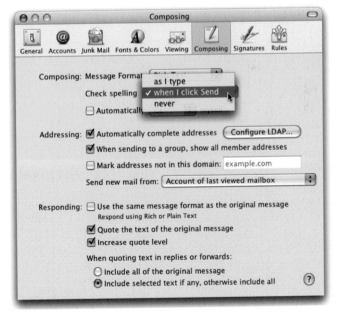

ing "As I Type," but you can change it to "When I Click Send" if you want to check it once when you're done. When you choose this method, after you click Send it will highlight any misspelled words (and underline them in red), and a pop-up spell-checking window will display a Guess of the proper spelling.

   MISSED A MESSAGE? MAYBE IT SHOULD HAVE BEEN BOLD

That little blue dot that lets you know that you've got a new mail message is easy to miss (especially if you're used to another email application where new messages appear in bold). If that's the case, you can have Mail display new messages in bold as well. Just go to Mail's Preferences (found under the Mail menu) and under Viewing, turn on the checkbox for Display Unread Message with Bold Font. From now on, any unread messages will be displayed in bold, which makes it even easier to quickly find which messages haven't been read.

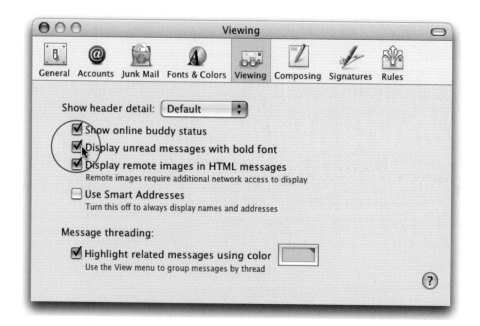

MAILBOX GETTING FULL? MAKE SOME ROOM FROM WITHIN MAIL

Is your email server's mailbox full? You can quickly delete old or unwanted email right from within Mail (rather than having to access your mail server directly). Here's how: First, click on the name of the Mail Account where you want to delete some excess mail, then press Command-I to bring up the Account Info dialog. If it's a standard POP mail account, select the Messages on Server tab to see a list of the email messages stored on your email server. Now select the message you want to delete (Shift-click to select a contiguous group of messages, or if you want to be more selective, Command-click on just the email you want to delete). Once you've got the ones selected you want to delete, just click the Remove From Server button in the lower-right corner of the dialog. That should free up some space, and you're back in business (well, at least you can get more email).

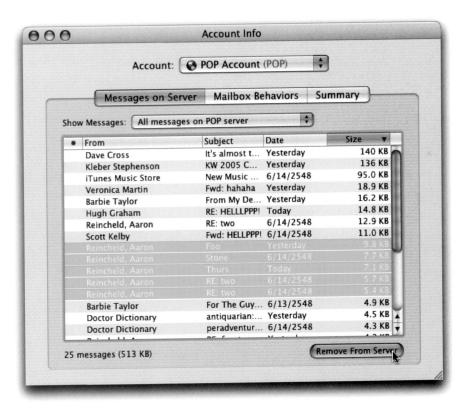

FITTING MORE IN YOUR MAILBOX PANE

If you have a lot of mailboxes, your Mailbox pane can get pretty crowded. If that happens, just Control-click within the pane and choose Use Small Mailbox Icons from the contextual menu that appears. These smaller icons will create much more room, enabling you to fit more in your pane.

QUICKLY BACKING UP YOUR EMAIL

If you want to archive (or backup) your email (I often back up mine to a FireWire drive just in case things go south), here's an easy way: Make your Mailbox pane visible (choose Show Mailboxes under the View menu), then click the little gray right-facing triangle to the left of your Inbox icon. This expands the Inbox listing your email accounts. Just click on the email address you want to archive, and either drag it right out onto to the desktop, or if the hard drive or server you want to back up to is visible, drag it right there for an instant backup.

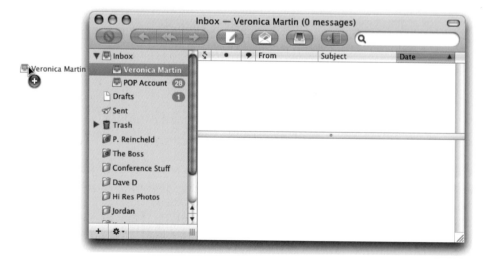

Content

ACCESS MAIL COMMANDS FROM THE DOCK

If your Mail app is running, but you're working in another application, you can save time by accessing a number of Mail's commands right from the Dock by just clicking-and-holding (or Control-clicking) on Mail's Dock icon. A pop-up menu of commands will appear, including shortcuts for checking your mail and composing new messages.

CUSTOMIZE MAIL'S TOOLBAR

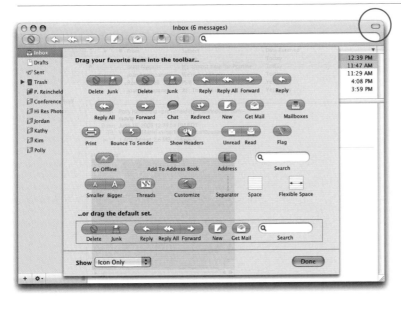

This is another place you can customize the toolbar, and probably one of the most useful because most people will only take advantage of a few tools, so why clutter the toolbar with tools you won't ever use, right? As usual, Control-clicking on the toolbar brings up a contextual menu where you can choose the size you want for your icons, and whether you want them displayed as icons and text, or just icons or just text (and which size you want for both). If you Command-click on the white pill-shaped button in the upper right-hand corner of the title bar, you'll step through the various toolbar icon/text configurations. Hold Option-Command and click the same button, and the all-important Customize Toolbar dialog will appear.

QUICK WAY TO ADD WORDS TO YOUR DICTIONARY

If you're typing a message in Mail and run across a
word that should be in your Spell Checker's dictionary
(such as your name, your company's name, etc.), you
can quickly add it to your Mail dictionary (then it will
recognize the name in the future, instead of flagging
it as misspelled). Here's how: When you come to a
word you want added to your dictionary (such as the
name "Kelby," which seemingly should be in every
dictionary, but sadly is not), Control-click on the word
and choose Learn Spelling from the pop-up menu.
Now it's added, and it will no longer be flagged as
unrecognized (unless you misspell it).

THREADING SHORTCUT

If you have your email organized by threads (under the View menu), there's a nice, simple
keyboard shortcut for opening and closing the threads. Just click on the thread to highlight
it, then press the Right Arrow key on your keyboard to open the thread, and the Left Arrow
key to close it.

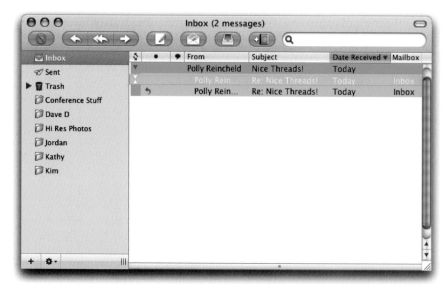

EMAIL ATTACHMENTS MADE EASY

I mentioned this in the Dock chapter, but since you might go looking for Mail-related stuff in this chapter, I thought I'd repeat it here too: If you want to attach a file to an email message, you can drag the file directly to Mail's icon in your Dock. This opens Mail and creates a brand-new email message window with that file already attached. Sweet! Better yet, even if you drag multiple attachments, they all attach to just one email message (rather than creating one message for each attachment, as in previous versions of Mac OS X).

   SENDING HUGE ATTACHMENTS

Most email servers have a limit to how large an attachment they'll accept. Most limit an attachment size to 5-MB (some even less), and if you email somebody a 6-MB file, it's probably going to get "kicked back" to you as undeliverable. Want to get around that? Use iChat instead. Once you have an iChat session started with someone, you can go under the Buddies menu and choose Send File. Navigate your way to the file you want to send, click OK, and the file will be sent to the person you're chatting with (and a link to download your file will appear in their iChat window). No matter how big the file size is, it'll get there.

  ⬤ **ABOUT TO EMAIL? WOULD YOU RATHER CHAT?**

When you open a New Message window and type in the recipient's email address, if you've got iChat running, Mail instantly checks to see if this person is available for an iChat. (After all, who wants to wait for email, when you can instantly talk face-to-face?) If they're available, a little green button appears right before their name, letting you know they're online and ready to talk. Click on their name and an iChat window will appear, where you can invite them to chat with you (at which point, they'll politely decline, but hey—it was worth a try). *Note:* This same "green-button-for-chat" feature is activated in Address Book, so if you go searching there for an email address, you'll see if they're ready to chat.

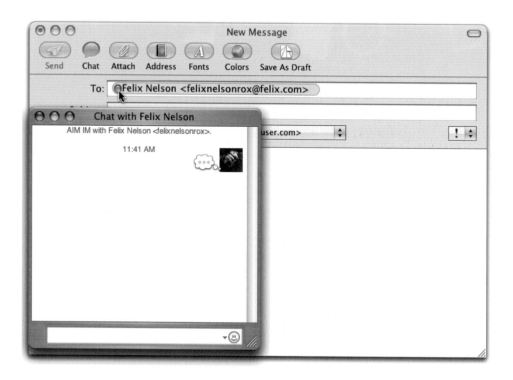

ADDING CUSTOM MAIL SOUNDS

If you don't like Apple's built-in Mail alert sounds, you can use your own custom sounds (I downloaded the AOL classic "You've Got Mail.aiff"). Once you've got the audio file you want to use for your alert, go to your Home folder, open your Library folder, then open your Sounds folder and drop it in there. Then, go back to Mail, and under the Mail menu choose Preferences. In the Preferences dialog, click on the General icon. In the New Mail Sound pop-up menu, you should see your new sound at the bottom of the list. (If not, choose Add/Remove. This opens your Sounds folder, where you'll find the alert sound you put there moments ago. Click on it, then click Done, which adds your sound to the New Mail Sound pop-up menu). Now that it's in the list, you can choose it as your new mail sound. Dig it.

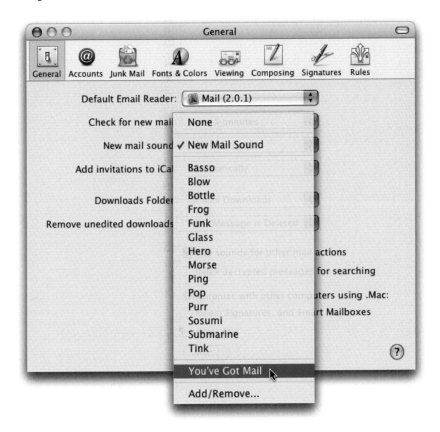

   SEEING MULTIPLE MAILBOXES IN THE SAME WINDOW

If you want to see the contents of multiple mailboxes displayed in the same window, just click on the first mailbox you want to see (they're nested under your Inbox), then Command-click on the second mailbox, and you'll get a merged list in the main window. This is really handy for things like looking for an important incoming email when you have multiple email accounts. By Command-clicking on the different accounts, you can see all your new mail, from all your accounts, in one window at the same time. Think about it. It boggles the mail. Uh…the mind.

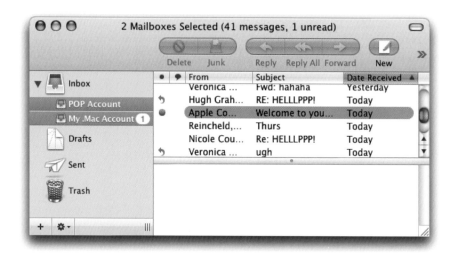

Takin' Care of Business

BUSINESS APPS THAT COME WITH MAC OS X

I know what you're thinking: Does Address Book really count as a business application? I mean, if you're using it for storing

Takin' Care of Business
business apps that come with mac os x

personal contacts (like your bookie, your pharmacist, your bail bondsman, etc.), then it's really not a business application, true. But, if you gave your bookie some Darvocet you got from your pharmacist to pay off a bad debt, but then he got busted and looked to you to bail him out (which is a surprisingly common turn of events), then it's all business, baby. Yeah, what about TextEdit? It's total business. Unless you wind up using TextEdit to methodically detail your plans for a gold heist. Then it's a fun caper-planning application. Well, it is until you're caught, and your bookie has to bail you out; and by that time he's had to pawn your iBook to raise your bail money, and now all you have is a spiral-bound notebook and a piece of chalk. Address Book doesn't seem so bad now, does it, Bunky?

   Address Book: **GETTING SMART ABOUT GROUPING**

Let's say you're the coach of your kid's soccer team, and you have all the parents' numbers in your Address Book in case you have to call them and cancel a game because of rain or extreme apathy. Of course, you could create a Group of just the parents' names, and then drag their addresses into this Group one by one, or you can create a Smart Group that will not only do it for you, but every time you add another kid to the team, you can have his parents' contact info jump right into that Group automatically. Here's how it's done: Hold the Option key and click on the little plus (+) sign in the bottom-left corner of the Address Book window (this is the shortcut for creating a Smart Group). A dialog will appear from the top of the Address Book, where you can choose who will make up your Smart Group. In the topmost field that appears, give your Group a name, then in the next field down, type "Soccer" and every card that has the word "Soccer" in it will appear in that Group. Now when you add any card with the word "Soccer" in it, it will automatically be added to your Smart Group.

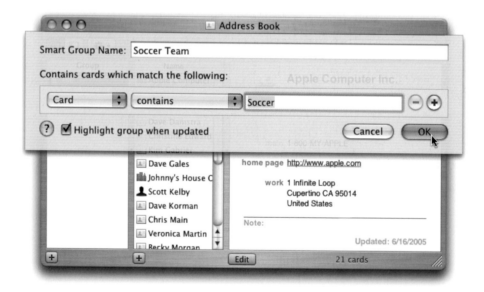

Address Book: **CHECKING FOR DUPLICATES**

If you've got more than one entry for the same person in your Address Book, you don't have to track them down manually. Just go under the Card menu and choose Look for Duplicate Entries. When you run this search, Address Book will report on what it found (duplicate cards for the same person or duplicate information in multiple cards), and it will tell you exactly how many it found of each. If you click Merge, it merges the info on those cards, which gets rid of the dupes, or if you don't want to merge the cards, just click Cancel.

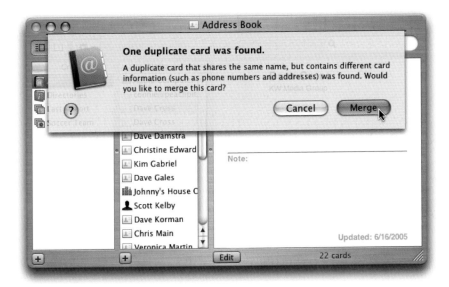

   Address Book: **SMART GROUP IDEAS**

Here are some ideas for Smart Groups: (1) Create one for your co-workers and have the Group created using your company's name. That way, as new people are added to your company, they'll automatically be added to the Group. If someone gets laid off, when you update their card, they'll move out of that Group and into your Federal Witness Protection Program Smart Group (Kidding. I hope). (2) If you enter birthdays for friends and co-workers in your Address Book, why not create a Smart Group of all the people who are having a birthday in the next 30 days. You do that by Option-clicking on the plus (+) sign at the bottom-left corner of Address Book, then when the dialog appears, in the first field enter a name, then in the first pop-up menu choose Birthday. The second pop-up menu will change to "is in the next," and you just type "30" for the amount of days and click OK. What's particularly cool is that you only have to do this once—it will automatically update every day.

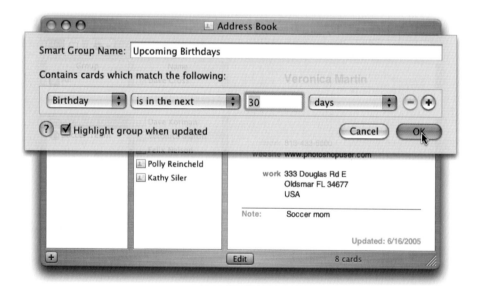

Address Book: **PRINT A MINI-ADDRESS BOOK**

If you've ever wanted a nice, small printout of all the contacts in your Address Book (maybe you want to keep it tucked away in your iPod case), it's easy. Just go to Address Book, click on the word "All" in the left column, and make sure no individual contacts have been clicked on (or you'll get an Address Book with just one address). From the File menu choose Print. When the Print dialog appears, in the Style pop-up menu, choose Pocket Address Book, hit Print, and in a minute or two you'll have your own printed mini-address book.

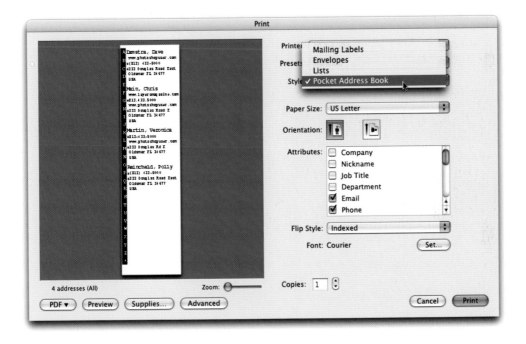

  Address Book: ADDING BIRTHDAYS TO YOUR ADDRESS BOOK

People love it when you remember their birthday, so it's very important to write them down. Where (you might ask) should you write them down? Right with their contact info in your Address Book. Just go to the contact, then go under Address Book's Card menu, under Add Field, and choose Birthday. This puts their card in Edit mode and adds a new field that's already highlighted and ready for you to enter a birth date (you can just enter the month and day, and then click the Edit button again to leave Edit mode—it will fill in the rest for you). That's it—you've got their birthday entered, but this is just the first step in making sure you remember it.

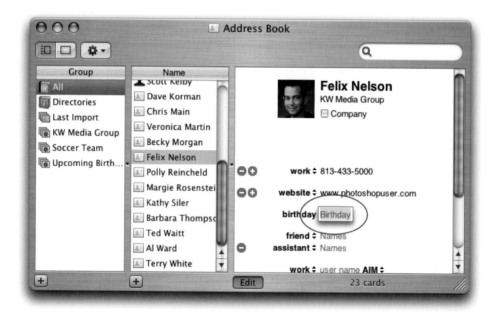

Address Book: **RUN A QUICK SEARCH ON YOUR CONTACT**

If you're looking at a contact in your Address Book, and you want to quickly find an email or a file someone sent you, just go under the Actions menu (that's the little button with a gear on it in the upper-left corner of Address Book) and you'll see the word "Spotlight" followed by the person's name. (For example, if you were looking at my contact, you'd see "Spotlight: Scott Kelby.") If you choose that, it runs a Spotlight search for all instances of that name on your computer (not just within Address Book, since chances are there's only one instance anyway, and you're already looking at it).

   Address Book: **GIVING OTHERS ACCESS TO YOUR ADDRESS BOOK**

Let's say you want to share your Address Book with a co-worker. For example, I share my Address Book with my Executive Assistant, the wonderful, and highly amazing, Kathy Siler. We work on a lot of projects together, so when she makes a contact we both need, rather than emailing it to me, she just adds it directly to my Address Book herself. Here's how: First, go the Address Book menu, choose Preferences, and click on the Sharing icon. This brings up a Sharing panel, and if the person in your Address Book that you want to share with has a .Mac account (they have to, to make this work by the way), then their name will appear in the list. If you want this person to be able to edit your Address Book, turn on that capability by clicking the Share Your Address Book checkbox, then click in the checkbox in the Allow Editing column to the right of the person you want to share with. Now, the person you're sharing with can open Address Book, go under the File menu, choose Subscribe to Address Book, and they'll enter your .Mac address. Then, as long as they're connected to the Internet, they'll be able to access your Address Book (from their Group column) and make entries and changes directly. How cool is that! (Very.)

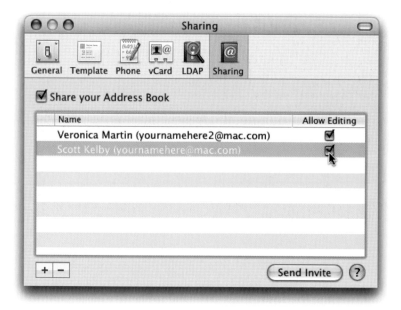

Address Book: **HIDING YOUR PRIVATES**

If you're sending someone your vCard, depending on who they are, you might want to limit how much info you give them. For example, if this contact is a business contact, you might not want them to have your private email address (these are all the rage right now, thanks to spam), or your home phone number (more and more people have one), or credit-card number. Well, luckily, you can decide which fields are saved as your vCard, and which are kept private, by going under the Address Book menu, under Preferences, and then clicking on the vCard icon. Then, click on the Enable Private "Me" Card checkbox. Now, go back to your vCard in the Address Book, click the Edit button, and a series of blue checkboxes will appear. The info in any "checked" fields will be included in your vCard, so uncheck any field you want kept private. It's as easy as that.

   Address Book: **SENIOR-SIZED PHONE NUMBERS**

Okay, the phone numbers in the contact window are pretty small, but don't sweat it; you can make the numbers so large that senior citizens who are standing a good 15 to 20 feet from your monitor could make them out. Just click-and-hold directly on the name of the field for the number you want to read (Work, Home, Mobile, etc.) and choose Large Type from the pop-up menu that appears. The menu item should really read "Huge, Gigantic, Billboard-like Type" because it plasters the number in giant letters across your entire screen. (Try it on an Apple Cinema Display—it's stunning.) To make the huge numbers go away, just click once on them and they disappear, back into a giant cave.

Address Book: WAS IT KAL-IB-RA OR KAL-EEB-BRA?

If you enter a new contact and you're concerned that when you call them again, perhaps months from now, you won't remember how their name is pronounced, Address Book can help. Just go under the Card menu, under Add Field, and choose Phonetic First/Last Name. This adds a tiny field right above your contact's name where you can enter the phonetic spelling of their name, so when you do call them back, you sound like a genius (or at least, someone with a good memory).

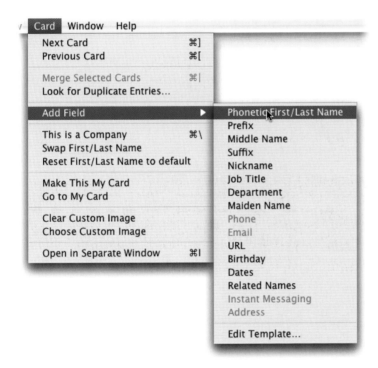

   Address Book: **GETTING VCARDS IN FAST**

vCards (Virtual Business Cards) are getting so popular that they now have an "industry standard" format. Luckily, Address Book not only supports them but also makes it easy for you to enter vCards. If you've received a vCard via email, just drag-and-drop it from your email right 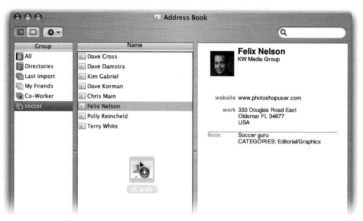 into the Address Book Name window, and Address Book will automatically format the information into a contact for you.

  Address Book: **GETTING VCARDS OUT FAST**

Getting a vCard out of Address Book got much easier in Tiger. Just go to the contact you want, and when you're there, if you look up in the Address Book's title bar, right before the words "Address Book," you'll see a little rectangular icon. That's a "mini vCard." There are two ways to use it: (1) If you hold the Option key, click on it, wait just a second, then drag it out to your desktop, it makes a freestanding vCard for whatever contact is highlighted in the Name column. You can then attach it to email, send it to friends, etc. (2) If you don't hold the Option key—you just click-and-drag it to your desktop—it creates an alias to that Address Book contact. Either way, the choice is yours: to Option-pause or not to Option-pause.

Address Book: **MAKING YOUR OWN VCARD**

I know, I know, you want to be all trendy and hip, so here's how to make your own vCard. *(Note: The first step in being trendy and hip is not to use the 1970s word "hip.")* Here's how: First, set up your own personal card the way you want it, then go under the Card menu and choose Make This My Card. This will change the icon for your personal contact to a silhouette of a person rather than a square photo icon, letting you know which card is "your card." If you've got a lot of contacts and want to get to your card fast, choose Go to My Card from the Card menu. If you want to email your card to somebody (to show you're trendy and that other thing), first choose Go to My Card from the Card menu, then go under the File menu and choose Export vCard. Save your vCard file (I save mine right to my desktop), then send it as an attachment to any Mail message. You can also drag-and-drop your card's silhouette icon right from Address Book onto Apple's Mail icon in the Dock, which opens a New Message window with your vCard attached. Or if you're using iChat, you can send your vCard to someone you're chatting with by going under the iChat Buddies menu and choosing Send File.

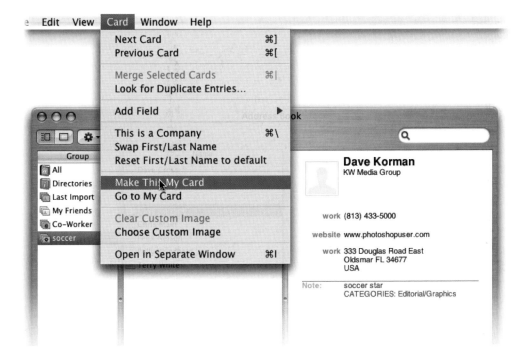

Address Book: **IS YOUR CONTACT AVAILABLE FOR CHATTING?**

If you're getting ready to send somebody an email, wouldn't it be better to get an answer right away, rather than waiting for them to reply to your email? Address Book can help, because when you go to a contact to get their email address, if they're using iChat and they're available for chatting, you'll see a little green dot next to their picture (consider that a green light for chatting—they're online, and available!). All you have to do now is click directly on that little green circle to bring iChat to the front, and then you can ask them if they will accept a chat from you. They probably won't, but that's an entirely different issue.

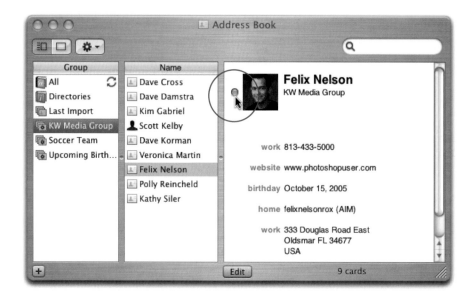

Address Book: **SEE WHICH GROUPS THEY'RE IN**

If you have a contact that appears in more than one Group, you can instantly see which of your Groups this individual appears in by simply clicking on his or her contact and holding the Option key. When you do this, every Group that they appear within will become highlighted. This is handy if you want to clean up your Groups by deleting extra instances of people who appear in multiple Groups.

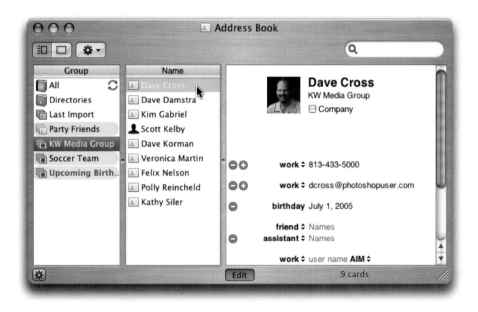

  ● Address Book: **SEND AN EMAIL TO EVERYONE IN YOUR GROUP**

Once you've created a Group (like friends, or co-workers, or perhaps Total Mac freaks), you can send that entire Group an email with just one click. Simply Control-click on the Group (in this case, we'll Control-click on our Group named "Business"), and then choose Send Email to "Business." It will open Mail and a New Message window, with your contacts' email addresses in the To field. Put in your subject, write your email, and when you click Send, everyone in your Business Group will receive the email. Not bad, eh?

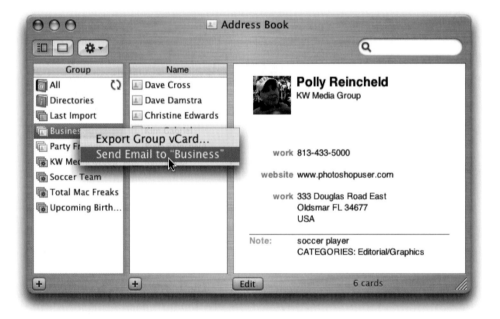

Address Book: **SENDING NOTES WITH YOUR VCARD**

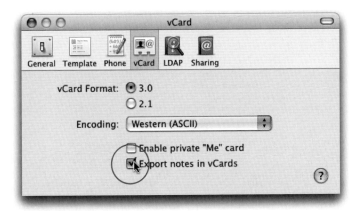

For some freaky reason, when you send someone your vCard, by default it sends them every single field except the Note field. Why? I have no earthly idea, but it doesn't have to be that way. To send your Note field along with your vCard, go under the Address Book menu, under Preferences, and click on the vCard icon at the top. In the vCard panel, turn on the checkbox for Export Notes in vCards, and from then on, your Notes will be sent along as well.

   Address Book: **THE WORLD'S EASIEST BACKUP PLAN**

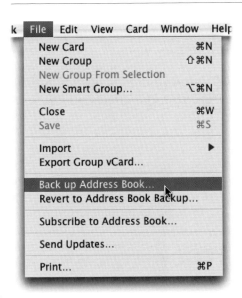

If you're not using a .Mac account to sync your Address Book (and if that all sounds very foreign, then you're not), you'll definitely want to make a backup copy of your contacts just in case anything unspeakable happens to your Mac (from being dropped, stolen, confiscated by the FBI, or just a really nasty hard disk crash). And since backup is so incredibly simple, there's no excuse not to—just go under the File menu and choose Back Up Address Book. This exports a copy of your entire Address Book (you should then put this copy on a removable drive, burn it to a CD, email it to a close family member, etc.) just in case the unimaginable becomes manageable (that doesn't make much sense, but it would make a great tagline for a company: "We make the unimaginable manageable").

Address Book: **GET DIRECTIONS TO THEIR OFFICE**

Now this is really cool—you can have Address Book automatically get a map and local directions to your contact's physical address. Just click-and-hold on their address field (not the address itself, the field title before it) and choose Map Of from the pop-up menu that appears. It will quickly go online (if you're connected to the Internet) and get a map and directions to their location for you. Seriously, how cool is that?

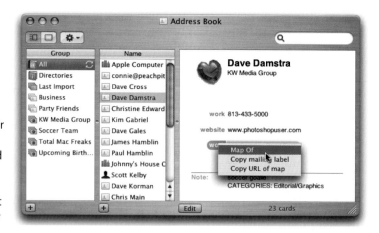

Address Book: **MERGING TWO RECORDS**

If you have two contacts for the same person (it happens more than you'd think—at least to me), you can have Address Book merge the two into one contact. First, press Command-1 to make sure your mode is set to Card and Columns view. Then use the Search field (in the upper right-hand corner) to find the two redundant contacts. Then, in the Name column, click on the first contact. Hold the Shift key and click on the second to select them both. Then, go under the Card menu and choose Merge Selected Cards, and the two shall become one (like the way I switched writing styles there? "The two shall become one." Hey, if nothing else, I'm versatile). If any of the information is re-dundant (two of the same phone numbers, etc.), just press Command-L to go into Edit mode, highlight the duplicate info, and press Delete. When you leave Edit mode, not only will the duplicate info be gone, but the duplicate field will also be deleted.

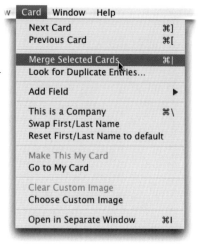

iCal: **KEEPING RELATED CALENDARS TOGETHER**

If you have a number of calendars that are related, you no longer have to sort through them all individually. (Let's say, for example, that you've subscribed to calendars for your NFL team and the other teams in your conference. Hey, there are freaks out there who care about this stuff. Like me.) Now you can group related calendars together, which makes keeping track of them easier and more convenient. Just hold the Shift key then click on the plus (+) sign in the bottom-left corner of the iCal window (its icon will change into mini-calendars with a plus sign), which creates a collapsible Calendar Group. Now just drag-and-drop your NFL calendars (within the Calendars list on the left side of the iCal window) into this Group. Then, click on the Group's right-facing arrow to collapse the Group, removing the clutter and bringing some sense and order into your otherwise chaotic list of calendars.

   iCal: **AUTOMATICALLY CREATE A BIRTHDAY CALENDAR**

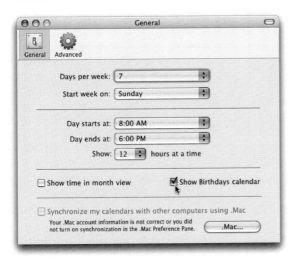

If you've been including people's birthdays with their contact info in your Address Book, then you can use iCal to automatically create a calendar of their upcoming birthdays for you. Here's how: Go to the iCal menu, under Preferences, and when the Preferences dialog appears, turn on the option for Show Birthdays Calendar. This adds a special calendar to your list of Calendars with all the birthdays you've dutifully entered in your Address Book, and now since they're on your iCal calendar (rather than buried in your Address Book), there's a better chance you'll remember to send them a lavish gift.

   iCal: ARE YOU "MEETING THEM TO DEATH?"

Want to find out if you're "meeting someone to death"? Just go to the Search field at the bottom of the iCal window and type their name. A window will pop up with a list of all the meetings you have invited them to attend. If you see dozens of listings, you might want to ask yourself, "Do I really need to have them there?"

(You might want to ask yourself other questions, like "Do I have a life outside of meetings?" "Have I become codependent on iCal?" Things along those lines.)

   iCal: HAVE ICAL CALL YOUR CELL PHONE

If you're like me, you sometimes need "extra" reminders about things like appointments, birthdays, meetings, etc. If you do, you can actually have iCal send an email to your cell phone reminding you of that important meeting (provided, of course, that you have a cell phone that accepts email). The first thing you need to do is put your phone's email address in your Address Book (not in iCal—in the Address Book application), in the card that you have designated as "My Card." Then, go to iCal and double-click on a date to create a new event (something like "Fight with a PC user—playground @ 10:00 a.m."), and in iCal's Info panel, click on the word "None," which appears to the immediate right of the word "Alarm." A pop-up menu of alarm notifications will appear. Choose Email. Then a new field will appear with a

list of email addresses that you have in (guess where?) your Address Book application in your My Card contact (that's you). Choose your cell phone's email address, choose how long before the appointment you want that email reminder sent, and you're good to go. As long as (a) your cell phone's turned on, (b) your Mac is still on, and (c) you have an Internet connection, it'll do it.

iCal: **GETTING A LINE BREAK IN YOUR HEADER**

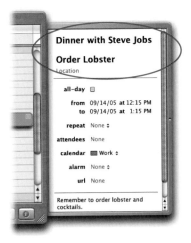

When you're entering a new event in your calendar, you've probably already noticed that hitting the Return key to add a line break in the Info panel doesn't work—instead it just thinks you've finished typing and closes the field (that's because by default iCal doesn't allow multiple lines—go figure). But there's a little-known keyboard shortcut that lets you create a line break. Instead of pressing just Return, press Option-Return, and you get that so well-deserved line break.

  iCal: **HAVING A MEETING? LET ICAL DO THE INVITES**

If you're scheduling a meeting, you can have iCal send out an email invitation to the people you want to attend. Start by adding your meeting to your calendar. Then, go under the Window menu and choose Address Book. This brings up your Address Book. Just drag-and-drop the people you want to invite right onto the Attendees section in the Info panel. When you're ready to send your invitations, click on the Send button at the bottom-right corner of the Info panel, and they're on their way! (*Note:* This only works if you have each attendee's email address in your Address Book, so make sure you do first.)

 iCal: **KEEP TABS ON YOUR LOCAL APPLE STORE**

If you have an Apple Store nearby, you probably already know that they hold lots of free seminars and special events. But how do you know which one is coming up next without going to their website to check? It's easy—just go to Apple.com/retail, click on the link for your local store, and subscribe to their iCal event calendar. This will add their calendar of upcoming events to your iCal so you can know what's happening next at your local Apple Store.

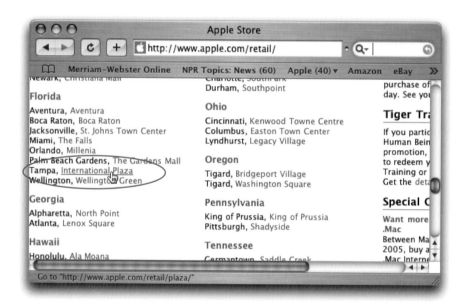

iCal: ADDING LIVE WEB LINKS TO YOUR CALENDAR

If you're leaving yourself a note to check a website, you can embed a live link to that site right in your iCal header (you could always embed a URL into a note, but not into the header that appears in the calendar itself). For example, let's say your message would have been "New Ricky Martin CD comes out today. Visit CDNOW.com to order." If you add angle brackets around CDNOW and include the full Web address like this:

<http://www.cdnow.com>

the link will be live. You can click on that header from within iCal's main calendar and be taken directly to that webpage (if you're connected to the Internet). If you look in the main Calendar window, you'll see that the link that appears is clickable and live.

iCal: **SETTING YOUR ALARM TO PLAY A SONG**

Why just have an annoying alert sound as your iCal alarm, when you can have it play your favorite song as your alarm? It's easy. All you have to do is click on the event you want to set an alarm for, then in the Info panel, click-and-hold on the word "None" that appears to the immediate right of the word "Alarm." In the pop-up menu that appears, choose Open File. This puts the entry Open File in that field, but it adds a new field directly below

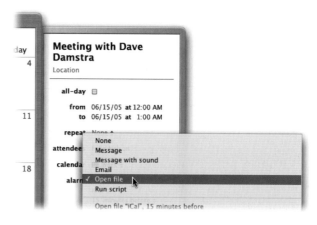

it. Click on that field and choose Other. Then, in the standard Open dialog that appears, navigate to the song you want played as your alarm (I use the 1980s club mix of Kano's "I'm Ready"), then click the Select button. In the bottom field, choose when you want the alarm (the song) to "go off." That's it—when your alarm goes off, you get the jams!

   iCal: **UNLEASH THE SCROLL WHEEL'S POWER**

If you're using a multi-button mouse with a scroll wheel, it's time to "unleash its power" by taking advantage of using your scroll wheel with iCal, because it lets you jump from field to field in the Info panel by simply moving the scroll wheel back and forth. This makes quick work of entering alarm times, status settings (just about anything in the Info panel), and if you bring up the To or From date fields, you can even scroll through the dates. It's "wheely" great (sorry, that was lame).

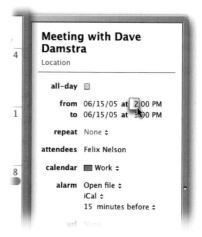

iCal: **CUSTOMIZING YOUR ICAL INVITE MESSAGE**

If you're inviting people to a meeting using iChat, it sends them a pretty straightforward, business-sounding email invitation. However, if you'd prefer iCal's invitation to read something like: "If you have any hopes of keeping your job, you'd better be at the 4:00 p.m. meeting today," you can do it pretty easily.

STEP ONE: Go into your Applications folder and Control-click on the iCal application's icon. Choose Show Package Contents from the contextual menu that appears. This brings up a folder named Contents. Look inside that folder and you'll find another folder named Resources. Look inside this folder for a folder named English.lproj, then look inside that folder for a file named iTIP.strings.

STEP TWO: Open this iTIP.strings in TextEdit (you can also open it in Microsoft Word if you like).

STEP THREE: As you look through this file, you'll see a line that reads "/* Mail body when sending an invitation to an event (IP 56)." Directly below this line, you'll see the default text that iCal uses when inviting someone to a meeting. This is the text you'll edit. However, iCal customizes part of this invitation with the recipient's name, the time you want your meeting, etc., so don't erase any characters that look like this: "%@"—leave those in place and work around them. For example, the default invitation reads "%@ has invited you to the iCal event %@, scheduled for %@ at %@ (%@)." You could change that to "%@ is warning you to get your lazy butt into gear for my meeting about: %@, and if you have any hope of keeping your miserable job, you'd better be there at %@ in the %@." Now you can close the file, save changes, restart iCal, and scare the hell out of your employees.

   TextEdit: TEXTEDIT AND THE WEB

TextEdit in Tiger has some Web features that might not be apparent at first glance. First, it opens and reads standard HTML webpages, and it saves any document you create (even one with graphics) as an HTML Web archive (just choose Save As from the File menu, and for File Format choose Web Archive). Plus, you can make any text a live URL link by highlighting the text, then going under the Format menu, under Text, and choosing Link. Enter your site, click OK, and it's live. Also, if you know how to write HTML code, you can use TextEdit as a code editor. Just choose Ignore Rich Commands in the Open dialog when you're opening an HTML document, and it will convert the page into code. When you're done, it saves the code back out as HTML (with the .html extension).

 TextEdit: **ADDING TABLES**

Want to add a table to your document? Just go under the Format menu, under Text, and choose Table. This brings up a floating Table palette that lets you choose how many rows and columns you'd like for your table, and as it soon as it appears, your table appears in your document (at the current location of your cursor) so you can see what it looks like while you're making changes in the palette. You can choose border thickness and color (just click on the gray color swatch in the Cell Border section), and the background color for your table all within the palette. There are also buttons for how your text will be aligned within your tables (top, center, bottom, etc.). When the table looks good to you, just close the floating palette. Once your table has been created, you can edit the cell width and depth by simply grabbing the divider lines and dragging.

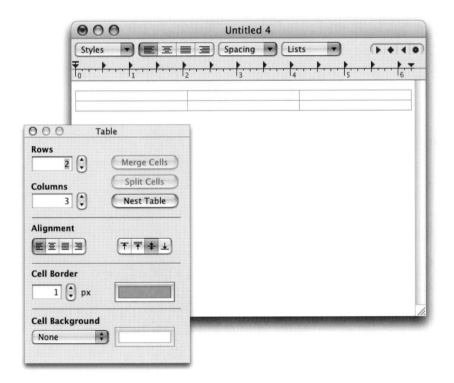

TextEdit: HAVE TEXTEDIT DO THE WORK WHEN CREATING LISTS

If you're creating a list (with bullet points, numbers, etc.), you can have TextEdit do most of the work for you. Just enter the items in your list with a simple return between each item, like this:

Monday
Tuesday
Wednesday

Then highlight whatever you want to be in your list and go under the Format menu, under Text, and choose List. A palette will appear, where you can choose which type of bullet you want for your list from the Bullet/Number pop-up menu. If you choose a standard round bullet (for example), your list will now look like this:

• Monday
• Tuesday
• Wednesday

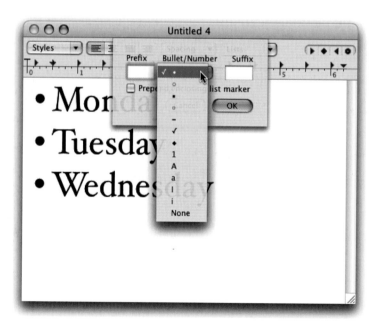

TextEdit: HOW DOES MY LETTER FIT ON A PAGE?

To see TextEdit's page boundaries, press Command-Shift-W (the shortcut for the Wrap to Page command) and the page margins will appear onscreen. Another thing that will make TextEdit behave more like the word processor it really is, is to go under the Format menu and choose Allow Hyphenation, so when a word extends to the page's edge, it gets automatically hyphenated and split by syllable to the next line, like you'd expect in a standalone word processor.

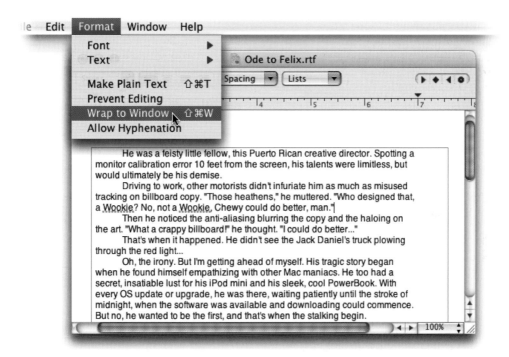

   TextEdit: COPYING FONT FORMATS

I mentioned this elsewhere in the book, but I thought it bore repeating here because this is such a cool tip and TextEdit totally supports it (not all Mac OS X apps do). If you've got a block of text formatted just the way you want it (font, type style, size, color, etc.), you can copy just that formatting (not the words themselves) by highlighting the text and pressing Command-Option-C. Then, to apply that copied formatting to another block of text that's formatted with different font styles, sizes, etc., just highlight the other text and press Command-Option-V. That text will now have the same font formatting as your original text. Big, big timesaver.

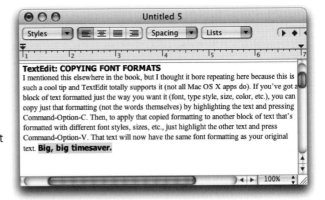

   TextEdit: COPYING PARAGRAPH FORMATS

Another typography tool usually found in page-layout applications and full-powered word processors is paragraph styles. Instead of the font-format copying we talked about in the previous tip, in this instance you'll be copying the paragraph formatting (first line indents, justification, tabs, etc.). To do this, highlight part of the paragraph that has the formatting you want, then press Control-Command-C to copy that formatting. Then switch to another paragraph, highlight that paragraph, and press Control-Command-V to paste that formatting onto this paragraph.

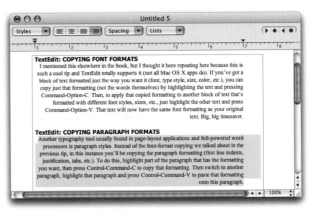

TextEdit: ADJUSTING THE SPACE BETWEEN LETTERS

Kerning is the act of adjusting the space between letters. (When it's called kerning, that usually refers to adjusting the space between only two letters. If you're adjusting more than two letters at once, it's usually called tracking.) At standard text sizes like 10, 11, and 12, you don't normally worry about kerning, but when you start creating display-sized type (like 72-point type), sometimes wide gaps appear between letters. (The space between a 72-point capital W and the small letter "a" is a perfect example.) To tighten the space between letters, highlight the two letters, then go under the Format menu, under Font, under Kern, and choose Tighten. This is a very slight adjustment, so you'll probably have to run it more than once (okay, probably more than five or six times). To Loosen the space, choose Loosen as many times as you need.

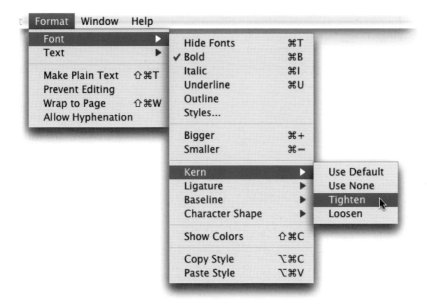

  TextEdit: **FONT CONTROL CENTRAL**

TextEdit gives you surprisingly robust control over your font formatting. Press Command-T to bring up the Font panel. You can choose the font Family, Typeface style (bold, italic, etc.), and point Size, and then you can see your choice in a large preview at the top of the Font panel (just choose Show Preview from the palette's Actions button, in the bottom left-hand corner of the panel). Just under the preview is a toolbar where you'll find everything from controls for colorizing your text to adding drop shadows.

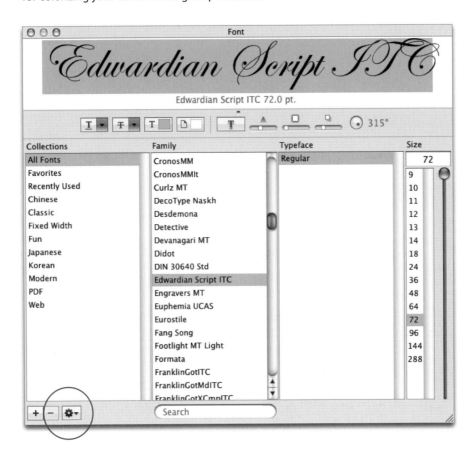

TextEdit: **CREATING SOFT DROP SHADOWS**

Okay, I know this sounds like a Photoshop technique, but the ability to create a soft drop shadow effect behind your type is built into TextEdit. Here's how to "drop it." Create your text (large type sizes work best) and highlight it. Then press Command-T to bring up the Font panel. At the top of the panel is a button with a large letter T with a slight drop shadow on it. Click on this to turn the shadow feature on (if you don't see this button, choose Show Effects from the Actions pop-up menu in the bottom-left corner of the panel). The three sliders to the right of the T control the Shadow Opacity (how dark the shadow will be), Shadow Blur (how soft it will be), and Shadow Offset (distance the shadow appears from the letter), respectively. To create a soft drop shadow, drag the middle slider (Shadow Blur) to the right (dragging it to the center looks pretty good). You can also control the angle of the light source using the Shadow Angle circle to the immediate right of the three sliders. Just drag the small dot in the circle where you want your light source. Cool!

 TextEdit: POP-UP SPELL CHECKING

If you want to check the spelling in your
TextEdit document, save yourself a trip to
the menu bar. Simply Control-click right
within your document and a contextual
menu will appear where you can take
control of the spell-checking process.
This works particularly well if you have
a word in question—just highlight that
word, Control-click on it, and the proper

spelling (if it's misspelled) will appear in the menu. By the way, in Tiger the Spell Checker checks
as you type, flagging misspelled words as soon as they're created. If you find this annoying, go
under the TextEdit menu, under Preferences, and in the Options section, turn off Check Spelling
As You Type (or to change this setting for just the document you're working on, Control-click in
the document and choose the same option from the Spelling submenu).

TextEdit: ALWAYS WRAP TO PAGE

Want to see those page margins every
time you create a new document? Go
under the TextEdit menu and choose
Preferences. In the TextEdit Preferences,
click the New Document tab, check the
box marked Wrap to Page, and from then
on, every new page will automatically
display the page margins.

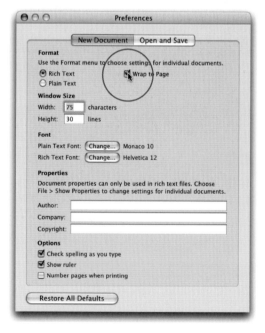

TextEdit: **CHANGING YOUR PAGE COLOR**

Want to change the color of the background area of your TextEdit document? No problem—you just do it in a place where you probably won't think to look—in the Font panel. Just press Command-T to bring up the Font panel, and in the toolbar at the top of the panel, the fourth button from the left has a tiny page icon with a square color swatch. The swatch is white by default, but you can change your page color by clicking on this button and a Colors panel will appear, in which you can choose the page color of your choice.

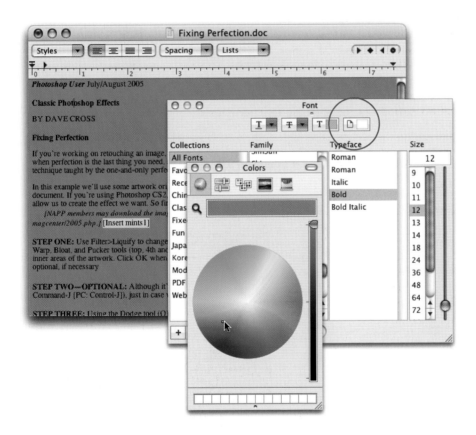

  TextEdit: CAN'T THINK OF THE RIGHT WORD? TRY THIS

TextEdit has a very cool feature that can help you out of a word logjam or spelling mishap. As you're typing, when you come to a word you're not sure how to spell, or you can't quite remember the word you want to use, take a stab at it by typing the first few letters, then press F5 on your keyboard. A pop-up menu will appear with a list of the words TextEdit thinks you might be trying to conjure up. All you have to do is click on the word that looks right, and it's entered into your document.

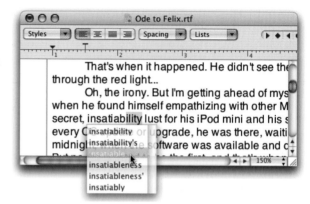

   TextEdit: SAVING FILES AS WORD DOCUMENTS

If you love TextEdit, but routinely send text files to people on other platforms who don't have TextEdit, but surely have Microsoft Word, you can make things easy for them by saving your TextEdit files in Word format so they can easily read them. Here's how: When you go to save your file in the Save As dialog, the default saves your file in Rich Text Format (RTF), but if you click-and-hold on the File Format pop-up menu, you'll see that you can also save the file in Word Format. Choose that, and your worries are over. (Well, you'll still have worries, just not about how other people will open your text files.)

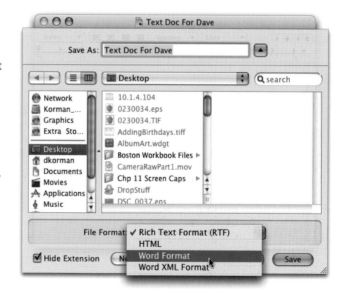

Preview: **FILLING OUT PDF FORMS**

Preview snuck in a little feature from Adobe Acrobat this time around, because now you can actually fill out and complete PDF forms right within Preview. Just click in any form field, start typing, and when you want to jump to the next form field, just press the Tab key. When your form is complete, you can print it like any other Preview document.

   Preview: **HIDDEN SORTING OPTIONS**

When you open multiple images in Preview, they appear in the Drawer. You can sort them manually by dragging them up and down the list, but there's another way—if you Control-click on one of the images in the Drawer, a contextual menu will appear, and you can then sort by name, size, keyword, and more.

   Preview: **SORTING DIGITAL CAMERA IMAGES**

Now you can use Preview to sort your digital camera images, by keeping the good ones and trashing the bad ones. Just open your photos in Preview, and when you come to a photo you don't want (it's out of focus, underexposed, etc.), just press Command-Delete to send that lame photo directly to the Trash. There is no undo (besides dragging the photo out of the Trash), so make sure you really want to delete it, because pressing Command-Z won't bring it back.

©SCOTT KELBY

Preview: **COLOR CORRECTING PHOTOS IN PREVIEW**

I know, it sounds crazy, but Preview actually has some pretty decent image-editing controls (very much like iPhoto's new image-editing controls, except believe it or not, Preview lets you set custom White and Black Points, whereas iPhoto doesn't). To unlock the photo-editing power of Preview, just go under Preview's Tools menu and choose Image Correction, which brings up a floating palette. Here are a couple of tips on correcting your images: The Gamma slider controls the midtones, and dragging it to the left brightens the midtones. To make a black-and-white image, drag the Saturation slider all the way to the left, then drag the Contrast slider to the right.

  ● Preview: **SEEING A PHOTO'S EXIF METADATA**

When you take a photo with a digital camera, a boatload of background information is embedded into the file (called EXIF metadata), including when the photo was taken, the make and model of the digital camera, the exposure, shutter speed, lens focal length, whether the flash fired, and a host of other related info. Believe it or not, Preview can display all this EXIF metadata—you just have to know where to look. To see the EXIF data for the current image, just press Command-I, then click on the Details tab, and if you scroll down a bit, you'll see a header for EXIF Properties, along with the full scoop on your image.

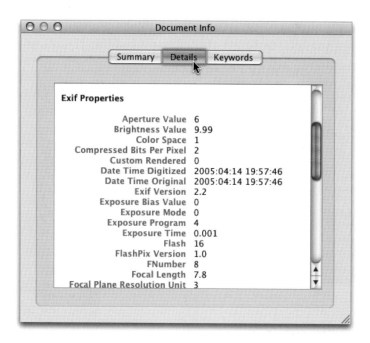

   Preview: **GIVING YOUR PHOTOS KEYWORDS**

If you're using Preview to sort your digital camera images (an advantage of doing it here, rather than iPhoto, is that it doesn't automatically copy of all the photos onto your hard disk like iPhoto does—it just displays them), here's another helpful feature—the ability to add keywords to your photos. These keywords will even show up in Spotlight, so if you want to search your hard disk for images using keywords, you can. Here's how it works: When you have an image onscreen that you want to rate, just go under Preview's Tools menu and choose Get Info. Click on the Keywords tab, then click the Add button to add a field. Enter your keyword in the highlighted field, click in the white space to finalize your keyword, and you're done.

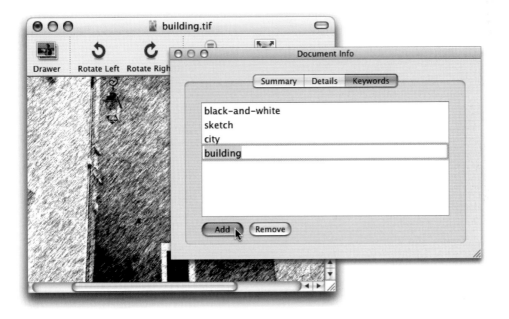

   Preview: **ASSIGNING COLOR PROFILES**

Here's another thing that Preview does that iPhoto doesn't—color manage photos. You can assign an ICC color profile for any open JPEG or TIFF image by going under the Tools menu and choosing Assign Profile. This brings up a dialog with a pop-up menu of available

color profiles. To assign a specific profile, just choose it from the pop-up menu, then click OK. If instead you want to change the color profile to match a specific ColorSync profile, then go under the same menu, but instead choose Match to Profile. A dialog will appear where you can choose the source, and which profile you want to match.

   Preview: **MARKING UP PDFS**

The ability to mark up Acrobat PDF files is a main feature of Adobe Acrobat Pro, but in Tiger you can mark up and annotate PDFs now as well. For calling attention to something, you can draw a red oval (like you're circling it in red) by first going under the Tools menu, under Annotation, and choosing Oval Annotation (it saves time if you choose the style first, then use the tool). Now that you've selected what kind of annotation you want, press Command-4 to

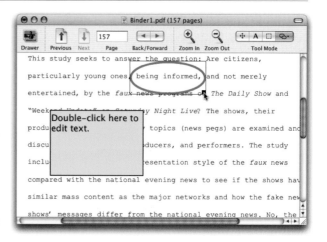

get the Annotation tool, and click-and-drag a red oval right where you want it within your PDF document. Once drawn, you can resize it by grabbing the right corner point. You can move the entire oval just by clicking-and-dragging within it. If you want to leave a little Post It-like note instead (like the one in Acrobat), go under the Tools menu, under Annotation, and choose Text Annotation. Press Command-4, then click-and-drag your little yellow note.

Preview: **CUSTOMIZE PREVIEW'S TOOLBAR**

Like the Finder itself, Preview's toolbar is very customizable, and you can easily adjust it so that only the tools you want will appear in the toolbar in the order that you want them. You do this by Control-clicking anywhere in Preview's toolbar (with a file open), and a pop-up menu will appear in which you can choose Customize Toolbar. A dialog will slide down with various tool icons that you can drag-and-drop right up to the toolbar (the options that appear depend on the type of file you have open—try applying this tip to a PDF and you'll see what I mean). If there's a tool you don't want in the toolbar, just click-and-drag it off the toolbar while this dialog is still open.

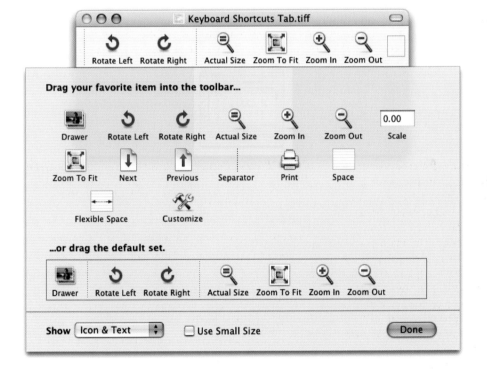

   Preview: **THE NON-MAGNIFYING GLASS TRICK**

If you're used to Photoshop's Zoom tool, which allows you to click-and-drag a selection around the area you want to zoom in on, you're probably frustrated with how the Preview Zoom In tool (it looks like a magnifying glass) works. There's no dragging—you just click on the Zoom In tool in the toolbar and it zooms in. But, you can get the same "drag-a-selection-and-zoom" effect by simply clicking-and-dragging a selection (you don't have to select a tool for this, just click-and-drag) around the exact area you want to zoom in on, then choose Zoom to Selection from the View menu. That area will zoom in, filling your window. Nice.

Preview: **STEP THROUGH TOOLBAR VIEWS**

Command-click on the white pill-shaped button in the upper right-hand corner of Preview's title bar, and each time you click, you'll get another view that's smaller than the default toolbar view (which is large icons and large text). Click once, you'll get smaller icons. Click again—icons with no text, smaller icons with no text, then just text, and then really small text. Of course, if you don't want the toolbar visible at all, simply click once on the pill-shaped button, and it will hide it from view.

Default view

Text view

   Preview: **PRINTING FINDER WINDOWS**

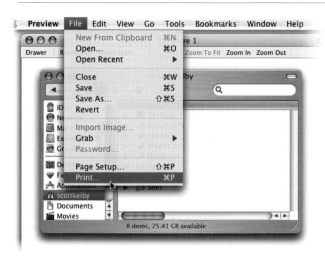

Since Mac OS X doesn't have the ability to print Finder windows (as in previous versions of the OS), here's a popular workaround: Make a screen capture of the window (Command-Shift-4 and drag a marquee around the window), which saves the capture as a PDF file on your desktop. Double-click on your PDF screen capture to open it in Preview, and then you can print the image from within Preview, producing a printed view of your Finder window (just like in "the old days").

  Preview: **CONVERTING TO TIFF, JPEG, OR PHOTOSHOP**

Want to change most any graphic into a Photoshop file? Just open the file in Preview, go under the File menu, and choose Export, where you can export your graphic in Photoshop format. But you're not limited to Photoshop format—Preview will also export your file as a JPEG, PICT, BMP (for sharing files with PC users), PICT, Targa (for video), and more. If the format you're saving in has options (such as quality and compression settings for JPEG and TIFF images), they will appear near the bottom of the dialog.

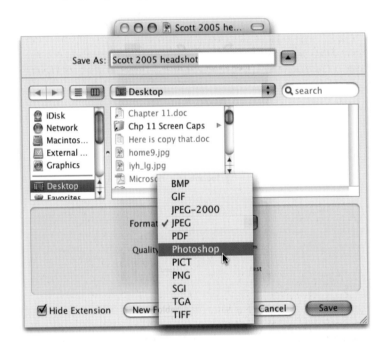

   DVD Player: **GETTING TO THE MAIN MENU DURING THE MOVIE**

 One of the most important keyboard shortcuts to me is the ability to get back to the main DVD menu while the DVD is already playing. To get there, just press Command–~ (that's the Tilde key just above the Tab key), and it will cycle you back to the DVD's main menu.

DVD Player: **THE SUBTLE CONTROL DIFFERENCES**

It seems that it would make sense for Apple's DVD Player to share the same keyboard shortcuts as the QuickTime Player, since they're both motion-graphics players, and they're both from Apple. Ah, if life were only that simple. While the Up/Down Arrow keys work for controlling the volume in the QuickTime player, you have to press Command-Up/Down Arrows to control volume in the DVD Player (the same volume shortcuts as iTunes). And while you mute the QuickTime Player by pressing Option-Down Arrow, you have to press Command-Option-Down Arrow to mute the DVD player. Thankfully, one important command is the same no matter which Player you're using—pressing the Spacebar starts or pauses movies in DVD Player.

   DVD Player: **CONTROLLER MAXIMUS (THE HIDDEN CONTROLS)**

If you're wondering whether DVD Player is missing some DVD functionality, you're only half right. It does have the ability to access DVD controls, such as slow motion, subtitling, camera angles, language, etc., but for the sake of space considerations, they're tucked away. To bring these buttons into view, double-click on the little vertical gray lines on the right center of the Player, and the Player will expand to show two additional rows of buttons. If that's too much work, press Command-] (Right Bracket key) to show/hide the options.

DVD Player: **HIDING THE CONTROLLER**

Want the Controller to quickly go away? Just press Command-Option-C and the Controller fades peacefully away. To return to the Controller, press the same shortcut.

The Controller fading away…

⬤ ⬤ ⬤ DVD Player: **BOOKMARKING YOUR SPOT**

One of the coolest things Apple added to the DVD Player is the ability to bookmark your spot while you watch a DVD, and if you have to stop or eject the DVD, when you re-insert the disc, it gives you the option of starting from the beginning or starting where you bookmarked. To bookmark a particular spot while a DVD is playing, just press Command–= (Equal Sign key on your numeric keypad) and that spot is bookmarked. A dialog will appear asking you to name your bookmark. Enter a name, click OK, and when you insert that DVD again, you'll have the option to start from your bookmarked spot.

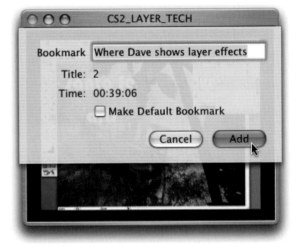

DVD Player: **USING AND EDITING BOOKMARKS**

You can actually set more than one bookmark, and there's even a Bookmarks submenu, so you can set multiple bookmarks and jump to your favorite bookmarks any time. Once you've saved some bookmarks, to use them, just go to the DVD Player's Go menu, under Bookmarks, and choose the bookmark you want. You can also edit and manage your bookmarks by going under the Window menu and choosing Bookmarks. This brings up a dialog where you can rename, delete, and choose one bookmark as your default, so when you reinsert the DVD, you have the choice of jumping to that default bookmark.

  DVD Player: **GOING VERTICAL**

Are you tired of the boring horizontal player? Maybe it's time to get vertical. Go under the Controls menu and choose Use Vertical Controller—a vertical version of the Controller appears. To return to the horizontal view, choose Use Horizontal Controller from the same menu.

DVD Player: PUTTING CAPTIONS IN THEIR OWN WINDOW

Imagine having the ability to put captions in their own separate windows. Then imagine why in the world anyone would want to do this? Not coming up with anything? Me either. Nevertheless, here's how to do it: Go under the Controls menu, under Closed Captioning, and choose Turn On (if it's not already on), then under the same Closed Captioning menu choose Separate Window.

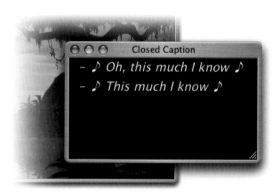

DVD Player: CONFIGURE THE PLAYER FOR DVD TRAINING USE

If you use your Mac's DVD Player mostly for educational purposes (like watching Photoshop training DVDs from PhotoshopVideos .com, hint, hint), you probably want to be able to jump back and forth between the DVD and whichever application you're learning, so you can watch a technique and then try it yourself. If that's the case, you can configure your DVD Player so it doesn't go "full screen" but instead displays the video in a floating window, so you can easily jump back and forth between it and any open applications. To set up this mode as the default, go under the DVD Player menu, choose Preferences, click on the Player icon, and where it says When DVD Player Opens, turn off the checkbox for Enter Full Screen Mode (it's on by default). Then the next time you insert a training DVD, it will appear in a floating window.

284   CHAPTER 11 • Business Apps That Come with Mac OS X

Sherlock: **STEP THROUGH SHERLOCK'S TOOLBAR VIEWS**

Sherlock has a new job—just Web searches (hard drive searches are now relegated to the Find command using the shortcut Command-F or using the Spotlight search menu in the menu bar). Although this has changed, it shares many of the same toolbar controls as other Mac OS X apps. For example, if you Command-click on the white pill-shaped button in the upper right-hand corner of Sherlock's title bar, you'll get another Icon/Text view that's smaller than the default toolbar view (which is large icons and large text). Click once, you'll get smaller icons. Click again—icons with no text, then smaller icons with no text, then just text, and then just really small text. To hide the toolbar altogether, click once on the white pill-shaped button in the upper right-hand corner, and it will hide itself from view. Want to customize its toolbar? Just Control-click anywhere within the toolbar itself and choose Customize Toolbar.

Regular toolbar

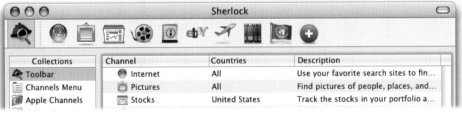

Icon toolbar

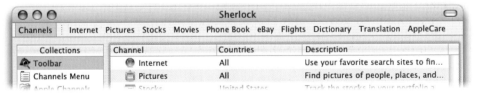

Text toolbar

   Sherlock: **TARGETING CHANNELS THE FAST WAY**

Know which Sherlock channel you need next? Don't waste time—jump right to it by Control-clicking (or clicking-and-holding) on Sherlock's icon in the Dock. A pop-up menu of channels will appear and you can jump right to the one you need fast. (*Note:* If you quit Sherlock after your last search, this won't work—it has to be running, but it doesn't have to be the active application, meaning you could be running Adobe InDesign and jump right to the Sherlock channel you want directly from the Dock.)

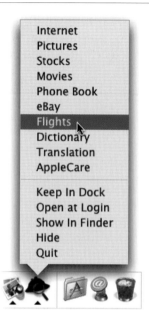

   Sherlock: **YOUR CHANNEL JUST ONE CLICK AWAY**

If you were thinking, "There's got to be a faster way to get to the channel I need," there is. At least after you do this one thing. Open Sherlock and double-click on the channel you want (so, if you find yourself using the Phone Book a lot, double-click on Phone Book). Then go under the Channel menu and choose Make a Shortcut. This brings up a Save dialog, and I recommend you save this file to your desktop (and/or drag it to your Dock). Once you've done that, you can close Sherlock. The next time you want to get to the Phone Book, just double-click this file and it will launch Sherlock, taking you right to the Phone Book. One click to get right where you want to go.

Sherlock: MOVING THE NAME COLUMN. WHAT??!!

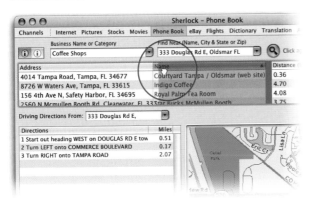

I know what you're thinking—moving the Name column—it can't be done. Mac OS X just doesn't let you do that. Oh sure, you can click, hold, and drag to reorder columns in any Finder window, and many other applications, but as a rule Mac OS X never lets you move the Name column out of its safe, comfy home at "first column on the left." Well, that age-old rule is broken in Sherlock, where you're actually allowed to click-and-drag directly on the first column and drag it to a different location. Do it once, just because you can.

  Sherlock: SAVE THAT SITE FOR LATER

If Sherlock finds a site that you think you might want to save for later (kind of like a Favorite), just click on it (in the results window) and drag it right to your desktop. It will create a file that you can use (by double-clicking) to get back to that webpage any time.

Sherlock: **REMOVING CHANNELS**

If there's a channel that you just never see yourself using, you can Command-click on it and drag it right off the toolbar. It will disappear in a puff of smoke (an Apple-approved, fully animated puff, with accompanying sound effect).

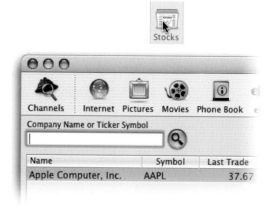

Sherlock: **PERFORMING MULTIPLE SEARCHES**

Let's say that while you're checking on the details of an arriving flight, you also need to find out what time the latest Harry Potter movie is playing at the local AMC, and you need to be simultaneously searching for "Think Different" posters on eBay. How do you pull off this "miracle of multiple searches?" It's easier than you'd think. Just start one search in motion, then choose New from the File menu to bring up another search while the previous one's still chuggin' away. I told you it was easy.

Stickies: **STICKIES WILL SPELL IT FOR YOU**

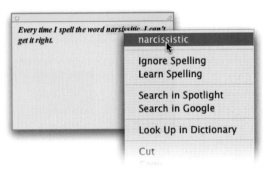

If you're working in Stickies and you're not sure you've spelled a word correctly, just Control-click on the word and a contextual menu will appear. At the top of this menu will be choices for what it believes to be the proper spelling of that word (if it's actually misspelled and it recognizes the word in the first place). If you agree, just move your cursor over that word, release your mouse button, and your misspelled word will be replaced. Mighty handy.

   Stickies: **KEEPING YOUR NOTE UP FRONT**

You probably already know how frustrating it can be if you have to toggle back and forth between an open Sticky and another application (let's say you're copying some text from a website into Stickies). Well, now the toggling is finally over: Just press Command-Option-F (the command for Floating Window) while Stickies is your active app, and this will make your current Sticky note float above your foreground application. That way, you can clearly see your note while working in another application (like Safari) because it'll be floating above it. Try this once, and you'll be using it daily. Provided, of course, that you use Stickies daily. And use your Macintosh daily. And that you use Stickies with another application daily. And that you bathe daily. (I just threw that last one in as a subtle personal hygiene reminder. See, I care.)

   Stickies: SEE-THROUGH NOTES

One of my favorite
Stickies features is
the ability to make
a sticky translucent.
Just click on a sticky
and press Com-
mand-Option-T
(Translucent Win-
dow). Then you can
see right through
your sticky to the
items behind it. This
is really handy if you
want to see items in
Finder windows that

would normally be covered by any open Stickies. To turn off the transparency (pardon me,
translucency), just press the shortcut again when Stickies is active.

   Stickies: SAVING YOUR TEXT COLORS

You've been able to colorize text in Stickies since at least Mac
OS 10.1, but did you know that you could save your favorite
colors and apply them with just one click? (Obviously, I'm
hoping you didn't or it really kills this tip.) To do so, just highlight a word, then go under the Font menu and choose Show
Colors. When the Colors dialog appears, choose the color
you'd like. Then, click-and-hold in the horizontal color bar up
top (where the color you've created is displayed), and start
dragging slowly—a tiny square will appear under your cursor.
Just drag-and-drop this square onto one of the white square
boxes at the bottom of the Colors dialog. This saves that color
for future use, so when you want it, all you have to do is click
once on that square (no more messing with the color wheel).
This is a great place to save commonly used colors like red,
solid black, white, etc.

Stickies: **PUTTING STICKIES IN MOTION**

Actually, this tip really should be called "Motion in Stickies," because believe it or not, you can put a QuickTime movie into a Sticky. Just locate the QuickTime movie you want (don't open the movie, just find it on your drive), and then open Stickies. Drag out your Sticky's window so it's big enough to accommodate the physical dimensions of your movie, and then drag-and-drop your movie right from the Finder window (or desktop) into your Sticky note. You'll get a dialog asking if you want to actually copy it, or just place an alias of it there. Choose Copy (or Alias), and within a few moments it will appear within your Sticky with a standard embedded-style QuickTime Player bar beneath it. Click the Play button, and your QuickTime movie will play right within your Sticky note. Why would you want to do this? I have no idea.

   Stickies: **JOT DOWN A QUICK NOTE ANY TIME**

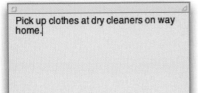

Working in the Finder and need to jot something down real quick? Just press Command-Shift-Y and Stickies will instantly launch and open a new sticky for you. It's super-fast and pretty darn handy.

CHAPTER 11 · Business Apps That Come with Mac OS X   **291**

   Stickies: SETTING FONT, STYLE, SIZE, AND COLOR DEFAULTS

If you have a favorite font, font size, Sticky size, and color you like to use for your Stickies, you can quickly change the defaults so every new Sticky will use your favorites. Just open a new Sticky, press Command-T to bring up the Font panel, and set your font, type style, and size just the way you like it. Choose which color you'd like for your

default Sticky by going under the Color menu and choosing a color. Then, go under the Note menu and choose Use as Default. Now, when you open a new Sticky, it will use your new custom default settings.

   Stickies: FROM STICKY TO TEXTEDIT IN ONE CLICK

If you get carried away in a Sticky and you wind up writing more than you expected, you can instantly convert your Sticky note into a TextEdit document by selecting all your text and then going under the Stickies menu, under Services, under TextEdit, and choosing New Window Containing Selection. This will immediately launch TextEdit and open a new document with the contents of your Sticky within it. You can now save your file in TextEdit format and use all of TextEdit's features as if your file had been created in TextEdit to begin with.

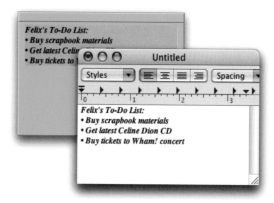

Stickies: **TURN YOUR SELECTION INTO A STICKY**

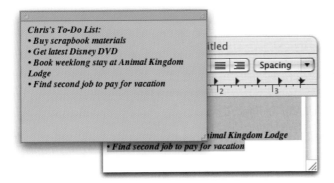

If you've selected some text in a Mac OS X application such as TextEdit (a phone number, Web address, etc.), you can turn that selected text into a Sticky in one click. Just go under the TextEdit menu, under Services, and choose Make New Sticky Note. Stickies will launch and open a new note with your selected text. The keyboard shortcut for this automation is Command-Shift-Y.

   Stickies: **THE ONE PLACE WINDOW SHADE STILL LIVES**

In Mac OS X, Apple did away with the popular Window Shade feature that appeared in previous versions of the OS, where you could double-click on a window's title bar and it would roll up like a window shade, leaving just the title bar visible. But in Stickies, a Window Shade feature still exists—just double-click the Sticky's title bar (or press Command-M) and the current Sticky rolls up—just like a window shade.

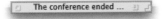

  ● Font Panel: **CHECKING FOR BAD FONTS**

If there's one thing that can bring a document (or your system) to its knees, it's using a corrupt font (meaning a font that accepts bribes—sorry, that was lame). Anyway, finding out which fonts on your system might be corrupt was no easy task, but in Tiger, it just got a whole lot easier. Here's how to search for rampant font corruption: Go to your Applications folder and launch Font Book. You can either click directly on any font that you might think is suspect (look to see if the font is sweating), or Command-click on the fonts you want interrogated,

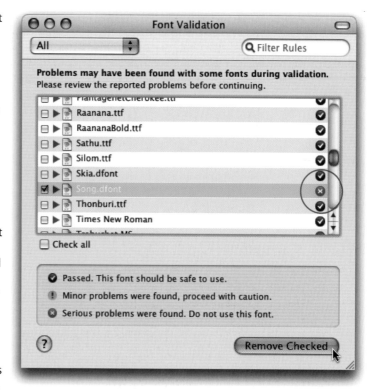

then go under Font Book's File menu and choose Validate Fonts. This brings up a Font Validation window and if your fonts are on the up and up, you'll get a little round checkbox beside them. If there's reason to believe something may be wrong, you'll get a yellow warning icon beside a font. If it's corrupt, you'll get a round icon with an X in it, telling you not to use this font. Click the checkbox beside that font, then click the Remove Checked button to remove this font from your system.

Font Panel: FINDING WHERE THE © AND ™ SYMBOLS LIVE

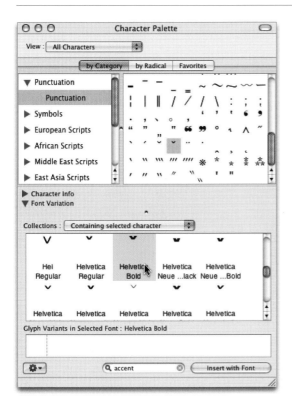

Since nearly the beginning of Mac-dom, when you wanted to find out which key combination produced a font's special characters (stuff like ©, ™, £, ¢, ‰, ƒ, etc.), you used a utility called KeyCaps. More than a decade later, KeyCaps is still a part of Mac OS, but a better way to access these special characters is through the Character Palette. You can access it two ways: (1) From within Mac OS X business apps (like Mail, TextEdit, Stickies, etc.), just go under Edit and choose Special Characters or click on the Actions pop-up menu at the bottom of the Font panel and choose Characters; (2) add Character Palette access to your menu bar, so you can access it when you're working in other applications (like Word or Adobe InDesign). You do this by going to the System Preferences in the Apple menu, under International, and clicking on the Input Menu tab. Turn on the checkbox for Character Palette and it will appear in the menu bar along the right side. Either way you open it, here's how you use it: When you open the Character Palette, choose All Characters from the View menu, then click on the By Category tab. The left column shows a list of special character categories and the right column shows the individual characters in each category. To get one of these characters into your text document, just click on the character and click the Insert button in the bottom right-hand corner of the dialog. If you find yourself using the same special characters over and over (like ©, ™, etc.), you can add these to your Favorites list, and access them from the Favorites tab in the Character Palette. To see which fonts contain certain characters (they don't all share the same special characters), expand the Character Palette by clicking on the down-facing arrow next to Font Variation on the bottom-left side of the palette. This brings up another panel where you can choose different fonts. You can also ask that this list show only fonts that support the character you have highlighted.

   Font Panel: ACCESS SPECIAL CHARACTERS FROM THE MENU BAR

If you need a quick special character (such as é, or °, or ˆ) but don't know which keyboard combination you need to create it, you can have the Character Palette (a list of every character) added to your menu bar. Here's how: Go under the Apple menu and choose System Preferences. Click on the International icon. When its pane appears, click on the Input Menu tab, and turn on the checkbox for Character Palette. This adds a little icon (that looks like the flag of your chosen native language) to the far-right side of your menu bar, where you can quickly choose Show Character Palette without going through the Font panel.

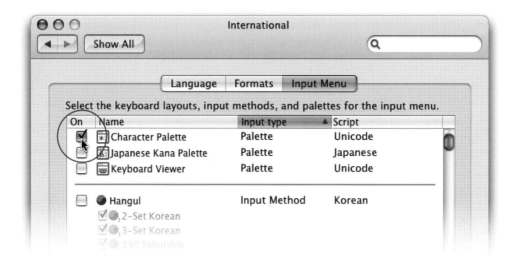

Font Panel: SEEING YOUR FONTS BEFORE YOU USE THEM

Apple has heard your plaintive cries, and finally they've included a preview of your fonts so you can actually see what they look like before you decide which one to use. You access this new wonder of modern science in any application that uses Mac OS X's built-in Font panel (apps such as TextEdit, Stickies, Mail, etc.). Press Command-T to bring up the Font panel. When it appears, click on the Actions pop-up menu at the bottom of the panel and choose Show Preview. A font preview pane will appear at the top of the dialog, and as you click on different fonts, their previews will appear in that pane. It also works for type style and font sizes.

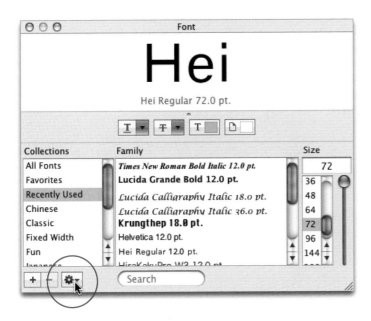

   PDF: THE SMALLER PDF SECRET CONTROL

This is another one of those "secret, buried-in-a-vault" killer tips that addresses something Mac OS X users have complained about: The file sizes of PDFs that Mac OS X creates are sometimes too big (vs. Adobe's Acrobat PDFs). Believe it or not, there's a way to get smaller PDFs. Here's how: Launch TextEdit, then choose Print from the File menu. From the PDF pop-up menu in the bottom-left corner of the dialog, choose Compress PDF. That's

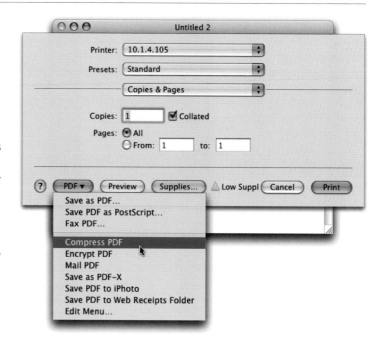

it. It'll compress the PDF and call it a day. However, if you're charging by the hour, and let's pretend you are, you have a wonderful time-consuming option: Choose Print from the File menu, and from the second Presets pop-up menu choose ColorSync. From the Quartz Filter menu that appears, choose Add Filters. Click on the three-oval icon in the top-left corner of the dialog that appears, click on the filter named Reduce File Size, and then click-and-hold on the arrow button to the right of the filter and choose Duplicate Filter. This creates an un-locked filter you can edit. Now click on the triangle to the left of the duplicate filter to show its options; this is where you choose what you want. I recommend clicking on the arrow to the left of Image Compression and dragging the magic slider that lets you control the amount of JPEG compression your PDF images receive. For smaller file sizes, drag the Quality slider toward Minimum. Now go back to TextEdit and in the Print dialog, choose ColorSync from the second Presets pop-up menu, choose your new filter from the Quartz Filter pop-up menu and click Print. That's it. (Whew!)

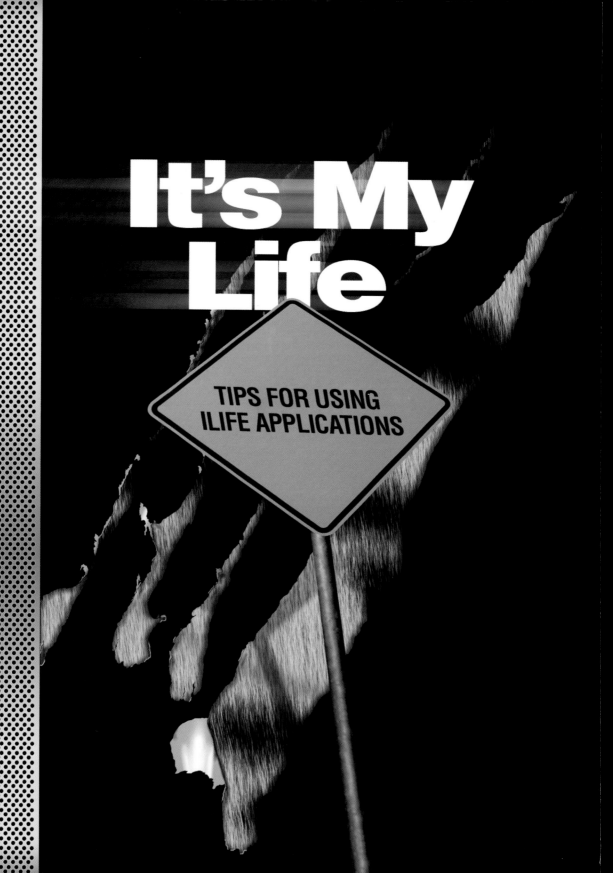

It's My Life

TIPS FOR USING ILIFE APPLICATIONS

When you hear the word "multimedia," what does it really mean? Isn't "multimedia" one of those buzzwords that

It's My Life

tips for using ilife applications

are now so "mid-'90s" that they belong with other lame mid-'90s terms like "Information Super Highway" and "Cyberspace?" Absolutely. So, isn't iTunes (which isn't in this chapter) considered one of the "multimedia" iLife applications? Well...yes, but I've covered it so extensively that it gets more than its own chapter—it gets its own book, well, two books actually—The iPod Book and The iTunes for Windows Book. So, if you want to pretend, just for the sake of this exercise, that The iPod Book and this chapter are really just one big chapter in this book, that's perfectly fine by me. Yes, but couldn't you lump the two together and use the all-encompassing term "Multimedia Applications" as a chapter head? No. Were you even listening at the beginning of this intro?

   iMovie HD: **MOVING MULTIPLE CLIPS WITH A DRAG SELECTION**

Although you probably know that you can select multiple clips and drag them to the Timeline (and if you didn't, you just learned another tip), you might not have known that you can select these clips really fast by dragging a selection around them (rather than Command-clicking on each individually). The only trick is—where to start. Just click your cursor in that gray area behind the clips and start dragging. Any clips that fall inside your dragged area will be selected. Now just click on any one of those selected clips and you can drag them right to the Timeline.

iMovie HD: **QUICK TOGGLE BETWEEN CLIP AND TIMELINE VIEWERS**

Want to quickly toggle back and forth between the Clip Viewer and the Timeline Viewer (I guess you do, or you wouldn't be reading this tip, right?). Just press Command-E.

Clip Viewer

Timeline Viewer

iMovie HD: **VISUAL TIP TO SEE IF A CLIP IS TRIMMED**

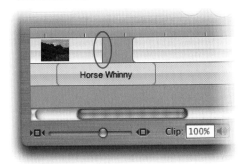

Here's a quick way to tell in an instant if a clip in the Timeline has been trimmed or not—just look at the corners of the clip itself. If the corners are square, it's been trimmed. If they're rounded, it hasn't—it's the full-length clip.

  iMovie HD: **BOOKMARKING YOUR MOVIE WHILE IT'S PLAYING**

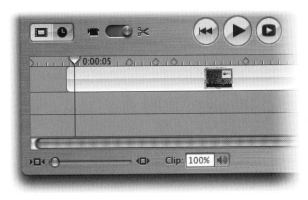

Bookmarking lets you flag any part of a clip as a reminder that something needs to be done at that spot (let's say you want to flag a part of a clip so you remember to add a sound effect, or you want to mark a spot where the background music should be softer, etc.). The cool thing is you can add these little green diamond-shaped bookmarks while your movie is playing. When you see a spot you'd like to mark, just press Command-B. Once you've got your bookmarks in place, you can jump to the next bookmark by pressing Command-[(Left Bracket key) or the previous bookmark by pressing Command-] (Right Bracket key). You can have the Playhead jump right to any bookmark by just clicking directly on the bookmark.

  iMovie HD: **GETTIN' SNAPPY**

Tired of guessing whether the clip you're dragging on the Timeline is really butting right up against the clip before it, with no gap? Just hold the Shift key while you're dragging, and your clip will "snap" to the clip as soon as it gets close. You can also use this trick for snapping to markers or audio clips, or just about anything worth snapping to. By the way, if you fall in love with this snapping (you get "snapinitis"), you can have it on all the time—just

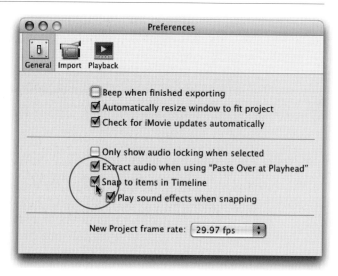

go to the iMovie HD menu, choose Preferences, and in the General section of the resulting dialog, turn on the checkbox for Snap to Items in Timeline.

  iMovie HD: **STRETCH THAT CLIP WITHOUT MESSING UP**

Wouldn't it be cool if you could stretch the length of your current clip without moving the other clips in your movie? That's would be great, but obviously, that can't happen. But how about the next best thing? How about stretching your current clip so it only af-

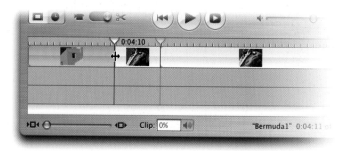

fects the clip immediately following it? Okay, that we can do. Just hold the Command key, then drag your current clip. This automatically shortens just the clip following it without messing up the other clips after it on the Timeline.

iMovie HD: SLO-MO AUDIO SCRUBBING

Want to hear your audio track (or sound effect) in "slo-mo"? Just hold the Option key as you drag the Playhead, then as your video scrubs along, so will your audio. This can be helpful if you're trying to sync a particular sound with a particular event in your clip.

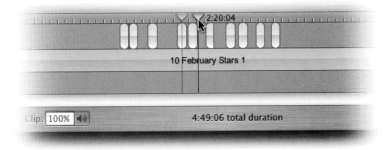

iMovie HD: KEEPING AN EYE ON THE TRASH

When you're editing, it's usually not long before your iMovie HD's Trash starts filling up with clips, and that's a good thing, because there's no sense in taking up loads of space with clips you're definitely not going to use. However, if you're like me, sometimes you want a clip back that you trashed. Well, as long as you haven't emptied iMovie HD's Trash yet, you can rescue it. Luckily, finding which clip to rescue (and which clips are okay to delete) is easier than ever. Just click on the Trash icon in the bottom-right corner of the iMovie HD window, which brings up a dialog that not only lists what clips are in the Trash, but also allows you to preview any clip by clicking on it and hitting the little Play button. If you do decide you want that clip, just drag it from that Trash window back into the Clips pane.

iMovie HD: **NO MORE BLACK BACKGROUNDS FOR TITLES**

Are you tired of having all your titles appear over a black background (which does tend to give your movies a "Made in iMovie" look to them)? Here's what to do: You're going to have to build your title between two existing clips (you can move it later if you like), so in the Timeline, click on the clip on the right and drag it a little to the right, which creates an empty space between the two clips. Now Control-click right in that empty space on the Timeline, and from the contextual menu that appears choose Convert Empty Space to Clip. This puts an empty black background there, but you're not stuck with black—just double-click directly on that clip and the Clip Info dialog will appear. In that dialog you'll see a Color swatch. Click it and the Colors dialog appears, where you can choose the color you want. Once that's done, you can add your title right over that new background color.

iMovie HD: **MAKING PRECISE EDITS TO YOUR EFFECTS**

©SCOTT KELBY

If you've applied an effect to a clip, you can edit the in/out points of the effect by dragging the slider, but if you know where you want your in/out points to be, you can enter those values yourself (instead of playing around with the sliders until you get the right settings). Just click on your clip in the Timeline (or Clip Viewer), click on the Effects button in the toolbar, then go up to the little effects preview, click on the Effect In (or Effect Out) numbers, and enter the values you want using your keyboard.

   iMovie HD: **GO DIRECT: CAMERA TO YOUR TIMELINE**

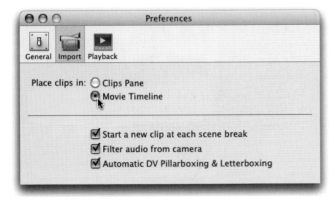

By default, when you import clips from your video camera, those clips are placed in the Clips pane, but because iMovie HD lets you arrange the order of clips right in the Timeline (you just click-and-drag them), you can save time by skipping the Clips pane altogether and have the clips appear right on your Timeline from the start. To do that, just go under the iMovie HD menu, under Preferences, and click on the Import icon. When the Import preferences appear, where it says Place Clips In, choose Movie Timeline.

iMovie HD: SHUTTLING THROUGH YOUR MOVIE

The Rewind button in iMovie HD takes you all the way back to the beginning of your movie, but if you want to back up just a little bit, there's a keyboard short-cut that will give you a live rewind (and by that, I mean it will play your movie in reverse) until you get to the spot where you want to be. Just press Option-[(Left Bracket key) to start the backwards playback, then press it again to stop. For a live fast-forward, press Option-] (Right Bracket key).

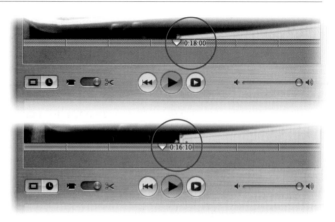

   iMovie HD: THE CLIP VIEWER'S VISUAL CUES

If you've adjusted the speed or direction of a clip, the Clip Viewer gives you a visual cue with tiny icons just above the clip itself (in the upper-right corner of the clip's "slide mount") to let you know just what you did. If you've added a built-in iMovie effect (like Black & White, Sepia, etc.), a little checkerboard pattern appears. If you add a title to your clip, expect a "T" to appear.

iMovie HD: **UNDO, UNDO, UNDO, UNDO, UNDO, UNDO +4**

Edit	View	Markers	Advanced	Win
Undo Apply Effect			⌘Z	
Can't Redo			⇧⌘Z	
Cut			⌘X	
Copy			⌘C	
Paste			⌘V	
Clear				
Select All			⌘A	
Select Similar Clips			⌥⌘A	
Select None			⇧⌘A	
Crop			⌘K	
Split Video Clip at Playhead			⌘T	
Create Still Frame			⇧⌘S	
Special Characters...			⌥⌘T	

If you realize you've made a mistake while in iMovie, as long as you catch your mistake fairly quickly (and before you empty the iMovie HD's Trash), you may be in luck. That's because iMovie gives you 10 undos. Just press Command-Z again and again until you come to your mistake, or you reach the 10th undo (which ironically is usually just one step before your mistake). (*Note:* In Tiger the undos seem to be actually unlimited, but if you get to 10 and it stops, you didn't hear that from me.)

   iMovie HD: **GETTING BACK CROPPED-OUT SCENES**

Revert Clip To Original

This will restore the underlying media that was trimmed or split from this clip. (0:05:29 available at the end of the clip). Would you like to revert?

Cancel　OK

When you crop a clip in iMovie, you can't access those cropped-away areas. That is, unless you know this little secret—if you need to get back to the original clip you imported, perfectly intact, believe it or not you can. Just click on the cropped clip in the Timeline or Clip Viewer, then go under the Advanced menu and choose Revert Clip to Original (or choose the same option by Control-clicking on the selected clip). A dialog will appear telling you how much you'll get back, and asking you to OK the process. Click OK, and the original clip is back, in its entirety. *Note:* If any effects were applied to the clip, these may be lost when you do this.

   iMovie HD: **LOCKING YOUR SOUND EFFECTS INTO PLACE**

If you've meticulous-
ly added sound ef-
fects to your movie,
and you've synced
them to events in
your clips, you might
think twice about
inserting a clip in
your movie because

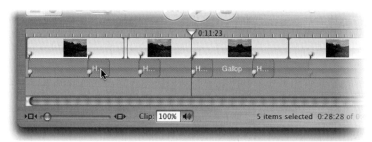

it would slide all the video clips that come after your insertion point down to accommodate
this new clip—making your movie longer—but leaving all your audio clips in their original
spots. Now all your sound effects will be out of sync by the amount of time your imported
clip takes. To get around this, before you import your clip, Shift-click on each sound effect
in your audio track, then press Command-L to "lock" your audio clips to your video clips
(if you're in the Timeline Viewer, you'll notice tiny yellow "pins" indicating the tracks are
locked). That way, when you insert your new clip, and all the video clips move over to accommodate the new track, all the sound effects clips will move right along with them.

   iMovie HD: **MOVING CROP MARKERS WITH PRECISION**

Once you have Crop Markers in place, you can be very precise in their placement by using
the Arrow keys on your keyboard to position them right where you want them.

iMovie HD: **MULTIPLE CLIPS IN THE SAME MOVIE**

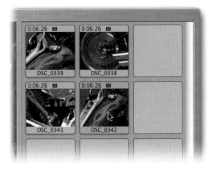

If you want the same clip to appear in multiple places within the same movie, here's a quick trick to make it fast and easy. Click on the clip in the Clip Viewer, then press Command-C to copy the clip into memory. Then go up to the Clips pane, click on any random clip up there, and press Command-V (Paste). Don't worry—it doesn't paste over that clip, instead it pastes a copy of the clip right beside it. (In the example shown here, I copied a clip from the Clip Viewer, then I clicked on the second clip down on the left in the Clips pane, and pasted the copied clip.) Now you can drag this copy down to your Clip Viewer. If you need more copies, use the same trick.

   iMovie HD: **PRECISE NAVIGATION**

To fast forward one frame at a time, press the Right Arrow key. To rewind one frame at a time, press the Left Arrow key. To move 10 frames at a time, just add the Shift key.

Before

After pressing Shift-Right Arrow

CHAPTER 12 · Tips for Using iLife Applications   **311**

   iMovie HD: CONTROLLING AUDIO FADE-INS/FADE-OUTS

In iMovie HD, if you want to fade in (or out) your background audio track, you've got pretty decent control over exactly when and how long it takes for that fade-in/out to happen. The first step is to press Command-Shift-L while the Timeline Viewer is visible to show the audio controls. When you do this, a line will appear in the center of your audio tracks. This line represents the volume of your audio track, so to create a fade-in, click once at the point where you want the audio to be at full volume (and a point will be added at that spot along with a tiny purple square at its left). Drag the little purple square down to where you want the fade-in to begin (usually at the beginning of your audio track). The length of time between the beginning of your audio track and the little yellow point is how long your fade-in will be. If you want a longer fade-in, drag the yellow point to the right.

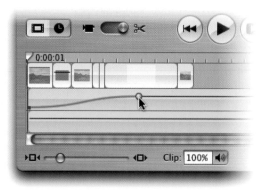

   iMovie HD: CONTROLLING SOUND EFFECTS VOLUMES

If you import sound effects (or use the built-in sound effects), you can control the volume of each sound effect individually. Just click directly on the sound effect you want to adjust (in the Timeline Viewer), then move the Volume slider (that appears to the right of the Clip field near the bottom-left side of the iMovie HD window) to the level you'd like the effect to play. iMovie will keep track of each sound effect's individual volume and adjust them accordingly as your movie plays.

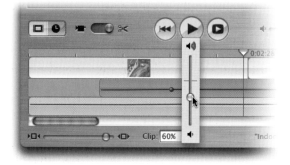

iMovie HD: SEND IMPORTED CLIPS STRAIGHT TO THE TIMELINE

By default, imported clips appear on the Clips pane, and then once imported, you can drag them individually to the Timeline Viewer. However, if you'd like, you can change one Preferences setting and iMovie HD will send your clips straight to the Timeline Viewer instead. You do this by going under the iMovie menu, under Preferences. In the Import section, under Place Clips In, choose Movie Timeline, and from now on, all imported clips will appear in the Timeline Viewer, rather than the Clips pane.

   iMovie HD: CONTROLLING HOW LONG STILLS STAY ONSCREEN

When you import a still image into iMovie HD (from Photoshop, a scanned image, a screen capture, etc.), you can determine how long the still image will stay onscreen. Just click on the image in the Timeline or Clip Viewer, and then click on the Photos button in the toolbar right above the Timeline, and in the upper portion of the Photos panel you'll see the Hare & Turtle slider (that's its official name, I think). Drag that slider to adjust the duration for that image (or to make your image look like a turtle—kidding). You can also determine how much you'd like to zoom in on the photo. After you choose the amount of time and zoom you want, click on either the Apply or Update button (it's Apply the first time you make a change to a photo). When you're there, you can turn off the Ken Burns Effect for that still (if you like) using the checkbox at the top of the Photos panel. From now on when you import a still, it will come in at that duration and zoom. You can easily change the settings by going back to the Photos panel.

iMovie HD: **VISUAL TRANSITION CUES**

Once you drag a Transition into your Timeline or Clip Viewer, the Transition icon sometimes gives you a visual cue as to which Transition you dragged. Just look at the little arrows in the square window in the center of the Transition icon for a hint. To see the name of the Transition, click on it. If the default name doesn't help you (like the name "Push"), double-click on the Transition and enter a new name (like "1st clip slides 2nd clip over") in the Clip Info dialog.

iMovie HD: **GETTING MORE AUDIO TRACKS**

In the Timeline, there are three tracks where audio can go. The top Timeline where the video clips are located also supports any audio from your digital camcorder's microphone that was captured when you shot your clips. The second track is usually used for sound effects or a narrator track. The third is usually used for background music. So you'd think you'd be limited to three tracks; but actually, iMovie HD lets you continue to import and lay multiple audio tracks right over one another. For example, if you have a music score on the bottom track and you import a sound effect, you'll notice that its little bar icon appears right on top of your score track's icon. It also plays right over it—not knocking it out—but playing right along with it. This enables you to use more than just the three tracks it appears you're limited to.

 **iMovie HD: BEATING THE SORTING SLUDGE**

If you've got a movie with a lot of different clips in your Clip Viewer, dragging a clip from one end of your movie to the other can take what seems like forever, while you sludge through clip after clip dragging your way down to where you want it. But there's a much faster way—instead, drag the clip out of the Clip Viewer and drop it on an empty space up in the Clips pane. Then use the scroll bar below your Clip Viewer to move quickly to the spot where you want your clip to appear. Now you can simply drag-and-drop your clip from the Clips pane back down to the Clip Viewer—right where you want it—in less than half the time.

   iMovie HD: MUTING YOUR CAMERA'S AUDIO TRACK

If you're putting a music track behind your movie and you don't want to hear the audio that was captured by your digital camcorder's built-in microphone, you can turn off the audio track for your camera clips. Just go to the Timeline Viewer, and at the far-right side, uncheck the top checkbox.

   iPhoto: **TRACKING DOWN UNUSED PHOTOS**

If you use albums, here's a trick for quickly finding all the photos in your Library that you didn't think were good enough to wind up in one of your albums (in other words, this is a quick way to gather all the photos that didn't "make the cut" and delete them so they stop taking up space on your hard disk). Hold the Option key and click the plus (+) sign in the bottom left-hand corner (when you hold Option, it changes from a plus sign into a gear icon). This brings up the Smart Album dialog. In the first pop-up menu, choose Album. In the second menu choose Is Not, and in the third menu choose Any. When you click OK, it will create a new Smart Album made up of just the photos that didn't make the cut. Now, you can delete those photos knowing they won't disturb any of your existing albums.

iPhoto: **FAST SORTING IN FULL SCREEN MODE**

One of the first things you're probably going to want to do when you get back from a shoot is separate the "keepers" from the "losers." But doing this by looking at tiny thumbnails is sometimes pretty tough (depending on the subject matter). You could create a full-blown slide show, but do you really want to create a full-blown slide show? Nah. Instead, do this "down and dirty" slide show so you can rate your images fast, while still viewing them full screen. First, click on Last Roll to isolate only the photos you just imported. Then click the Display Slideshow button at the bottom left of the iPhoto window (it's directly below the Source list. This brings up a simple Slideshow dialog. When the options appear, turn off Repeat Slideshow and click OK. Now click the Play button (it's sortin' time!). As each image appears onscreen, simply press a number: 5 to give it a five-star rating, 3 to give it a three-star rating, etc. When you've gone through all the photos, the slide show will end. You'll have your photos rated (and thereby sorted) in no time. To see your ratings appear below your thumbnails, click back on your Last Roll in the Source list on the left of the iPhoto window, and press Command-Shift-R.

   iPhoto: RATING YOUR PHOTOS FAST

In iPhoto, you can rate photos on a scale of one to five stars, but it can take a while to rate an entire import of photos from a digital camera. That's why you'll want to "batch rank." To do that, click on the first photo you want to have a 5-star ranking. Then press-and-hold the Command key, and as you search through your photos, click on every other five-star photo. Once you've gotten through your imported photos, just press Command-5, and every selected photo will instantly be rated with five stars. You can continue doing four-star, three-star, etc., using the same fast technique.

   iPhoto: GETTING TO THIS MONTH'S PHOTOS FAST!

If you're using iPhoto's built-in calendar to view photos by the month and date they were imported into iPhoto, here's a quick trick for getting back to the current month's photos—just click directly on the word "Calendar" in the Calendar panel. *Note*: Make sure you're in month and date view first.

iPhoto: **FIT YOUR SLIDE SHOW TO THE LENGTH OF YOUR MUSIC**

If you don't want the music to loop during your slide show, you can make the slide show adjust to the length of the music; that way it's not as annoying listening to the same song over and over again. So, select the album you want to use as your slide show from the Source list, and then click the Slideshow button at the bottom of the iPhoto window. When the slide show options appear, click on the Settings button, and in the resulting dialog, turn on the option to Fit Slideshow to Music and click OK. Once you click Play, iPhoto will adjust your slides' duration time so that each image appears onscreen once as the song plays, without the annoying "loop" factor.

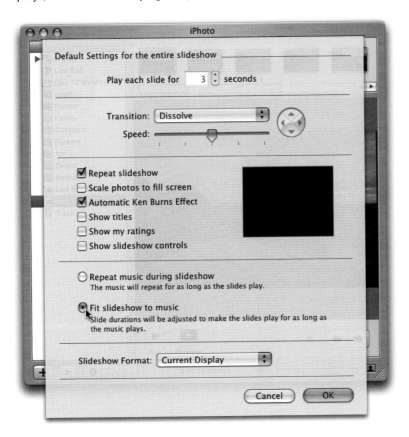

iPhoto: **A FASTER WAY TO IMPORT PHOTOS**

Want to get your digital camera photos into iPhoto fast? Just plug in your digital camera's memory card, then select the photos you want to import on the card. Now just click on any one of the selected photos, drag-and-drop them right on iPhoto's Dock icon, and they'll be imported, without going through the whole import process normally associated with importing photos into iPhoto.

   ### iPhoto: **CREATING MULTIPLE LIBRARIES**

If you have a huge iPhoto Library, you might want to create multiple libraries, and then you can decide which of these libraries you want to open in iPhoto

for today's editing. Here's how: Just hold the Option key, then launch iPhoto. When you do this, a dialog will appear asking you if you want to create a new Library, or open an existing Library. If you want to create a new one, click the Create Library button and a new separate Library will be created. The next time you open iPhoto, you can decide which Library you want to open by simply holding the Option key before you launch iPhoto (you'll get the same dialog again).

iPhoto: **THE "WHITE BALANCE" SECRET SETTING**

©SCOTT KELBY

You can set the white balance for any photo in iPhoto by entering Edit mode (click the Edit button at the bottom of the iPhoto window), then once you're in Edit mode, hold the Command key and click your cursor on something that's supposed to be light gray (that's right—don't click on something that's supposed to be white—click on something light gray). You'll see the Adjust panel appear, and the Temperature and Tint sliders (which control the white balance) will already be adjusted.

   iPhoto: **DELETING PHOTOS TRICK**

By now you already know that if you delete a photo from an album, it just deletes it from the album—the original file is still intact in your Library. So, if you really want that photo deleted that you just removed from your album, you have to now click on the Library in the Source list, find the same photo, and remove it there as well. That is, unless you know this shortcut—just click on the photo in the album, and press Command-Option-Delete. This removes it both from the album and the Library at the same time.

   iPhoto: **PHOTOGRAPHER'S BASIC BLACK**

There's a background that's very popular with photographers for organizing their photos. It's basic black. Using black as your background gives you that "artsy photographer" look that artsy photographers love. To get that look, go under the iPhoto menu and choose Preferences. Click on the Appearance icon and drag the Background slider to the far left (to Black). Then it's up to you whether you want your thumbnails to appear with a white border (choose Outline in the Border section) or without (by deselecting all Border options).

   iPhoto: **MAKING SLIDE SHOW MOVIES**

This is one of my favorite iPhoto tips because it lets you create a self-contained QuickTime movie slide show, complete with music and transitions, and the file size of this movie is surprisingly small, making it great for posting slide shows on the Web. Here's how it's done: Just click on the album you want for your movie slide show (or you can click on an existing slide show in the Source list). With your album selected in the Source list, go under the Share menu and choose Export. In the Export Photos dialog, click on the Quick- Time tab and set the options for how you'd like your movie to look, and then click Export. That's it—iPhoto automatically saves this as a QuickTime movie slide show, complete with music (if you chose this option).

iPhoto: LISTING YOUR MOST RECENT PHOTOS FIRST

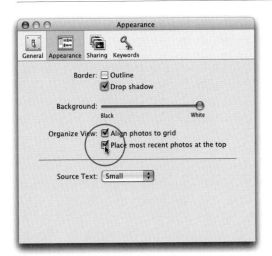

For some reason I can't figure out, by default iPhoto displays the thumbnails of your oldest photos at the top of the main window, so to get to the most recent photos you imported, you have to scroll all the way to the bottom. If you'd like the convenience of having your most recent photos at the top, go under the iPhoto menu, under Preferences, click on the Appearance icon, and then click on Place Most Recent Photos at the Top.

   iPhoto: DUMP THE SHADOW

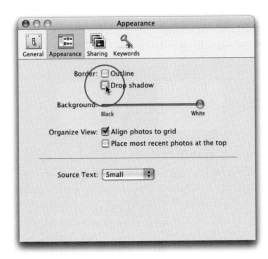

You know that little drop shadow that appears behind your thumbnail images in the iPhoto window? If it gets on your nerves, you can ditch it by pressing Command–, (that's the Comma key) to bring up iPhoto's Preferences. In the Preferences dialog, click on the Appearance icon, and then click on the Drop Shadow checkbox to turn it off. If you like, you can replace the shadow effect with a thin black (or white, depending on your Background color) border around the thumbnail of your photo by turning on the Outline checkbox.

iPhoto: **EDITING IPHOTO IMAGES IN PHOTOSHOP**

iPhoto lets you adjust a variety of aspects of your image, from tonal adjustments to removing red eye, using iPhoto's built-in image editor. However, if you prefer to edit your images in another application (such as Adobe Photoshop or Photoshop Elements), you can configure iPhoto to launch the editing application of your choice when you double-click on the image inside iPhoto. You do this by pressing Command–, (Comma key) to bring up iPhoto's Preferences. In the dialog, click on the General icon, and where it says Double-click Photo, click on the Opens Photo In button, navigate to the application you want to designate

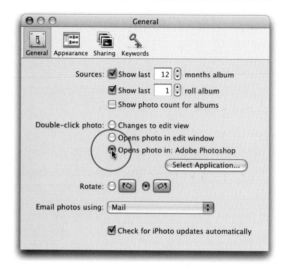

as your editing app, and then click OK. Now when you double-click a photo, your photo will open in your designated image-editing application.

   iPhoto: **SKIP THE NEW ALBUM BUTTON**

If you want to start a new album, skip the Create a New Album button. You can save time by just selecting one (or more) image that you want in your new album from your Library (or current Roll), and then dragging it over to the Source list—a new album will be created for you automatically. *Note*: Just don't drag them onto an existing album, as they will be added to that album.

iPhoto: **WHAT TO DO WHEN ALL GOES WRONG**

If you've edited, cropped, and otherwise adjusted an image in iPhoto and, after looking at the results, you wish you really hadn't, you can actually start over—from scratch—and get back your clean un-retouched original image. You do this by selecting the image, going under the Photos menu, and choosing Revert to Original. Okay, but what if you set up iPhoto to let you edit your image in another application, such as Photoshop? Believe it or not—Revert to Original still works.

   iPhoto: **ROTATING IN THE OPPOSITE DIRECTION**

When you click the Rotate button, by default it rotates your image counterclockwise. If you want to rotate your image clockwise, just hold the Option key before you click the Rotate button (you'll notice the arrow on the button is now pointing to the right, not the left). If you want to make this a permanent change, press Command–, (Comma key) to open Preferences, and in the General section, choose your default Rotate direction.

   iPhoto: DEALING WITH LONG COMMENTS

iPhoto lets you add comments to your photos, and you can use these comments to help you sort, categorize, or just make notes about a particular photo. These comments are entered in the Comments field, which appears in a field below the Information panel (if you don't see the panel, click on the button with the little "i" on it near the bottom left-hand side). If you add a long comment for a particular photo, iPhoto will accommodate you, but you won't be able to scroll down and see your entire comment because the Comments field doesn't have scroll bars. There's only one way to see your entire comment—and that's to click on the little circle at the top center of the Information panel and drag upward to make more of your comment visible.

   iPhoto: PUTTING YOUR COVER SHOT INSIDE THE BOOK

There will be times when you want the photo you chose for the cover to also appear inside your book (perhaps because you want to add a different caption, or you want to pair it with another photo inside, or maybe you want to show it without a caption at all). To do this, all you have to do is duplicate the photo.

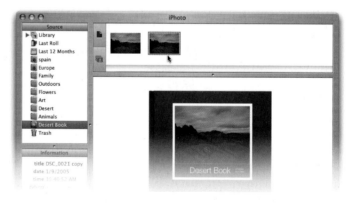

You do this by clicking on the photo you want to duplicate in the image well at the top of the Book window and pressing Command-D. This creates a duplicate of your image, which you can now drag-and-drop in your book's layout.

  iPhoto: CHANGING FONTS IN BOOK MODE

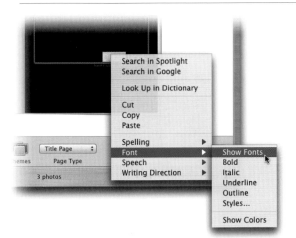

If you're creating a book in Book mode, you can edit the font used in any page by highlighting the text (by double-clicking on it) and then Control-clicking on it. In the contextual menu that appears, click on Font, and then choose Show Fonts. Now you can set the font, size, style, and color of your choice using the Font panel.

   iPhoto: INDIVIDUALIZED EDITING

©SCOTT KELBY

If you want more control over editing your images in iPhoto, press Command–, (Comma key) to bring up the Preferences dialog. Click on the General icon, and where it says Double-click Photo, choose Opens Photo in Edit Window. Then, when you double-click a photo to edit it, your image opens into a different environment, giving you more control over your editing process.

iPhoto: **EDIT IN PHOTOSHOP WITHOUT SETTING PREFS**

Earlier, I showed how to set up iPhoto to let you edit your photos in a separate image-editing application (such as Photoshop) by changing your iPhoto Preferences. But here's a great tip if you only occasionally want to edit your photos in a separate application— just drag the thumbnail of your photo right

from the iPhoto window onto the Photoshop icon in the Dock. Your image will be opened in Photoshop (or, of course, you can drag it to any other image-editing program just as easily, but really, why would you?).

   iPhoto: **SUPERSIZE THAT PHOTO**

If you want to quickly see a photo within an album at a very large size, just click on the image in the iPhoto window, and then in the toolbar at the bottom, click on the Desktop button. Your selected photo will be set as your desktop image and will take over the screen.

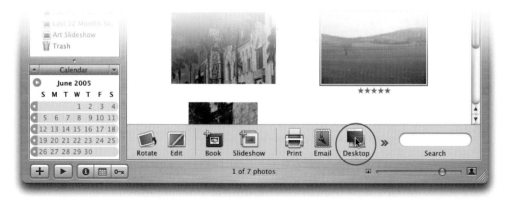

GarageBand 2: **PRINTING YOUR SCORE**

As amazing as the Musical Notation feature of GarageBand 2 is, the one thing it doesn't do is let you print it out. I know, it doesn't make sense. Don't get me started. But there is a bit of a workaround, if you don't mind jumping through a few flaming hoops (okay, they're not flaming, but non-flaming-hoop references don't sell books). Here's what to do: First, record a track by clicking on the red Record button, then when the track is complete, press Command-E to make the Editor visible. Now, click the tiny musical note button on the bottom-left side of the Editor to view the musical notation of your recorded track, which will appear to the right side of the Editor. Now, press Control-Command-Shift-4 once, and your cursor will turn into a crosshair. Drag this cursor over the visible part of your musical notation, then release the mouse (you should hear the default screen capture camera-click sound). Now launch Preview. Go to Preview's File menu and choose New From Clipboard. This creates a new document with the contents of your screen capture (your musical score). Now, you can print this snippet, and continue this process (of screen capturing and pasting into Preview) for the rest of your song. Hey, I never said it was an elegant solution. I said it was a workaround.

GarageBand 2: **THE 10 MOST ESSENTIAL SHORTCUTS**

Like most Apple applications, GarageBand 2 has a host (okay, a bunch) of keyboard short-cuts and there's no sense in memorizing them all, because you won't use them all (some you won't even want to use—ever), but there are a few essential shortcuts you'll need to start using now, before you pull your hair out. They include: (1) Pressing the Spacebar on your keyboard to start/stop your song. (2) Pressing the letter Z to jump back to the begin-ning of your song. (3) To delete the current track, press Command-Delete. (4) You can mute the current track by pressing the letter M. (5) Isolate just the current track (which mutes all the others) by pressing the letter S. (6) Press the letter C to turn cycling (looping of your song) on/off. (7) Press Command-U to turn the built-in Metronome on/off. (8) Command-L shows/hides the Loop Browser. (9) Start/Stop recording by pressing the letter R. And last but not least: (10) Press Command-D to duplicate any track. Learn those 10, and it will make your GarageBand life much easier.

Without cycle (looping)

With cycle (looping)

  GarageBand 2: ADDING REVERB TO YOUR ENTIRE SONG AT ONCE

You probably know by now that you can add reverb or an echo (along with a host of built-in effects) to any instrument track by double-clicking on the instrument's name in the Tracks column and then moving either the Reverb or Echo sliders to the right in the Details section of the resulting dialog. But what might have slipped by ya is that you can apply reverb (or echo, or effects in general) to your entire song, rather than instrument by instrument. Here's how: Double-click on any instrument, and when the Track Info dialog appears, click on the Master Track tab. Now click on the Edit icon to the right of Echo or Reverb and move the sliders to the right in the resulting dialog(s) (or click-and-hold on the word "Manual" and choose the effect you want from the pop-up menu). Close the dialog and you're set.

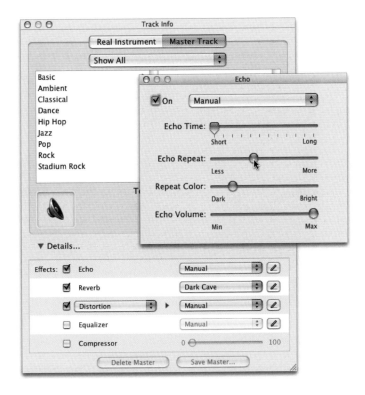

   GarageBand 2: **FADING OUT AT THE END**

If you can't come up with a good ending for your song, do what the pros do—fade out. To do that, press Command-B to make the Master Track visible, then scroll near the end of your song on the Timeline. Click once right on the Volume line (which appears about a third of the way down within the Master Track) right at the spot where you want your fade-out to begin, which adds a point on the Volume line. Then, click once more at the point in the Timeline where you want the music totally faded out to add another point. Now drag that second point downward, and you'll see the line slant down from the first point to the second point. The first point is where the music starts to fade; the second is where it's faded out. For a more gradual fade, drag the first point farther to the left (in other words, the steeper the slant, the quicker the fade).

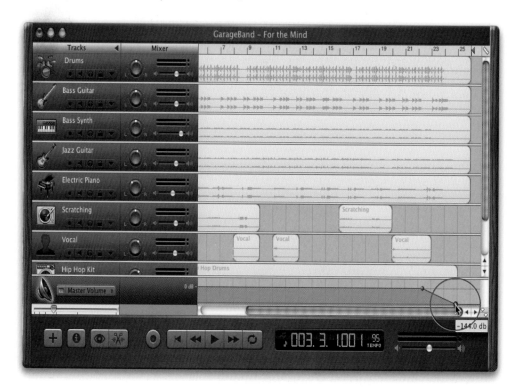

GarageBand 2: **FREE UP SPACE BY LOCKING DOWN A TRACK**

Once you've got a track laid down pretty much the way you want it, you can free up some of your hard disk space by locking down that track. When you lock down a track, Garage-Band temporarily renders that track to disk, so it doesn't take up a bunch of RAM. To do this, click on the track you want in the Tracks column, then click the Lock icon that appears in the group of five icons. Now play the entire track by clicking the Rewind button, and then click the Play button. As it plays, GarageBand will lock the track, securing it on your drive. To unlock a track so you can make changes later, just click the Lock icon.

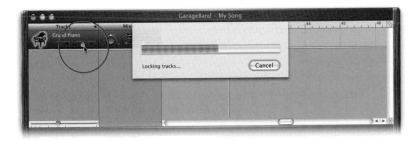

  GarageBand 2: **THE TIME DISPLAY DOES MORE THAN SHOW TIME**

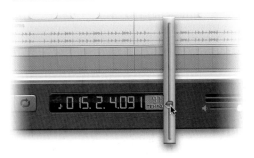

If you're just looking at the Time Display, you're only seeing a tiny bit of what it does. For example, click on the Tempo (it's in the far-right corner) and a pop-up slider appears where you can adjust the tempo. If you click-and-hold directly on the time readout, you can move the position of the Playhead by dragging left, right, up, or down (and the amount the Playhead moves depends on which readout you click-and-drag on). To see the length of your song in minutes and seconds (rather than measures), click on the musical note icon on the left side of the Time Display.

GarageBand 2: **CHANGING THE ORDER OF LOOP BUTTONS**

If you don't like the order of the loop buttons in the Loop Browser, you can easily change them. For example, if you want the Percussion loop button up top, just click directly on  that button and drag it to the top row. You can also rename the loop buttons. So if instead of the All Drums loop button, you'd like it to show Snares, just Control-click on the All Drums button, and in the contextual menu that appears go under Instruments, under All Drums, and choose Snare. You can use this same trick to change any Instruments button into either a Genre button or a Descriptors button.

 GarageBand 2: **REVEALING MORE LOOPS (AND BLANK BUTTONS)**

By default, you can see 30 loops—six rows wide and five buttons deep. There are more loops (and even some blank buttons waiting to be customized), but they're kind of hidden. If you 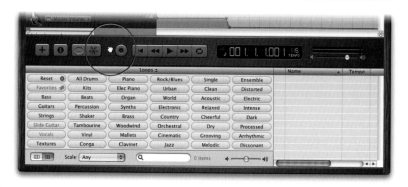 want to access them, just click-and-hold in one of these two places on the toolbar: (1) just to the left of the Volume slider, or (2) just to the left of the round red Record button, and once your cursor changes to a fist, drag straight upward until the loops are visible. This will reveal another three horizontal rows of buttons.

GarageBand 2: MEGASIZED KEYBOARD

In GarageBand 1.0, the little onscreen piano keyboard was just that—a little keyboard. But in GarageBand 2, you can make it "über-sized." First, make the keyboard visible by pressing Command-K, then click on the little green Zoom button in the top-left side of the keyboard and it will jump up in size. Then, click that same green Zoom button again, and it will jump up to the full size of your screen.

GarageBand 2: USING THE BUILT-IN TUNER

Believe it or not, GarageBand 2 has a built-in digital tuner that you can use to make sure your real guitar, bass, etc., is perfectly in tune. To use this tuner, first create a new Real Instrument track (go under the Track menu and choose New Track). Then click on the Tuning Fork icon that appears on the left side of the Time Display in the toolbar. This shows the tuning options.

    GarageBand 2: **TRY A LOOP WITHOUT COMMITTING TO IT**

Sometimes a loop sounds great by itself, but when you drag it up into your Timeline and play it with everything else, it just doesn't fit. Well, here's a great tip for trying out loops with your song, without having to add them to your song first. Just click the Play button for your song, then click on the loop you want to try (in the Loop Browser). In a second or two, you'll hear both your song and the loop, which is automatically synced to your playing song. That way, you can hear if that particular loop will work before you actually drag it up into your Timeline, find out it doesn't work, and then have to delete it.

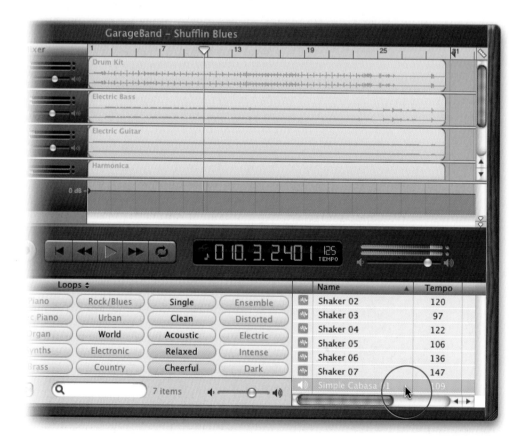

 GarageBand 2: **PANNING KNOB TIP**

When you adjust the Track Pan knob (that appears to the left of an instrument's volume in the Mixer column), it puts the audio of the selected track in the left speaker, the right speaker, or both. By default, it jumps to some preset settings. For example, as you "turn" to the right, it jumps to +16, then +32, then +48, and so on. But what if you want +11 or +22? Instead of grabbing the outside of the knob (where the little white "tick" line is), click on the center of the knob, and now it will move Left or Right in 1% increments. *Note:* You may have to click-and-drag beyond the knob to get the increment you want.

   iDVD 5: **CREATING YOUR OWN THEMES**

No doubt, iDVD comes with some fairly cool background themes, but you can also create your own (using a program like Adobe Photoshop). Just create a new document (from the File menu) in Photoshop at 640x480 pixels, and design your new theme. Save your theme as a Photoshop file by choosing Photoshop (PSD) from the Format pop-up menu in the Save As dialog. Launch iDVD 5, and click on the Customize button in the bottom-left corner of the iDVD window to make the Customize Drawer visible. Click the Settings button at the top of the Customize Drawer, and then drag-and-drop your Photoshop file onto the Background image/movie well. That background now becomes the current background theme. Or, if you don't have Photoshop, just drag a picture from your iPhoto Library.

iDVD 5: STOPPING THAT INFERNAL MUSIC LOOP

If you've used iDVD at all, you already know how short of a time it takes before the looping music track that plays over and over and over again starts to drive you mad. If only there were a way to stop it. Thankfully, there is: Click the Motion button (of all things) at the bottom-right corner of the iDVD window

to stop the infernal music loop until you want it on again (it's hard to imagine that time will ever come, but it will). When it does, click the Motion button again. *Note*: If you burn a DVD and you don't get the motion menus or motion backgrounds, here's an easy fix: Before you burn your DVD, make sure you have the Motion button turned on, or the motion menus, buttons, and audio won't be available when you try to play your disc.

iDVD 5: CHECKING YOUR DVD LIMIT

If you go to the Customize Drawer (by clicking on the Customize button) and click on the Status button, it shows a DVD Capacity amount by default. If you click on the capacity amount along the right-hand side, it will toggle between minutes and the file size you've used. Click on this to see if your movie will fit on your DVD.

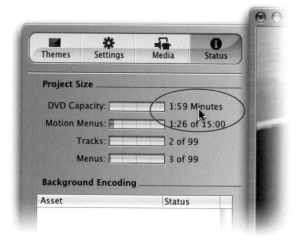

iDVD 5: **CREATING THEMES THAT WORK ON TV**

If you're creating your own custom iDVD themes, you have to be careful not to get your buttons or any other content too close to the edges, or when your DVD is played on a TV screen, the edges will be cropped off (that's just the way TV works). However, you can make certain that you don't enter this "no man's land" area (called the NTSC title safe area by the video crowd) by going under the Advanced menu and choosing Show TV Safe Area. This puts a backscreened border around the outside edges of your theme, indicating which areas to steer clear of.

   iDVD 5: **SETTING THE TRACK ORDER**

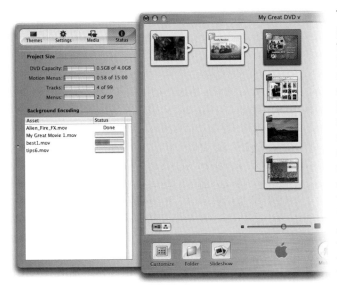

This one throws a lot of people, because moving the clips around in the iDVD menu doesn't actually change the track list order on the DVD. To put the clips in the order that you want them to appear on the DVD (so you can bypass the menu altogether and just shuttle from one track to the next), drag each clip (one at a time) to the iDVD window. Double-check the order by clicking Customize to open the Customize panel and then click the Status button. Your tracks will appear in order in the Asset column.

 iDVD 5: WHICH SETTINGS WORK BEST FOR IMPORTING

iDVD 5 supports most of the same video and image file formats that QuickTime does, so if your video-editing app can export to QuickTime, you can probably use these movies in your iDVD project. To get the best results, here are

some QuickTime export settings you can try: Choose DV/DVCPRO-NTSC with a frame rate of 29.97 (if you're creating video that will be viewed outside the US, use PAL-DV with a frame rate of 25). For audio, choose No Compression and set the rate to 48 KHz. Also, for best quality onscreen, don't use QuickTime movies that are smaller than the DVD standard size of 720x480 pixels.

 iDVD 5: GETTING RID OF THE APPLE LOGO WATERMARK

I'm never one to deny Apple its props, and I love the Apple logo (in fact I have an Apple logo sticker on my car and at least one-third of my clothing), but the one place I don't want it to appear is on my iDVD projects (where it appears by default as a watermark). If you're like me and want it to go away, just go under the iDVD menu, under Preferences, click on the General icon, and turn off the Show Apple Logo Watermark checkbox.

iDVD 5: MOVING YOUR IDVD 5 PROJECT TO ANOTHER MAC

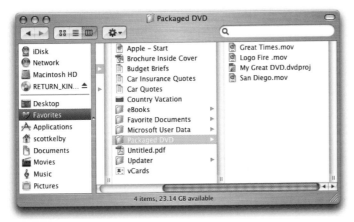

If you're thinking of moving your iDVD project from your Mac to another Mac, make sure you move all of the source files (both still images and movies) you used in your project right along with it. You'll need to, because iDVD references those files, and without them, you're pretty much out of luck. Your best bet is probably to store all your source files in the same folder as your iDVD project file; that way (a) you won't forget them when copying, and (b) you don't have to worry about iDVD going to search for them—they're right there.

   iDVD 5: BEATING THE SLIDE SHOW LIMIT

While it's true that iDVD limits your slide show to 99 slides, iDVD does allow you to have multiple slide shows on the same disc, so your only real limitation is that it can show only 99 at a time.

Talking Heads

ICHAT AV TIPS →

If you're not chatting, you need to be, because there should not be a single second of any waking moment that you're

Talking Heads
ichat av tips

not communicating with somebody about something using an electronic gismo of some sort. As far as electronic gismos go, iChat is among the coolest. So much so, that I have an entire chapter of cool tips for using it. In fact, I use iChat every day, and wind up talking to people I would never normally wind up talking to. But since they can see I'm online and available, I can't just ignore them, so I wind up wasting valuable time talking about how hot is it in Florida, and what I think about the whole Apple/ Intel thing. Sometimes it trashes my productivity for the entire day, but I keep reminding myself that chatting, video conferencing, and text messaging are necessary tools. Without them, I would be required to (gasp!) pick up the telephone. Unthinkable!

  iChat AV: WHICH TYPES OF CHATS ARE THEY UP FOR?

If you're wondering if someone in your Buddy List can do a particular type of chat with you, just click on their name in your Buddy List, then press Command-I to bring up their iChat Info dialog. From the Show pop-up menu at the top of the window, choose their buddy name, and at the bottom you'll see a header called "Capabilities," followed by a list of all the types of chats they're capable of participating in, so you'll know if they're "up" for a particular kind of chat.

   iChat AV: USE YOUR PHOTO, INSTEAD OF THEIRS

If you don't like one of your Buddy's iChat photos, believe it or not, you can replace it with one of your own (of course, I mean a photo you have of them—it would be pretty creepy to replace their photo with a photo of you). Here's how to play the ol' photo swap-a-roo: Click on their name in the Buddy List, then press Command-I to bring up the Info dialog on your buddy. Select Address Card from the Show pop-up menu. Now drag-and-drop the photo you want to use for them right onto the photo box, and then be sure to check the preference named "Always Use This Picture" (otherwise, the photo your buddy has set will reappear). That's it—from now on that photo will be displayed for them instead. By the way—unless you tell your buddy, they'll never know, as this change is only visible in your iChat—not theirs. So basically, if it's somebody you don't really like, you could replace their photo with a photo of Darth Vader and they'd never know (unless they had The Force, of course—then they'd sense a disturbance. Forgive me for this last part—I don't know what I was thinking).

iChat AV: **STAY LIVE EVEN WHEN YOU'VE QUIT**

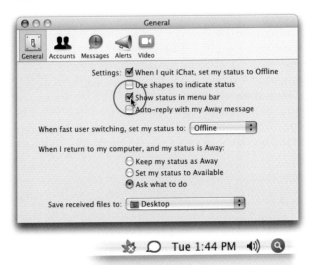

Just because you've quit iChat AV doesn't mean your buddies can't send you an instant message. Well, actually, that's exactly what it means, if you don't make one little change to iChat AV's preferences. Go under the iChat AV menu and choose Preferences, and under the General section, turn on the checkbox for Show Status in Menu Bar. That will add a tiny menu icon to your menu bar that looks like a "talk bubble." Click on it, and you'll see your status, and even your Buddy List (and their status) if you like.

   iChat AV: **A PICTURE'S WORTH A THOUSAND TEXT CHATS**

If you want to include a preview of a JPEG photo with your text message, just drag the JPEG file right onto the text field where you type your messages. This adds a little icon at the far left of the field, letting you know that a photo will be sent with your text. Now, when you press the Return key, the photo will preview in your iChat window along with your text.

iChat AV: SHARING YOUR MUSICAL TASTE WITH YOUR BUDDIES

If you listen to iTunes while you're chatting, you can give the people you're chatting with a glimpse into your musical genius, by going to your Buddy List, and under the Status pop-up menu, choosing Current iTunes Track. Now the song you're listening to will be displayed to the person you're chatting with, which basically tells them that they're not important enough to demand your full attention, and that you must do other things, like listen to music, to keep yourself occupied while mindlessly chatting with them. Okay, I'm not sure it does mean all that, but you get the drift. Okay, so what if they really like the song? They can click on it, and it will take them directly to that song in the iTunes Music Store, so they can buy it themselves, and then they'll be the one who looks cool. It's a vicious cycle.

iChat AV: YOUR BUDDY DOESN'T NEED A CAMERA

If your buddy doesn't have a camera connected, but you do, you can still have a one-way video chat. That way, your buddy gets to see and hear you on their end. The only down-side—you don't get to see them, but that's what you get for having friends that are too cheap to buy an iSight camera. Here's how it works: Click on your buddy's name in the Buddy List (they're probably named something like "El Cheapo" or "Save-a-buck," etc.), and then go under the Buddy menu and choose Invite to One-Way Video Chat. Again, they'll see and hear you, but not the other way around. Well, technically, if they have a microphone built into their Mac (it's an iMac, eMac, PowerBook, iBook, etc.), then you'll be able to hear them, too, but with your buddy being so cheap, they probably have a Mac mini, dontchathink?

   iChat AV: DROP 'EM A FILE

If you want to send a buddy a file—it doesn't get much easier than this—all you have to do is drag-and-drop the file you want to send directly onto their name in the Buddy List. For instance, say you'd like to send your buddy a full JPEG file, instead of just a preview. All you have to do is drag-and-drop that photo onto your buddy's name in the list. A dialog will appear asking if you'd like to send the file. Click Send and your buddy will be able to download the entire file.

iChat AV: **MANAGING LOTS OF BUDDIES**

If you're fairly popular with the iChat crowd (and my guess is you are, because only very cool people buy this book), you've probably got lots of buddies in your Buddy List, which means your life is filled with an awful lot of scrolling. But it doesn't have to be that way, because you can group related people together into Groups (just like you do with groups of people in Address Book). So, if you have a number of people you chat with from your office, you can have a Work Group, with all their buddy names appearing within a collapsible Group (which saves loads of space and scrolling time, and just generally makes your Buddy List easier on the eyes). To create a Buddy Group, first go under the View menu, and choose Use Groups. Then click-and-hold on the plus (+) sign in the bottom-left corner of the Buddy List window, and choose Add Group from the menu that appears. Next, give your new Group a name, and then in the Buddy List window drag-and-drop any buddies you want included into this Group.

iChat AV: **HOW LONG HAS THIS BEEN GOING ON?**

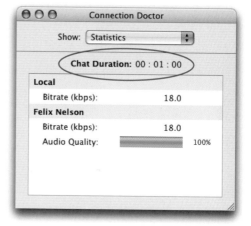

Audio chats are like phone calls— you can really eat up some time without realizing how long you've been chatting. If you'd like to know exactly how long you've been at it, go under the Audio menu and choose Connection Doctor. This brings up the Connection Doctor dialog (which you'd normally use to help fix bad connections), and at the top of the dialog is the duration of your current chat. Scary, ain't it? Now close that chat and get back to work! *Note:* The Audio menu will not be visible if you have a video peripheral installed (if you do, the menu will show Video options instead).

iChat AV: **AUDIO CHATTING? DROP IT TO THE DOCK**

If you're doing an audio chat, do you even need the iChat window open, just cluttering up your screen? Well, if you close it, you'll quit the chat, but if you minimize the chat window to the Dock instead (press Command-M), you can continue your chat, even though the window is no longer visible. When it's time to end your chat, just click on the minimized chat window in the Dock.

   iChat AV: **HAVE ICHAT ANNOUNCE YOUR BUDDIES**

If you want to have iChat automatically make an audio announcement when one of your buddies logs on, it's easy. Just click on their name in your Buddy List, then press Command-I to bring up their Info dialog. Choose Actions from the Show pop-up menu at the top of the Info dialog, and you'll see a list of alerts you can have go off when your buddy logs on. At the bottom of this list is a checkbox for Speak Text. If you turn that checkbox on, click in the text field and type the message you want spoken by your Mac.

  iChat AV: FIXING BAD AUDIO CHATS

This is an old trick, but I forgot to include it in the previous edition of this book…so…here it is: If you're having an audio chat, and the audio becomes garbled or is dropping out a lot, you can have iChat try to improve the connection using this simple trick. Just click the Mute button for a second, then unmute it by clicking it again. This causes iChat to reassess the connection and that will usually do the trick.

   iChat AV: GETTING A TRANSCRIPT OF YOUR CHAT

There are a dozen reasons why you might want a written log of your text chats: maybe someone gave you instructions, a recipe, or just typed a bunch of stuff that cracks you up. Well, luckily, you can ask iChat to keep a running log of your text chats—go under the iChat menu, to Preferences, then click on the Messages icon, and turn on Automatically Save Chat Transcripts.

iChat AV: **A BUDDY IN YOUR DOCK**

This is one of those things that just makes you smile—if you're chatting with someone and you minimize their chat window to the Dock (maybe they're taking a break for a moment, for a snack, etc.), their buddy photo shows up in your Dock as a Dock icon (as shown here, where my good friend and Creative Director Felix Nelson is killing some time in my Dock). When your chat buddy comes back and sends you a message, a tiny iChat AV icon slowly blinks on and off to get your attention.

   iChat AV: **KEEPING YOUR CAMERA FROM GOING TO SLEEP**

I picked up this great tip from Scott Sheppard over at OSXFAQ.com and it's for people who don't use iChat AV with Apple's iSight, but instead use their own digital camcorder. The problem: After about 5 minutes, most commercial camcorders go to sleep automatically to preserve battery life. The solution: Remove the DV tape from the camcorder and it stops the camera from ever going to sleep. I never would have thought of that. Thanks, Mr. Sheppard.

iChat AV: **AVOIDING UNWANTED CHATS**

If you have a lot of buddies in your Buddy List, you can wind up with a lot of incoming chats, which is cool if you're sitting around doing nothing; but if you're trying to get some work done, it can drive you crazy. Here's how to narrow the list of who can get through (so you can get some work done). Press Command–, (Comma key) to bring up iChat's Prefer-ences, go under Accounts, and then click on the Security tab at the top. You can go one of two ways: (1) Click on Allow Specific People, then click the Edit List button. Going this route, in the Edit List window you enter the email names of only the people you want to know you're online. To the rest of the people in your Buddy List (and the rest of the world), you're offline. Or (2) choose Block Specific People, and click the Edit List button to enter the people who, if they chatted with you, would drive you crazy. Either way, only the people you want to know you're online will know.

iChat AV: **BEATING THE 5-MB EMAIL LIMIT**

If you're sending someone an email with an attachment that's larger than 5 MB, you can almost bet that it's going to get bounced back because their server has a 5-MB limit for incoming email. So how do you get around this—use iChat AV to send the file, since it has no file size limits. Start a chat with the person you want to email, then simply drag-and-drop the file you want to send right onto their photo in your Buddy List. How cool is that!

iChat AV: **IGNORING THE FREAKS**

If you're in a public chat with several people, and one of them starts to really get on your nerves (in other words, they're a PC user), you can ask iChat to completely ignore their comments by going to the list of participants (in the sidebar), clicking on their name, and then going under the Buddies menu and choosing Block. From that point on, their comments will no longer appear in the chat window. In short, you dissed them (by using "dissed," I picked up incredible street cred with people still stuck in the '90s).

iChat AV: **PULLING SOMEONE INTO A PRIVATE CHAT**

If you've got a group chat going, and you want to pull someone aside into a private chat (so you can make fun of someone else in the chat), make sure you have the Participant pane open by going under the View menu and choosing Show Chat Participants. Then just double-click on their name in the list and they'll be invited to a private chat outside the current chat. You can also double-click on their name in the Buddy List to invite them to a private chat.

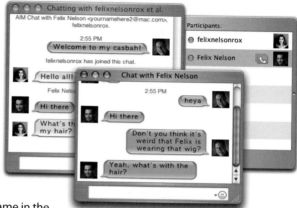

   iChat AV: **AVOIDING LATE-NIGHT AUDIO CHATS**

If you're working late at night and your spouse and kids are in bed, you may not want one of your buddies calling you for an audio chat. If that's the case, go under the Audio menu and turn off Microphone Enabled. Now, when they look at you in their Buddy List, the green Audio Chat icon will be hidden, and if they want to talk to you, they'll have to text chat.

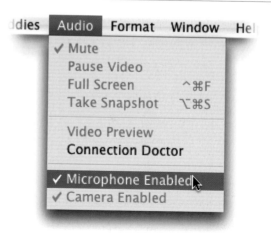

iChat AV: **ADD A BUDDY FAST (WITHOUT ALL THE EXTRA INFO)**

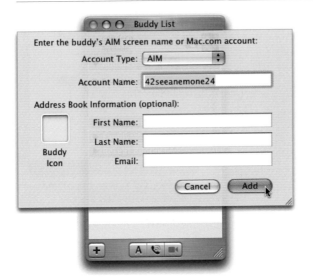

When you add a buddy to your Buddy List, it looks like you have to enter all their Address Book info, but in reality, that's totally optional. To add a buddy quickly, just click on the plus (+) sign at the bottom-left corner of the Buddy List, and when the Address Book dialog appears, click New Person. When the Add a Buddy dialog appears, just enter their chat name and click Add; you can skip all the other info.

iChat AV: **THE TRICK TO GETTING LINE BREAKS**

When you're doing a text chat, if you're typing and press Return, it doesn't give you a line break—it sends your message. If you want a line break, press Option-Return instead.

iChat AV: QUICK WAY TO CUSTOMIZE YOUR BACKGROUND

Want to put a background photo behind your
chat window in iChat? Under the View menu is an
option to Set Chat Background. Select it, and from
the resulting dialog choose the image file you'd
like to use as your background. To delete it (if it's
too busy—like the one shown here), go under the
View menu and choose Clear Background.

   iChat AV: POPPING THE BALLOONS (QUICK VIEW CHANGE)

Want to view just text, just photos, both at the same time, or toggle back and forth? Just
Control-click within your message window (where the bubbles appear). A contextual menu
will appear, and under the View submenu you can choose how you'd like your chat messages displayed.

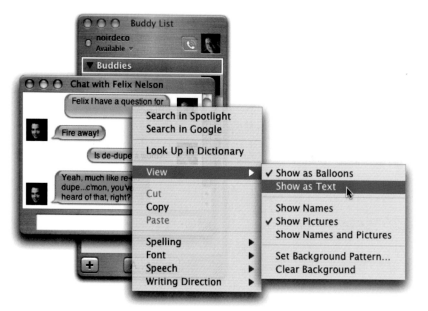

iChat AV: **A BUBBLE OF A DIFFERENT COLOR**

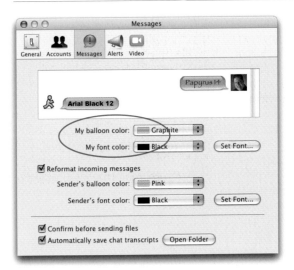

Don't like the default color of your dialog bubble? You can change it by going under the iChat menu and choosing Preferences. When the Preferences dialog appears, click on the Messages icon and in that pane, choose your desired color from the My Balloon Color pop-up menu. While you're there, why not pick a cooler font for your chat, and even your font color? You can also change the color of incoming chat balloons so they color-coordinate with yours. Be sure to tell your therapist about this aspect of your chat life. It will answer a lot of questions.

   iChat AV: **PUTTING LIVE LINKS INTO YOUR CHAT**

In previous versions of iChat, if you wanted to put a live link into your chat messages, you had to bring up a special screen. Now, all you have to do is type in the address of the site you want them to click on (you don't even have to add the "http://" to the address, but you do need the "www" part). When they see the link, they can click on it, which will launch their browser and load that site.

  iChat AV: **GETTING YOUR MESSAGES ONCE YOU'VE QUIT ICHAT**

One of the coolest things about iChat AV is that you don't have to have it up and running to get instant messages. Start by launching iChat AV, then go under the iChat menu, choose Preferences, and click on the General icon. When the General options appear, turn on Show Status Bar in Menu Bar to add an iChat pop-up menu to your menu bar. In this menu, choose Available as your status. Back in the iChat Preferences, click on the Alerts icon, then under Event, choose Message Received. That way, iChat will notify you when you receive a message, so you can close it. Now, how will it alert you that a new message has been received? That's where the fun begins. Click the Speak Text checkbox and iChat will verbally tell you you've got a message (there's even a field for you to type in what you want it to say). If you're afraid that won't get your attention, click on the checkbox for Bounce Icon in the Dock. If that's still not enough notification, click the checkbox for Send Repetitive 110-Volt Electric Shocks Via Keyboard. (Okay, that last one isn't really in iChat, but don't ya think it should be?)

Index

COLOPHON

The book was produced by the author and design team using Macintosh computers, including a Power Mac G5 1.8-GHz, a Power Mac G5 Dual Processor 1.8-GHz, a Power Mac G5 Dual Processor 2-GHz, a Power Mac G4 Dual Processor 1.25-MHz. We use LaCie, Sony, and Apple Studio Display monitors.

Page layout was done using Adobe InDesign CS. We use a Mac OS X server, and burn our CDs to our CPU's internal Sony DVD RW DW-U10A.

The headers for each technique are set in Adobe MyriadMM_565 SB 600 NO at 11 points on 12.5 leading, with the Horizontal Scaling set to 100%. Body copy is set using Adobe MyriadMM_400

RG 600 NO at 9.5 points on 11.5 leading, with the Horizontal Scaling set to 100%.

Screen captures were made with Snapz Pro X and were placed and sized within Adobe InDesign CS. The book was output at 150 line screen, and all in-house printing was done using a Tektronix Phaser 7700 by Xerox.

ADDITIONAL RESOURCES

ScottKelbyBooks.com
For information on Scott's other Macintosh and graphics-related books, visit his book site. For background info on Scott, visit www.scottkelby.com.

http://www.scottkelbybooks.com

Layers Magazine
Layers—The How-To Magazine for Everything Adobe—is the foremost authority on Adobe's design, digital video, digital photography, and education applications. Each issue features timely product news, plus the quick tips, hidden shortcuts, and step-by-step tutorials for working in today's digital market. America's top-selling computer book author for 2004, Scott Kelby is editor-in-chief of *Layers*.

www.layersmagazine.com

National Association of Photoshop Professionals (NAPP)
The industry trade association for Adobe® Photoshop® users and the world's leading resource for Photoshop training, education, and news.

http://www.photoshopuser.com

KW Computer Training Videos
Scott Kelby is featured in a series of Photoshop training DVDs, each on a particular Photoshop topic, available from KW Computer Training. Visit the website or call 813-433-5000 for orders or more information.

http://www.photoshopvideos.com

Photoshop Down & Dirty Tricks
Scott is also author of the best-selling book *Photoshop CS Down & Dirty Tricks*, and the book's companion website has all the info on the book, which is available at bookstores around the country.

http://www.scottkelbybooks.com

Adobe Photoshop Seminar Tour
See Scott live at the Adobe Photoshop Seminar Tour, the nation's most popular Photoshop seminars. For upcoming tour dates and class schedules, visit the tour website.

http://www.photoshopseminars.com

Photoshop World
The convention for Adobe Photoshop users has now become the largest Photoshop-only event in the world. Scott Kelby is technical chair and education director for the event, as well as one of the instructors.

http://www.photoshopworld.com

The Photoshop CS2 Book for Digital Photographers
This book cuts through the bull and shows you step by step the exact techniques used by today's cutting-edge digital photographers, and it shows you which settings to use, when to use them, and why.

http://www.scottkelbybooks.com

Photoshop Hall of Fame
Created to honor and recognize those individuals whose contributions to the art and business of Adobe Photoshop have had a major impact on the application or the Photoshop community itself.

http://www.photoshophalloffame.com

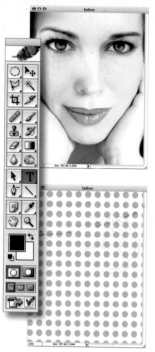

Before NAPP

After NAPP

How'd they do that?

You'll learn how and more from the National Association of Photoshop Professionals (NAPP)

You're invited to join NAPP, the most complete resource for Adobe® Photoshop® training, education, and news.

Member Benefits:

- Annual subscription to *Photoshop User* magazine
- Killer tips, video tutorials, action downloads plus more
- Free online tech support

- Discounts on educational books, training DVDs, and seminars
- Exclusive discounts on hardware, software and everything in between
- Individual online portfolios

The National Association of Photoshop Professionals
A one-year membership is only $99
(includes a one-year subscription to Photoshop User magazine)

Join today! Call 800-738-8513
www.photoshopuser.com

NAPP's Official Publication

Corporate, educational and international memberships available.
Adobe and Photoshop are registered trademarks of Adobe Systems, Inc.

Join today and get "Best of Photoshop User: The Seventh Year" DVD free ($69.99 value).
(Special new member discount code NAPM-1UM).

VYPER™
XS · M · XM · XL

Vyper. The First Truly Cool Laptop Sleeve. Fits Your iBook or PowerBook Like a Glove.
Choose the perfect size for your laptop at www.booqbags.com.

booq (b)

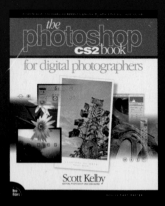
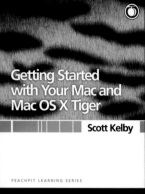